Ex Libris
Robert J. Augustt
1938
Wadhams Hall,
Ogdensburg, N.Y.

SCIENCE AND CULTURE SERIES
JOSEPH HUSSLEIN, S.J., PH.D., GENERAL EDITOR

Luther and His Work

By the Same Author

The Protestant Reformation in Great Britain: a Short History

St. Anselm: a Biography

St. Hugh of Lincoln: a Biography

Sir Thomas More: a Short Study

Luther
AND HIS WORK

Joseph Clayton, F.R.Hist.S.

THE BRUCE PUBLISHING COMPANY
MILWAUKEE

Nihil obstat: H. B. RIES, Censor librorum
Imprimatur: ✠ SAMUEL A. STRITCH, Archiepiscopus Milwaukiensis
March 22, 1937

(Second Printing — 1937)

Printed in the U. S. A.

To

W. F. P. STOCKLEY, M.A., D.Litt.
Emeritus Professor of English Literature
at the University of Cork
In Friendship

Contents

CONTENTS

CONTENTS

Chapter *Page*

Preface by the General Editor

VAST BEYOND computation has been the output of literature relating to Luther and his work. The printing press had just reached its effectiveness when the preaching of the New Evangel began and was used to full advantage for its defence and promotion. The number of writers who through the ensuing four centuries have essayed to give the world their contributions, friendly or adverse, on this central figure of the Reformation can be summed up in one word only, and that is, "Legion."

To add, then, a new volume to those already in existence might seem superfluous were there not a sufficient reason in the changed conditions of our time, and also in the need of a brief reliable history that shall cover the entire range not merely of Luther's life, but of his influence as well.

A new epoch in world history has begun. Like all enduring changes it has been long in preparation. Its earliest premonitions go back considerably beyond the period of the Reformation. Its more immediate developments manifested themselves with the coming of the Industrial Revolution, a century and a half ago, and with the attendant general advance in technological science.

Simultaneously with these two factors the results of the Reformation had been steadily working themselves out in ways little anticipated by its founder. For only too many of his previous followers or their descendants the path from Catholicism to private judgment in religion no longer ended there. Continuing further, it led on to scepticism and thence to the ultimate atheism so widespread and active in our day. Catholics, too, were thenceforth in peril of falling into the same abyss by way of the prevalent indifferentism. Only by special safeguards could men maintain their religious and social principles.

The modern atheistic movement has steadily advanced. The wave is cresting, and who can tell how it will break or when? In not a few countries the calamity has already descended.

My purpose here is not to play a Cassandra role in predicting evils, but rather to avert them while it is possible. But one thing is clear: the time has come when Catholics, Protestants, and all who still retain a spark of true religion must co-operate towards the common good. It is true that without a miracle of grace we cannot at this instant hope to see realised that unity for which Christ prayed and which Europe knew at an earlier age. But at least we must endeavour rightly to understand each other and so to join ranks in a common defence of what is sacred to us all. This need not imply a compromise in faith.

New problems are confronting us and a new division of spirits is taking place among the peoples of the earth. No longer are Catholicism and Protestantism facing each other in the embattled field, as in the endless wars that followed on the breaking up of Christian unity in the Western World, but instead religion of whatever kind to-day stands confronted by the alert, organised, and highly militant forces of atheistic action.

With exalted lip service to democracy and under the disguise of the United Popular Front, Communism everywhere begins its work, until it can safely cast off the sheep's clothing assumed by it and act in its own true nature. In Russia, Mexico, and Spain — to proceed no further — we have beheld it indifferent to the shedding of a veritable deluge of human blood in its relentless efforts to obliterate at all costs the very name of God from the mind and heart of man.

Under these conditions, obviously, it should be possible to view the Reformation in a new perspective.

The period in which we live is one in which an impartial evaluation of Luther and his work, by a man steeped in social and historic knowledge, should prove acceptable to Catholic and Protestant alike and most helpful to both. For that purpose it must not merely be written objectively, according blame and praise impartially, but the writer must be able to control whatever subtle influences of sympathy might in the least imperil his historic judgment or presentation. In a word, he must have but one single bias, and that in the author's own felicitous words must be "the bias for truth." This supreme quality of history Mr. Clayton has invariably sought at all costs to maintain.

His present book, calm, factual, and impartial, will meet the needs of our day.

JOSEPH HUSSLEIN, S.J., PH.D.,
General Editor, Science and Culture Series

St. Louis University,
May 11, 1937

Author's Preface

WE SEE it to-day throughout the world — that separation of Christian from Christian, that division between the Catholic Church and the multitudes that call themselves Christian and boast a Protestant ancestry. We are accustomed to this division; have indeed accepted it as normal, so plain is it that millions of people — all calling themselves Christian — are content to live and die, neither considering nor deploring the division. Hardly a town or city may be named where Christian people do not assemble to worship apart from the One, Holy, Roman, Catholic, and Apostolic Church. Hardly a land where Catholic missionaries to the heathen will not find the missionaries of Protestant societies in the field. And many of the numerous societies and congregations of Protestant Christians are as sharply divided from one another as they are sharply separated from all who acknowledge the authority of the pope and submit willingly to his jurisdiction.

From time to time the question forces itself on our attention: Why this division? The lively intelligent mind puts a further question: How did this separation of Christian from Christian, of Protestant from Catholic, come about?

To Catholic and non-Catholic alike these questions are of vital interest. Complacency is disastrous in the face of our unhappy divisions. Reposing in ignorance we are liable to fall into mortal error. Passion and prejudice — so often allied — play havoc when truth is denied admission, and honest enquiry baulked. Do we, in the cause of truth, dare say that disunity and the disorders that spring from disunity, are proper to the Christian religion?

Why then are Christians divided from Christians? Why do Catholics worship apart from all those who generally call themselves Protestant? Why, indeed, do they call themselves "Protestant" and what is the historic significance of the term?

Unity is the divine order of the Founder of Christianity to His first disciples. It is the very prayer of Christ to the Father. Unity is the recurring message of St. Paul in his letters to the earliest Christian churches. The notion that Christian men and women have been granted liberty to start a new church when and wherever they feel moved to do so has no countenance in the New Testament. It was not so at the beginning, is all that can be said when sects multiply and the denominations of separatist Christians extend. Indeed it was not so till four hundred years ago. True there are certain divisions already noted and strongly reprehended in Holy Writ. True, there existed Christians in Asia Minor and North Africa outside the Catholic unity, Armenians, Copts, Nestorians, and Eastern churches of the Greek rite who would not have the pope for their head. Doctrinal differences still keep the ancient and strictly local churches of Abyssinia, Egypt, and Armenia outside the unity of the Catholic Church. Their bishops and rulers have never accepted the definitions of Catholic Faith given by the ecumenical councils. Political considerations have sundered the Greek churches from the Catholic unity and from one another. From the time when Constantinople was founded as the New Rome and the seat of the Roman Empire, allegiance to the see of St. Peter was grudgingly given by Byzantine emperors and patriarchs. Obedience to the successor of St. Peter lapsed from unfulfilment into frank refusal.

Westward the course of Catholic missions took its way, and northward, till all Europe beyond the Greek empire became Catholic Christendom, with the pope for its chief bishop on earth. Christendom: owning one Lord, one Faith, one Baptism. For a thousand years this Christendom endured; the Catholic unity, threatened when rival popes claimed the prerogatives of the Holy See and the faithful were in open confusion as to who was the true pope and who the false, endured.

Then in Germany in the sixteenth century came that change in religion we call the Protestant Reformation and the unity of Christendom was broken; to remain broken to this day. The multitudes of non-Catholic Christians all over the world isolated from the Catholic unity are the descendants of the men who departed from the Catholic unity four hundred years ago and were the first to accept the title of "Protestants." The nations upon whom the change of religion was forced by their kings and princes are in their descendants still averse from submission to the papal authority. Scandinavians of Norway, Sweden, and Denmark, Prussians and Saxons, Dutch in Holland and South Africa, English, Welsh, and Scotsmen — these remain in the mass non-Catholic wherever found; as their forefathers were Protestant so they likewise inherit. But why they are the heirs of the Protestant tradition, why and how their forefathers departed from Catholic unity to set up new churches, are questions apt to be lightly dismissed as barren of fruitful result. The more so since criticism of the fundamental beliefs and dogma of sixteenth-century reformers has whittled away the once authoritative Protestant teaching, while the exuberance of private judgment has produced such strange and fantastic exhibits of human credulity as to make the old Protestant standards of faith and morals no longer recognisable.

One man, Dr. Martin Luther, of the order of Augustinian Hermits, is rightly discerned as the author of the sixteenth-century disruption. For it was Luther who preached and led the exodus from the Catholic Church, proclaimed the pope to be anti-Christ, and founded the new "evangelical" churches of Germany.

Far back in the eighth century an English monk, St. Boniface — a west countryman from Crediton in Devon — brought the Catholic Faith to Teuton heathens; revived the moribund communities of Germanic Christians and restored them to the unity of Christendom; recovered to the papal allegiance the semi-pagan tribes, and died a martyr for the gospel he preached, slain by savages who would have nothing of Christ and His Catholic Church. The martyred English monk, St. Boniface, is known to history as the Apostle of Germany.*

Eight hundred years later Martin Luther, from that very part of Germany that Boniface had evangelised, made an unexpected return for the gift that came from England. For Luther, by his writings and through his disciples, brought the Protestant teaching to Great Britain, and from England and Scotland this Protestant teaching spread to North America and to all British Colonies and dominions. John Calvin, a Frenchman, was to give from Geneva a positive and rigid dogma to Protestants dissatisfied with the vague Lutheran formularies, to lay upon the churches of "the reform" a doctrine and discipline of sterner stuff than Luther knew, to impose through what came to be called "Puritanism" a morality of its own on vast numbers of English-speaking nations. But it was Luther who first raised the cry, "To your tents O Israel!" and started the breakup of Christendom. It was Luther who preached that man was saved by believing that Christ had saved him and needed no sacrificing priesthood, nor Mass. And on Luther's doctrinal foundation, that man was justified solely by faith in Christ, all Protestants built their churches. Whatever the varieties

* "A man who had a deeper influence on the history of Europe than any Englishman who has ever lived. Unlike his Celtic predecessors he was not an individual missionary but a statesman and organizer, who was above all a servant of the Roman order." Christopher Dawson, *The Making of Europe,* 1932.

of Protestant teaching, they all derive from Luther. History takes it for indisputable fact that Martin Luther was the founder of the Protestant "evangelical" church of Germany and the source and fountainhead of all the reformed churches of Europe.

Hence it is that to this day Martin Luther is praised and his name revered in non-Catholic Christian denominations for having wrought deliverance from the authority of Rome, for bringing the gift of private judgment in faith and morals to all believers. Similarly on the other hand among Catholics, Luther is held in abhorrence as an apostate monk who drew countless souls into heresy and whole nations into schism; the evil of whose life has lived after him.

Thomas Carlyle extolled Luther as the "true great man; great in intellect, in courage, affection and integrity; one of our most lovable and precious men. . . . A right spiritual Hero and Prophet; once more, a true son of nature and fact, for whom these centuries and many that are to come yet, will be thankful to Heaven." Carlyle's panegyric may be read in that astonishing poetical medley of intuitive assertion and inaccurate information called *Heroes and Hero-worship* (1840).

In our own time the distinguished French author, M. Jacques Maritain, has supplied a portrait in *Three Reformers* (1928) that reveals another point of view. M. Maritain sees Luther "gifted with a nature at once realistic and lyrical, powerful, impulsive, brave and sad, sentimental and morbidly sensitive. Vehement as he was, there was yet in him kindness, generosity, tenderness, and with it all unbroken pride and peevish vanity. Reason was very weak in him. If by intelligence we mean capacity to grasp the universal, to discern the essential, to follow humbly the wanderings and refinements of reality, then he was not intelligent but shallow — stubborn especially. But he had the understanding of the particular and practical to an amazing degree, and an astute and vigorous ingenuity, skill to detect evil in others, the art of finding a thousand ways out of a difficulty and crushing his opponent."

Again, let the reader of *Martin Luther and the Reformation in Germany* by Dr. Charles Beard (London, 1889), compare that scholarly work by a non-Catholic minister with the one-volume edition of *Martin Luther* by Hartmann Grisar, S.J., adapted by F. J. Eble and edited by Arthur Preuss (Herder, U.S.A., 1930), and observe the startling difference in the estimate of Luther's character.

The name of Luther and the work of the founder of Protestantism must needs be honoured where it is counted a gain to the world that mankind in general, and Christian men and women in particular, no longer give allegiance to a supreme pontiff sitting in the chair of St. Peter at Rome, nor admit the existence on earth of an authority infallible in precepts of faith and morals, but rather display a freedom of private judgment that results in the present variety of creeds.

And as inevitably is the work of Luther deplored and his name a word of reproach where it is held that the unity of the Christian peoples of God — "one Lord, one Faith, one Baptism" — is part of the divine plan for the salvation of mankind, and that the guarantee of that unity resides in a common obedience to the spiritual authority of the pope.

For good then, as Protestants believe, for evil as Catholics maintain, Martin Luther started this sixteenth-century separation of Christian from Christian, this detachment of nations from the papal obedience and the Catholic unity; with vital consequences to civilisation that are apparent throughout the world to-day.

Not that Luther, when he began his campaign for reform of abuses, contemplated the setting up of a new church. He, no more than Pope Leo X, who excommunicated him, foresaw what loomed ahead, or supposed it possible or desirable to break the unity of Catholic Christendom. Coming events cast no shadows before in Wittenberg or in Rome, when Luther challenged the justice of the indulgence business and awaited Pope Leo's reply. Yet in the short space of forty years the work of cleavage we call the Protestant Reformation was accomplished. In that brief historic period whole nations were violently sundered from the Catholic unity, withdrawn from the papal obedience.

Who can study the course of those immensely fatal forty years of European history without being moved by the tragedy of the sixteenth century? Who can read of Luther's achievement in the story, unfolded by the patient research of scholars of many lands, and not be stirred? It is a story of tumult, of fierce passions, and grossest crime; of cruelty and folly, of pride summoning pride to mortal combat, of political ambition making havoc of the things of God. It is all this and more, the history of the Protestant Reformation in sixteenth-century Europe. The worldliness, the violence, the malignant hatreds, the intolerance are plain enough. The invective of the printed word, and the reported speech of foul-mouthed partisans still show the bitterness of anger and the murderous rage of the disputants.

But these are not the whole story. The dramatic episodes so frequently fastened upon and expanded by writers of history often turn out upon close and full investigation to be of no significance; often enough, indeed, to be no more than the later inventions of ingenious and imaginative commentators, anxious to improve the occasion and to tell what they think ought to have happened. By some, indeed, an emphasis on these dramatic or melodramatic episodes is accounted of high value, and perhaps even necessary if history is to be made attractive or party purposes and popular prejudice are to be served. Nevertheless, for the sake of historic truth all detected falsehood must be ruthlessly eliminated however picturesque its appearance, however endeared to us by repetition.

The visible evil is never the whole story in any just and

true account of human endeavour. Tales of crime and folly have a pleasing quality that excites and thrills, a quality that the literature of wisdom and purity rarely possesses. "Sin in some shape or other is the great staple of history." The charity that "is not puffed up"; that is "patient and kind" and is "not ambitious" is apt to be passed over by the historian. The charity that "seeketh not her own; is not provoked to anger; thinketh no evil; rejoiceth not in iniquity, but rejoiceth in the truth" is overlooked by the chronicler of world politics. The charity that "beareth all things, believeth all things, hopeth all things, endureth all things" is hardly taken into account when the historian is seeking the fearful incidents that will decorate the narrative, the alleged utterance that may point a moral or adorn the tale.

Holiness was not extinct, faith was not dead, the simple piety of uncounted multitudes had not vanished in the turbulent age of the reformation. Men and women, holy and humble of heart, still followed the ways of religion and sought to do the will of God though Christendom was breaking up. The very men who wrought the disruption and the men who opposed it are neither the heroes their admirers have acclaimed them, nor the villains their enemies have painted them. They were men like unto ourselves, whose temptations are our temptations, whose failings are our failings. To a few power gave the opportunity for imposing decisions of tremendous influence. When conspicuous ability is joined with political power the quite probable result is a considerable discomfort to mankind. Only by the grace of God is the possession of power in a strong man compatible with the fine scruple of a good conscience. Macchiavelli, the predominant political writer of the sixteenth century, allowed no room for scruple or conscience when he set out the implications of power in the state.

They were men like ourselves, these Protestant reformers and the Catholics who withstood them. Of complex character for the most part; no doubt often largely self-deceived, being without the rare singleness of mind, and purity of heart that is rewarded with unclouded discernment of the will of God. One fact may be noted, the Protestant Reformation with its breakup of the unity of Christendom and its repudiation of papal authority was the work of clergy and laity brought up in the Catholic Church, educated in the Catholic Church, and knowing nothing of any faith but the Catholic faith.

Not from without — though the sultan Solyman, the Magnificent, and his Turkish hosts were pressing hard on Vienna and overrunning the Mediterranean — but from within came this disaster to the unity of the kingdom of Christ. Catholic bishops and Catholic priests, Catholic princes and Catholic cities revolted from the supremacy of the pope, rejected the Catholic doctrine of the Mass, and plunged Europe into bloody wars; leaving to their descendants to carry on the strife throughout the centuries to come.

To the question "What does history teach us?" one answer may be given: *Vigilate!* It teaches us that men and women unwatching, off their guard, and unforeseeing, accomplish profound changes for good and for evil. Washington did not contemplate an independent United States when the American colonies revolted, neither did the British government. Luther and Pope Leo X were for years unaware of the revolution that was already at work.

To study profitably why this revolt occurred, to read that we may learn how the separation of Christians came about, it is well to exclude any natural bias that afflicts us, whether derived from ancestry or education, from association or from personal interest. Let the bias for truth possess us and our prejudices may cease to operate effectively. We cannot hope, perhaps in our study of history, for the total elimination of prejudice, but we may at least resolve that truth shall not be wilfully betrayed to serve the baser ends of the bigot or to palliate the mischief of the ignoramus.

AUTHOR'S PREFACE

Truth and truth alone, the whole truth and nothing but the truth, is the concern of the writer of this short history, in the belief that "truth is a greater good than the most picturesque story, that truth is more important than edification, that in reality truth is the highest edification."

In these pages of what is no more than an introduction to the history of the Reformation — so briefly for instance are the political and economic conditions of Europe and the Empire described — I have sought neither to justify nor condone, neither to praise nor reproach the deeds of Catholics and Protestants in that eventful era. But I have, after many years of study and much sifting of evidence, tried to set out why certain things of lasting significance were done, and how it happened in the sixteenth century that Catholics rose against Catholics; to explain as best one can to twentieth-century readers why the numerous Protestant churches, autonomous and self-contained, exist and are outside the One, Holy, Roman, Catholic, and Apostolic Church whose head is Christ and whose supreme governor on earth is the vicar of Christ.

That a lasting and profound hurt was done to the Catholic Church by the withdrawal of the genius of German- and English-speaking nations from its communion is a conviction that must always cause unhappiness and disquiet. That within that sixteenth century the Catholic counter-reformation checked the Protestant advance, recovered so much of the ground lost to the Protestant separatists, and brought with the reform of morals and discipline the restatement of doctrine so long desired by good men, is a testimony of history to the faith of Catholics — that the Catholic Church being of divine institution is not to be overthrown utterly by the devices of any man.

J. C.

Chipping Campden,
Glos. England.

Luther and His Work

I

The World of Luther's Youth: 1483-1505

MARTIN LUTHER was born Anno Domini 1483. In the years of his boyhood and youth took place the voyages of Columbus to the West Indies with discovery of America and the establishment of the Spanish empire beyond the Atlantic; grave events to mark profoundly — for better, for worse — the history of Europe and the world. Others besides Columbus sailed adventurously to claim vast territories by right of occupation for their respective sovereigns. Cabot from Bristol reached the North American coast. Brazil fell to the Portuguese, while Vasco da Gama in the east sailed round the Cape of Good Hope and landing in India at Calicut brought that station under Portuguese supremacy.

The years of Martin Luther's youth are the years of the beginning of modern imperialism and strife between nations for world markets. With the rise of the Fugger family at Augsberg, they were the years also of the beginning of international finance. A period of restlessness, of excited lusting after gold, of fresh and all-engrossing human interests and obvious preoccupation with material goods. A time of change. The end of the Middle Ages.

The sanctions of feudalism were cast off beyond recovery

with the appearance of trained professional soldiers, Swiss, German *Landsknechts,* and later Spanish troops. These were men engaged to fight for their paymasters in any land of Europe; men to be hired by the highest bidder. A doctrine that a balance of power must be preserved was already affecting the politics of Europe before the close of the fifteenth century, and wars were waged and treaties made and broken by rulers influenced by that doctrine. In Italy, especially, the contest between Spanish and French forces, involving the sovereign pontiff of the states of the Church, meant half a century of warfare. The possession of the duchy of Milan, and of the kingdom of Naples implied predominance in Italy. It is impossible to discuss the question of how Lutheranism arose in Germany without considering the question of Italy, and the intrigues, treaties, and battles for Milan and Naples. The popes of the renaissance were something more than patrons of the fine arts; they were secular princes and their wars and political alliances were made for very definite secular ends. The danger of being hemmed in by foreign powers was always imminent.

Conditions in Italy

The papacy of Luther's youth and early manhood was no longer the instrument of French ambitions, as many had held it to be during the years of exile at Avignon. The bad years of the papal schism, when even good and pious Catholics could not tell who was the rightful pope and who the intruder, were over, leaving the papacy with weakened authority in the sight of kings and cardinals. Not that such popes as the Spanish Roderigo, of the Borgia family, Alexander VI, or that intrepid warrior Julius II admitted a lessened authority. They were no weaklings these popes of the renaissance, no creatures of European monarchs. In their aggressive individualism they were true types of that period of personal assertion; assertion manifested in the artist, the statesman, the sovereign. Vital energy fiercely asserted itself in the Italy of the renaissance. It was ruthless in its will power; the energy of Alexander VI deciding that power could best be strengthened by the elimination of enemies and the enrichment of the family.

Great patrons of literature and the arts were both these popes, Alexander VI and Julius II, as were their successors Leo X and Clement VII, but they were also men of keen political purpose, bent on achieving an independence for Italy, or at least an independence for the states of the Church, that would exclude invasion of liberties by German emperors or kings of France or Spain. It was partly to assist this policy that the nephews and nieces of popes were loaded with riches and estates. For the sake of this policy the welfare of Christendom as a whole was neglected, and to this policy of papal enrichment and papal power the welfare of Christendom was sacrificed. Within Italy itself the fiercest enmities were aroused and the most bitter hatreds kindled between the great families by the Borgian rule. Vendetta, waged by hired assassins, did its foul and murderous work, and Rome itself was the very seat of corruption. The popes of the renaissance, of the period of Luther's early manhood, were the last people to achieve those reforms in the Church that decent men and women cried out for all over Europe. Until cleansed of its domestic foulness and disorders how could Rome summon the general reforming Council that was so badly needed and by the few so greatly desired?

At the same time while Christian piety was distressed and remains shocked at the sensuality and worldliness of the renaissance papacy it is certain that the people of Rome were cheerfully indifferent. For the brief reign of the cardinal of Utrecht, Pope Adrian VI (1522–23), a man of pronounced holiness and the last non-Italian pope, provoked expression of popular disapproval and his death was hailed with relief. The citizens of Rome had no good word for the scholarly and humble-minded Fleming whom the conclave chose on the death of Leo X.

There is no need to stress the corruptions of the papacy of the renaissance. The facts set out in history are common knowledge. A cult of beauty that produced glories of architecture, of painting, and sculpture; that drew as pilgrims to the cities of Florence, Rome, and Venice, all in quest of the unimagined achievements of the artist, was accompanied by abundant moral depravity. Violent desire prevailed above the sanctions of conscience.

Abuses in the Church that in their flagrance compelled the cry for reform were left uncorrected, because at the very centre of Christendom there was preoccupation with family interests, with patronage of art and cultivation of letters, with wars and alliances to secure political independence for the papal states, and freedom in Italy from external rule. For all these things money was needed, and from every land in Christendom — from Germany in particular — was money extracted for papal needs. They appeared as Italian princes, seeking like other princes their own ends, these popes of the early sixteenth century; and we still see them in that character to-day. The vicar of Christ was masked, his spiritual dignity concealed. The high office of the pope was forgotten. Few men questioned the pope's supremacy in the Church; fewer still thought about it. When it came to be openly questioned and then denied quite a number of Catholics found they did not believe in it, and saw no reason to hold it.

Yet during all that bad time the leaven of justice was working; men and women filled with fair love, and fear and knowledge and holy hope were working and praying for the Catholic reform that was to come, the renewal long referred to as the counter-reformation. To these men and women, holy and humble of heart, the Catholic Faith was objective truth. The doctrine that the Church of Christ was one and indivisible, its unity, assured by the headship of St. Peter's successor, could not be upset by deplorable failings in one or more of the duly elected successors. Nor was there a renaissance pope who did not recognise and fully acknowledge the sanctity in others while fully aware of his own shortcomings and irregularities. St. Anselm was canonised by Pope Alexander VI. St. Bruno, founder of the Carthusians, by Pope Leo X.

The works of charity, the renewal of discipline in the religious orders and among the clergy, the deepening of the spiritual life in the laity — the activity that in Italy itself was expressed in these various ways and is the seed of what now we call the Catholic Reformation, was never discouraged by the popes; and there were always cardinals of godly life to encourage it. But the popes of the renaissance needed money, and money they would have. They knew there was no serving of God and mammon, and preferring the latter, the service of mammon brought heavy punishment.

The feuds, ambitions, and rivalries of the powerful families of Borgia and Rovere, of Medici and Colonna belong to the history of the papacy and of Italy. Outstanding is the figure of Pope Alexander VI, that singularly handsome and dignified pontiff, as hard working as he was unscrupulous, no hypocrite (not for his personal holiness nor for his scathing rebukes of the pope's scandalous way of living was Savanorola, the Dominican friar of Florence burnt, but for his pro-French politics in opposition to Alexander's policy), self-indulgent to the expression of fierce primitive instincts, unconcerned to preserve the chastity required of a priest, using his position for the accomplishment of political ends, seeking as an earthly prince to raise his kingdom to an independence secure and lasting, "so blending," in the words of Lord Acton, "his spiritual and temporal authority as to apply the resources of the one to the purposes of the other." During his reign we find the papacy with its spiritual authority at the lowest.

His successor, Julius II, nephew of Pope Sixtus IV, was no friend to the Borgias, though he pursued the Borgian policy. Skilful and energetic soldier, Julius in alliance with

France and the Emperor Maximilian must needs make war on the Venetian republic and reduce its pride, because he judged that Venice, and Venice alone, stood in the way of a free Italy and the full independence of the papal dominions. When France threatened the political independence of the papacy then Julius made war on France. On the French cardinals summoning a general council at Pisa, the pope retaliated by calling a Council at the Lateran, and pronouncing excommunications on his opponents.

Julius was also moved to rebuild the great church of St. Peter's in Rome and make the eternal city all glorious by the immortal genius of the artists he employed. He, like Alexander, required money for his undertakings.

If Leo X — cardinal at 14 and not even a priest when elected pope — cared less for European politics and more for the literature of the past than his predecessor, he was all unaware of the crisis that approached and of the tragedy of Luther enacted in his reign. Fastidious in his tastes, extravagant in his admiration for the classics of ancient Greece and Rome, of Cicero in particular, Leo went his way while the German reformers took theirs. It was in the reign of Leo X the revolt started that broke up Christendom and separated so many nations from the unity of the Catholic Church. And in his reign the sultan Solyman, the Magnificent, advanced in Europe and took Belgrade.

Pope Adrian VI was too old and his reign too short for the reforms that might yet have saved the Church from the loss of its northern peoples and Europe from the Turkish advance and the Turkish supremacy in the eastern Mediterranean. He saw the evil and deplored it; the more because he had neither power nor influence to uproot financial abuses profitable to Rome.

When another member of the Medici family, Clement VII, nephew of Leo X, sat on the papal throne the Lutheran revolution was accomplished. The reign was disastrous for Christendom and to Clement. It saw the Turks at the gates of Vienna, and the pope's intrigues and alliance provoked the Emperor Charles V to a war that brought imperial armies into Italy and to the sack of Rome. With that appalling event — its horrors are hardly to be exaggerated — the renaissance was ended in Italy. In less than twenty years the long frustrated general council, the council of Trent, would hold its first session.

The characters and deeds of these popes of the renaissance, their blindness to the signs of the times, their indifference to all save personal or political advantage — such matters belong to the history of the papacy and of Europe. They are noted here because they help to explain why Rome was totally unable to initiate reform and equally unable to cope with the demand for reform when Luther began his protests.

Similarly must we judge of the treaties and alliances made by these popes and of their relations with the emperor and the kings of France and England. The papal foreign policy and diplomacy of the years of renaissance belong to the history of Europe. But they vitally affected the rise and course of the Protestant reformation in Germany because they made the pope appear in the sight of German princes as no more than a foreign and often an unfriendly power.

Conditions in Germany

Conditions in Germany, conditions political, social, economic, and religious, in the early years of the sixteenth century must also be considered. Amongst clergy and laity many minds were receptive to anti-papal propaganda, favourable to an anti-papal revolt. The conditions in Germany largely explain this receptiveness and account for the favour that Luther won with compatriots.

Politically the Germany that through its seven electors made Maximilian emperor and twenty-seven years later the youthful Charles V, was a conglomeration of independent states and free cities. The former ruled by princes, many of whom were bishops, absolute lords of vast territorial estates. These prince-bishops accepted the pope's spiritual supremacy with no more fervour than they admitted the emperor's political authority. Papal supremacy and imperial authority alike were part of the existing order.

The free cities were either self-governing republics owing allegiance to none save the emperor, or they were, in varying degrees, semi-independent communities placed within the dominions of secular princes and prince-bishops. In the Hanseatic League the cities had their own self-government, and were united for commercial ends.

Beyond principalities and prince-bishoprics and free cities were the free knights, living as robber chieftains in their castles. Nominally the emperor's subjects, these knights were in reality bandits; raiders of cities, plundering where they could. The disturbing and predatory existence of the free knights was only brought to an end by the employment of cannon.

Over this loosely bound confederation of states the Hapsburg emperors, Maximilian and his grandson Charles V, were elected to reign. It was an empire that had no common law, no common parliament. The imperial council and the diet which consisted of princes, electors, and the free cities, might meet on the emperor's summons and pass decrees; there was no power to enforce the decrees, no common will to desire enforcement.

The Hapsburg emperors, rulers of territories that sprawled all over Europe, sovereigns of vast Spanish dominions in the New World, had only a partial interest in the empire. Spain, the Netherlands, Burgundy with its long-standing antagonism to the royal house of Valois, brought military responsibilities to Maximilian and to Charles. The activities of the most Christian kings of France kept the Hapsburg emperors for ever on the alert, and deflected the forces required to oppose the Turkish advance. Charles, a youth of sixteen when proclaimed king of Spain and but twenty when elected emperor, inherited Hapsburg and imperial interests not always to be reconciled. Hence imperial interests suffered because Spanish and Austrian Hapsburg territories — the latter ceded to his brother Ferdinand — claimed the prior attention of Charles.

Charles indeed was always something of an alien in the empire. He never learnt to speak the German of his subjects. Though the danger from Islam was imminent, with the Turks pressing hard in Hungary, the emperor's nominal dependents could not be induced to levy troops for imperial purposes. Principalities and free cities acknowledged the danger from the Turkish advance and deplored the situation but gave no adequate help when the emperor called for assistance. Feudalism had crumbled beyond restoration. The feudal system was transformed into an unchecked tyranny of nobles who were absolute rulers within their own territories. From this tyranny whether exercised with justice and mildness or with harshness and rapacity the tenants of elector, prince-bishop, and duke, had no court of appeal. Princes and petty nobles alike were absolute rulers and allowed no imperial right of interference. They simply could not be persuaded to levy troops for the emperor, either for wars in Italy or for campaigns against the Turk.

As Charles V, great emperor that he was, put the good estate of the widely scattered realms of the house of Hapsburg before other political ends, giving a secondary consideration to the safety and prosperity of the holy Roman empire, so electoral dukes and prince-bishops with lesser nobles and burghers of free cities put each their local and territorial advantage first and gave imperial policy the second place. No common aim bound the rulers of these German estates and cities so that when Luther challenged the faith and unity of Christendom with his new "evangel" no common front opposed him. Princes — whether bishops or laymen — were as other territorial magnates in deciding for or against Luther. The cities of the Hanseatic League were as variously divided when the Lutheran conflict became acute. Politically then the ties of empire under Maximilian and under Charles V were insubstantial. Ecclesiastical disintegration became a rapid process in a land where political divisions were plentiful, where each ruler, jealous of his own sovereign rights, assented but tepidly to a theory of imperial overlordship. Loyalty to emperor as to pope was without warmth.

If politically the conditions in Germany were favourable to Luther's protest, social conditions were no less provocative of revolt.

Socially the nobles were widely separated from their tenants, and kept deeply apart from the peasants by laws and customs that meant serfdom for the labourer without hope of emergence to freedom. So resolute were the nobles to exclude from their caste persons of less exalted rank and ancestry that they were able to restrict the episcopate to members of the nobility. This was done by the canon laws that required all cathedral chapters — with whom rested the nomination of the bishop when a see became vacant — to be born of noble parents and to be able to prove the nobility of their grandparents. Hence it happened that the prince-bishops so nominated were generally no better and no worse than the rest of the ruling nobles.

If a scholar and zealous pastor can be named among the bishops of the empire in the early sixteenth century — as Berthold, archbishop of Mainz, is at once remembered — the majority were prelates who ignored Christian morals and cared nothing for Catholic theology. Assured of preserving the rule over their dominions and the emoluments of their office these bishops would cheerfully have resigned their ecclesiastical state. As it was they hunted and feasted and kept mistresses as their fellow nobles did, leaving the duties and obligations of their high spiritual calling for the most part unfulfilled. And then it often happened that cathedral chapters, their own birth certificates beyond reproach, were persuaded to nominate to vacant sees the illegitimate sons of princes. While these proceedings brought wealth and power to men otherwise unprovided with the good things of this world, it was obviously not to the advantage of the church to be thus ill-shepherded. Besides the old medieval way brought many a peasant's son to the priesthood and hindered no poor man's son from reaching the cardinalate or even the papal throne itself. The empire under Maximilian and Charles V revealed, in this exclusion of all but nobles from the episcopate, the existence of class feeling and class hatred that was bound to manifest explosive results. The revolutionary communism of Anabaptists was the reply to anti-social and unjust laws.

Yet while sorry abuses in the Church were evident in Germany there was far from general consent to the unhappy state of affairs. These abuses in fact were felt to be an intolerable reproach to the Christian people of God, by many a parish priest and devout layman. Acquiescence in the face of gross clerical disorders is disproved by the definite and irrepressible demand for ecclesiastical reform so frequently heard. Not a reform of doctrinal statement; of enlargement or curtailment of Catholic creeds; but a reform of clerical morals and church discipline. Such a reform could only be accomplished by a general council; but to call a general council was not to the minds of renaissance popes; since in the papacy itself reform must first begin. Besides Pope Julius II had held his general council of the Lateran and this council had only been dissolved by Leo X with the announcement that all necessary reforms had been completed. (The proceedings of this council of the Lateran were held of no account in the empire.) Again, had the popes been willing to call a general council; no general council could meet without the co-operation of the emperor and the French king and this necessary co-operation was absent.

Not till the sacred unity of the Church had been rent beyond mending could the general council on which men set their hopes be assembled.

To what extent, we may here ask, was the demand for reform within the Church a reform of morals and discipline, and not a restatement of doctrinal belief or credal change, influenced by the revival of learning in Germany?

Influence of the Renaissance

While in Italy the renaissance brought a neopaganism; and in England the revival of learning was bound up with a richer spirituality in the persons of Dean Colet, St. John Fisher, and St. Thomas More; in Germany the response to the renaissance was expressed in humanism. The keenness of a few for the classical learning we call the humanities, rather than any renewal of the Christian life, was the fruit of the renaissance in Germany. Four men may be named as conspicuous figures in the renaissance: Erasmus (1467–1536), John Reuchlin (1455–1522), Ulrich von Hutten, and Philip Melanchthon. Men sharply divided in theological opinions, unlike in character, and wide apart in any estimate of ability.

Erasmus, of European reputation in his own day, still holds and must for ever hold a high place in the history of learning. Reuchlin, appreciated for his scholarship by contemporaries and notably by the English humanists, was rather by accident than by choice brought into prominence.

The once popular epigram "Erasmus laid the egg that Luther hatched" suggested that but for the revival of learning there would have been no Protestant reformation. An opinion hardly to be justified when the evidence is examined. Luther built on no foundation of humanism. His revolt was no protest by a man of letters. The war he waged was something far removed from the quarrels of literary men, though these quarrels were acrid and scurrilous enough at times and vituperation is a mark of all renaissance controversy.

Erasmus it is true was a hostile critic of monks. He claimed that, as an orphan, he had been constrained to become a monk of the Order of Canons Regular of St. Augustine, and at nineteen was solemnly professed. The monastic environment never suited him. When a schoolboy at Deventer his unusual gift for scholarship had been noted and encouraged; the interest of the young Erasmus was directed to the study of the classics and the Fathers. Unfortunately the canons regular in the monastery of Stein, so far as we may credit his description,[1] were neither given to learning nor heartily inclined to the exercise of the intelligence. It was enough for them to keep the rule and attend to the external practices of the religious life. Erasmus thus came to be treated as many a youth at school or college may be treated who prefers study to games, and zealous for books, is contemptuous of the cult of athletics. There was unconcealed resentment, he tells us, in the monastery at Stein. Who was this young man that he should set himself up as a scholar-monk? Why should he want to be different from his fellows in religion?

Erasmus has described in bitter words the resentment and disapproval that surrounded him. To make matters worse he suffered horribly from the diet and his impaired digestion was still further weakened. Happily for Erasmus his reputation as a Latin scholar carried him from the priory at Stein to the post of bishop's secretary at Cambrai and there he remained five years. Nor was there any return to the priory and in due course of time the pope gave Erasmus full release from the obligations of the rule of the canons regular.

Whatever we may think of the monks at Stein, no array

---

[1]See *Erasmus* by Christopher Hollis (U.S.A., 1933) for an examination that throws doubt on the account given by Erasmus of conditions at Stein.

of terms can express adequately the contempt of Erasmus for the intellectual standards of contemporary monasticism. In fact it is only too certain that the earlier profound discussions of the eternal truths of theology had dwindled to arguments often as trivial as they were absurd. Scholasticism, the scholastic method, and philosophy — splendid triumphs of the mind in the middle ages — had fallen on evil days. With the loss of interest in things of the mind had gone decay in the spiritual life of the religious orders — a common experience in all ages. Erasmus was not alone in marking these defects. No doubt he wrote the more severely from memories of an unpleasant personal kind. At all events monasticism for Erasmus implied a deadly routine; religious services mechanically performed; meals that induced dyspepsia; conversation futile and irritating; parade of an ignorance as gross as it was ludicrous.

Now, of course, there was nothing remarkable in an attack on current monasticism by a Catholic writer. All through the later middle ages monks and friars had been lampooned both in prose and verse for their shortcomings. When Europe was Catholic, and it was inconceivable that the Christian church could be other than Catholic, many words were uttered, many things published in frank disparagement of contemporary manners and morals; more particularly of clerical bad manners and lax morals. Within the domestic circle the jest may go round, the joke be pointed, much be profanely spoken at the expense of members of the family that would be intolerable were strangers present, and would be highly resented as impertinence if delivered by an alien.

But Erasmus was a priest when he wrote and published with its dedicatory epistle to Sir Thomas More the *Encomium Moriae,* "In Praise of Folly," and he had been a monk. It is true the book was in Latin and not for popular consumption, though it became the most popular of all the writings of Erasmus. So far was the book from being taken seriously at the time (1512) that Pope Leo X was delighted with it and graciously accepted the dedication of Erasmus's Greek Testament which followed a few years later. Nevertheless when Luther started the disintegration of the religious orders in Germany, when the work of destruction came to be pursued by Henry VIII in England and by rulers in the Scandinavian countries, it may be urged that the biting satire of the *Encomium* had both assisted in many quarters the anti-monastic prejudice and discouraged the display of sympathy for an institution held in reverence from the first centuries of Christianity. The monastery and the convent were as old as the Catholic Church in Germany. Yet the show of indifference was pitiful when monks and nuns mocked at their vows and turned Protestant, surrendered their houses or were forcibly dispersed on the Lutheran advance. Erasmus, the most forcible because the most distinguished critic, attacked the enfeebled spiritual life of the time, the formalism of religion, as he and others saw it. There was no attack on the religious orders in themselves. They needed a new spirit rather than new constitutions. Erasmus proclaimed the disease, he propounded no cure.

Reuchlin was never an outstanding figure in the world of letters, neither did he exercise the influence of Erasmus. A typical scholar of the renaissance, a German humanist, with an abiding interest in philology rather than in theology, Reuchlin, by profession a lawyer, was no pioneer of Lutheran doctrine. As a lover of the literature of the ancients, as an earnest student of Hebrew, he won the friendship and respect of Erasmus, and of Bishop Fisher, of Sir Thomas More, and of Cardinal Pole; only by accident did Reuchlin achieve the prominence thrust upon him. Collision with that exceedingly active person John Pfefferkorn, a converted Jew, broke up the peace and quiet of Reuchlin's judicial and studious life. For Pfefferkorn, raging fiercely against the faith and morals of Judaism, demanded the destruction of all Hebrew books wherever found in Germany, and the right to search for them. The Emperor Maximilian was persuaded in 1509 to give Pfefferkorn a mandate for this inquisitorial work, but the imperial mandate was modified by the attitude of Ulrich, archbishop of Mainz, and Reuchlin with other learned men from the universities of Mainz, Cologne, Erfurt, and Trier, was called upon to deliver opinions on the matter.

Reuchlin, absorbed in Hebrew studies and immensely preoccupied with the *Talmud* and the mystical books of the *Cabbala,* found this anti-Semite campaign utterly repellent. Against his will he was dragged into public controversy with Pfefferkorn and a war of pamphlets went on for years with appeals to Rome for Reuchlin's condemnation. Against his will Reuchlin was made to appear as the champion of free learning and his opponents as upholders of ignorance and bigotry. That the humanists could write with all the violence and bitterness of the men who traduced them, and with far more skill, was manifest when the *Epistolae Obscurorum Virorum,* "Letters of Obscure Men," were published in 1515 and 1516. Ulrich von Hutten is the principal name in connection with the savage and entirely pitiless satire of the letters. And von Hutten, himself a knight with neither money nor lands, hating the dull dislike of the clergy to the newer studies, hating the power of the clergy, hating the heavy financial payments to the curia at Rome, hating also the restraints of authority and the discipline of the Catholic Church, naturally, being the anti-clerical that he was, gave Luther wholehearted support and died outside the Church.

Reuchlin, from the mere fact that he was assailed by Pfefferkorn and the ruck of nonliterary ecclesiastics, was extolled, long after his death, as "the father of the German Reformation." No title is less deserved or more inaccurate. Reuchlin had no quarrel with authority and was content in the controversy with Pfefferkorn that the pope should judge the dispute. Neither had he the least inclination to question or doubt the articles of the Catholic Faith or criticise current church practices. The abuses and corruptions of the age provoked no censure from Reuchlin. No man was less inclined to meddle with the moral delinquencies of his neighbours or sit in judgment on his fellows. Primarily a scholar, essentially a man of study and the lecture hall, Reuchlin, in his old age professor of Hebrew in the recently created University of Tübingen, was by no means attracted to the Lutheran revolt. So repugnant were the doings at Wittenberg to Reuchlin that when his great-nephew, Philip Melanchthon, joined Luther, the professor of Hebrew was as profoundly vexed as he was deeply disappointed, with the result that Melanchthon did not inherit the library of books his uncle had spent a lifetime in collecting. While Reuchlin thus expressed positively a dislike and disapproval of the Lutheran outbreak, Ulrich von Hutten in reply voiced the disappointment of the younger anti-clerical humanists at Reuchlin's attitude.

The truth probably is that John Reuchlin, thrown on his defence by Pfefferkorn and writing not in Latin but in German, did help to discredit ecclesiastical authority that would have silenced him if it could. But that authority was already widely discredited by its rapacity, ignorance, and lack of spirituality. The great mass of the clergy in Germany, with some notable exceptions, did not regard sympathetically that general love of secular learning we call humanism, while the humanists generally did not include theological knowledge in their range of studies. Into the theological conflict, therefore, the humanists were dragged unwillingly and unwittingly. If various current practices in the Church against which Luther first inveighed were obnoxious to the humanists they were ill-prepared to defend Catholic doctrine when Luther passed from attacking abuses to the assault on Catholic unity. In fact theological strife was the one thing to be avoided by humanists, who pursued the paths of learning for learning's sake and sought enlightenment by patient study. To promote culture not breed discord was their aim. And like all philosophers in a time of war, the humanists were ignored and insulted when the issue of Luther versus Rome was set.

Erasmus wrote sympathetically of Luther and nothing against him, till, driven by the latter's repudiation of free will, he came out in defence of the orthodox Catholic philosophy. An ill-disciplined anti-clerical layman, von Hutten for instance, could openly rejoice at the schism in the Church caused by Luther's campaign. But Melanchthon, coming as a young man under the personal influence of Luther at Wittenberg and remaining under that influence, was no preacher of revolt. Melanchthon indeed lived to be a pillar of strength to the new evangelical church of Germany; but his very moderation was his power, for it gave the note of comprehensiveness to the Lutheran creed and appealed to common-sense men, baptised and brought up in the Catholic Church but never trained in the Catholic Faith or taught the significance of Christian doctrine and the elements of church history. Lutheranism expounded by the moderation of Melanchthon was made acceptable as a "religion of all sensible men," to the wrath of the stricter sects of Calvinists and Zwinglians, who abhorred such compromise as Puritans abhorred the comprehensiveness of the Church of England. Melanchthon would never have initiated revolt. Neither zest for theological controversy nor zeal for the overthrow of papal authority and departure from the established unity of Christendom can justly be attributed to Philip Melanchthon. But humanism could produce men eminently susceptible to emotional appeal, and Luther's invitation to abandon the old Catholic order, with its restraints and traditional discipline, for what was called "the liberty of the Gospel" was not displeasing to men like Melanchthon.

The Hussites

Two other contributions to unrest must be included in the outline of conditions in Germany in the years of Luther's early manhood. Danger to the very existence of the empire was always present from the Turkish advance, and there was also the threat to Christian unity from Bohemia, where the followers of Huss maintained an organised resistance to Catholic authority and were in time to become a definitely Protestant society. The Brethren, as the Bohemian Hussites were called, while politically within the empire were in race and speech apart from the rest of Germany. The memory of the burning of Huss at the council of Constance and of the horrors of the wars that followed were cause enough for silence and the avoidance of all open profession of Hussite doctrine outside Bohemia. Yet that doctrine, theologically vague, ill defined, a bundle of personal beliefs, had stray adherents in numerous places, and when Luther first read the works of Huss — to whom he was in no way indebted for his own doctrine—he declared that all unknowing he had long been a Hussite.

The politico-social doctrine of Huss, akin to Wycliff's dominion of grace, that wealth pertained only to the good, had also its disciples among forerunners of the leaders of Anabaptists and warring peasants. Numerically of no account, and without influence among humanists or the princes of the empire, the people who inclined to the Hussite doctrine within the empire could be relied upon to support any movement that was anti-papal and anti-clerical. Inevitably they rallied to Luther in his hour of revolt.

Witchcraft and Sorcery

With the decline of the middle ages, in the fifteenth century, the existence in Germany of a belief in witchcraft is apparent. Under the sinister influence of this belief men and women were brought to trial and condemned as witches or sorcerers. Suspected and denounced by their neighbours it was hard to get an acquittal. Not that Germany alone allowed and encouraged the persecution of witches, for in other lands in Europe there is evidence that fear and hate wrought similar work. But the witch trials in Germany were far worse than elsewhere and the persecution far more extensive.

Nor did Luther and the setting up of his evangelical church help matters, while Calvin's reform at Geneva produced ultimately the worst persecution of all. Protestantism appealed to the Old Testament in support of its belief in witchcraft and in justification of its penal code. (But the imperial diet under Charles V at Ratisbon, in 1532, pronounced sorcery a criminal offence.) Fear and hate allied with ignorance and superstition are apt to run eagerly to cruelty when empowered by the prejudices of those in authority and protected by a callous and indifferent public opinion. The renaissance with its love of letters and its enjoyment of beauty disproves the notion that mental culture and pride of intellect can either banish superstition or extinguish that lust for inflicting torture, that pleasurable excitement in the suffering of others we now call "sadism."

The bull of Pope Innocent VIII, issued at the end of 1484, though it initiated nothing not already widely accepted in Catholic Europe, did untold harm in Germany. This bull and the Witch Hammer, *Malleus Maleficarum,* published in 1486, encouraged persecution, and the Emperor Maximilian supported the two inquisitors sent by the pope. It was of one of these inquisitors (Henry Institoris) that the bishop of Brixen wrote gravely: "I am distressed about this monk. I find in the pope's bull that he has been inquisitor before, under a number of popes, but he seemed to me when I heard him here at Brixen with the chapter, to have become quite childish through old age." The University of Cologne regarded the bull unfavourably.

Only four professors could be found to give even a qualified approval.

Malleus Maleficarum, the work of the other inquisitor, James Sprenger, was received with satisfaction by all who wanted official sanction for the hunting to death of witches. The mischief done by this book is not to be estimated. It gave the stamp of authority to the base credulities that raged in so many German towns and villages. The first part of this deplorable treatise dealt with the reality of witchcraft, which was defined as heresy and worse. The third part was concerned with the conduct of the witch trials. Heresy was not made the central point of the offence; it was *maleficium,* the sorcery, that worked injury and was to be punished; hence it was advised that witch trials should be generally relegated to the secular courts. The animus against women was not hidden and for every one man burnt ten women suffered at the stake. Statistics of the number of victims in the first twenty years of the sixteenth century do not exist, and the figures collected are quite inadequate. The rack was the form of torture commonly employed. Half a century later when witch trials and the preliminary torture were prevalent all over Germany, a German Jesuit, Frederick von Spee, could write: "Woe to the poor wretch who has once set foot in the torture chamber! He will not be let out again till he has confessed everything imaginable. I have often thought to myself that the reason why we are not all of us avowed sorcerers is only that torture has never fallen to our lot. Very true is the boast recently made by the inquisitor of a great prince, that if the pope himself should come under his hands and his torturings, even his Holiness himself would end in confessing himself a sorcerer."

From their first coming to Germany and throughout the Catholic counter-reformation the Jesuits never gave the slightest encouragement to the witch trials, and Protestant pastors can be named who played an equally honourable part in withstanding the current ideas of sorcery and witchcraft. But in general the superstition that witches and sorcerers did hold criminal intercourse with evil spirits for the accomplishment of superhuman deeds was a fixed idea with most of the inquisitors and judges. So that at the outset of a witch trial they were convinced of the guilt of the accused and equally convinced that it was their duty to wring out a confession of guilt by persistent torture.

The belief in magic and sorcery was amazingly widespread, and the crimes commonly alleged against accused persons were usually injury to their neighbours. Destroying crops by hailstorms, stealing and killing children, and changing themselves and others into black he-goats were the charges that most frequently brought conviction.

Jannsen's summary of the whole shocking business may be quoted:[2] "The number of innocent victims was out of all proportion to the guilty. In the first place in the witch trials, in many cases, it is a question of mentally afflicted persons, suffering from illusions of sight or hearing, and all that they say about the devil and his dominion over all mental and bodily life, about devil's arts and devil's brides and devil's sabbaths and orgies is simply what they had heard from their youth up and had come in consequence to think they had themselves experienced. Of mental diseases however the people of that age, speaking generally, had little understanding; they regarded such diseases as something contrary to nature, as evidence of punishable magic or necromantic influences; not seldom also other diseases, epilepsy, hysteric seizures or somnambulism were treated as sorcery and witchcraft and their victims burnt to death.

"The belief in witchcraft and sorcery, by which all brains were possessed, and the concomitant terror of witches that had become a regular popular craze were perpetually fed and strengthened on the one hand by the growing demoral-

---

[2] *History of the German People,* English translation, Vol. VI.

ization around, while on the other hand they were an abundant source of vice and depravity, of greed, calumny, faithlessness, bloodthirstiness and murder. In trials innumerable the moral depravity of the torturers, the officials, judges and clerks play a disgraceful part, whilst in case after case, the whole judicial procedure against the witches was conducted in such a manner that many thousands of innocent victims were driven, mad with torture, to the stake, and out of every funeral pile rose a fresh crop of witches."

With hardly an exception it was the poor and the old, not the rich and the young, who suffered.

It is necessary to recall both the belief in witches and the sanctions awarded to that belief by the papal inquisitor and the *Malleus Maleficarum* to appreciate the conditions in the Germany of Luther's youth. Perhaps the more necessary, since in the histories of the Protestant reformation and of the life and times of Martin Luther the witch trials and the century of horrors that followed the bull of Pope Innocent are not commonly intruded.[3] The ignorance and cruelty that feasted on the torture of the unhappy persons charged with witchcraft and sorcery — ten women to one man, old rather than young, poor rather than rich — are not to be dismissed as "medieval." They appear with the decay of theology and the rise of humanism at the end of the middle ages, and reveal the low estate of Catholic faith and Christian morals. Nor did Protestantism bring enlightenment or greater charity. Protestants burnt few heretics but they prolonged and extended the torture and killing of witches. From Great Britain the witch trials were carried to America by Puritans seeking liberty of conscience.

To sum up. It is the end of the middle ages and the breakup of feudalism for Europe at the beginning of the sixteenth century. A time of unrest, a time of change, and of engross-

---

[3]How much has been written concerning the Spanish Inquisition, how little, of the victims sacrificed at the German witch trials!

ing human activities everywhere. Voyages westward had discovered America with results incalculable. The wealth of gold and silver imported to Spain from her new conquests brought economic consequences that affected all Europe. With the discoveries made by English and Portuguese explorers may be recorded the beginning of modern imperialism, of contest for world markets and of international finance.

Similarly, in Italy, may be noted the beginning of the doctrine that a balance of power must be preserved in Europe, with France, the Hapsburg emperors, and the papacy, by alliances, treaties, and wars, straining to adjust and preserve that balance. Emperors and French kings — Hapsburg and Valois — aware of old hostility the one to the other, were in the meantime both seeking territorial dominion in Italy, while the popes remained resolutely determined not to be hemmed in by king or emperor but to strengthen papal independence.

It is also the time of the renaissance. The popes are not merely political sovereigns playing their part in the politics of Europe, they are also great patrons of art and letters, by no means conspicuously interested in moral theology or distressed at corruption and abuses in the Church.

Always on the east the Turkish advance threatens Christendom and becomes increasingly powerful in the Mediterranean Sea.

In Germany political and economic conditions in the loose confederation of the empire are not favourable to a papacy perpetually calling out for money, often at war with the emperor, and when challenged by the demand for reform ignoring both challenge and demand. Socially the German hierarchy consisting of secular princes, not all of exemplary private character, was utterly aloof from peasants and townspeople. Theological studies in monasteries and priories were at the ebb. Scholasticism had petered out in trivialities and futile questions. The laity thus shepherded were but scantily taught the rudiments of Christian faith and morals. In fact while millions of God-fearing Germans held loyally to the Catholic Faith, multitudes grew up in ignorance.

The renaissance in Germany did not mean an outbreak of neopaganism as it did in Italy; neither did it mean a deepening of the Christian life. Its expression was a revived interest in classical studies and that learning we call the humanities. It was naturally regarded with aversion by a priesthood, unlearned and not trained to desire learning. Erasmus, pre-eminent in Europe, enjoyed no great esteem among clerical compatriots; and Erasmus and other German humanists were ill prepared for the theological controversy raised by Luther.

Within the empire there was little tendency beyond the frontiers of Bohemia to follow or take an interest in the doctrines of Huss. But those doctrines had adherents; men and women attracted by mystical visions of a Christian communist society were alienated from Catholic creeds and discipline.

The ignorance and superstition of all classes of the empire were exploited by a minority not less ignorant, not more superstitious, but more cruel in the persecution of witches and sorcerers from the close of the fifteenth century.

In this Europe of excited secular interests, in an empire of conflicting ambitions, among a Catholic people suffering under the disability of a worldly episcopate and an ill-taught clergy, Martin Luther, an Augustinian monk at Wittenberg, emerged from his priory at Wittenberg to accomplish in his own lifetime the breakup of Christendom, and cause (in the words of Maritain) "that immense disaster for humanity, the Protestant Reformation." For humanity an immense disaster; for the Catholic Church the call, not disregarded, to awake to righteousness.

Luther and the men who helped in the work of disruption looked for the complete and speedy extinction of the papacy, and awaited confidently the general acceptance by Christians of the new reformed confession of belief. Protestants, as the members of reformed churches came to be called, felt assured that the pope being anti-Christ must quickly be banished from the earth; then throughout Europe the reformed religion would triumph.

This confident hope was swiftly shattered. Protestants divided from the first into many sections and subsections were soon violently separated from each other on vital questions of dogma and discipline, and have never been joined in one communion and fellowship. The papacy renewed its strength; cleansed of disorders, healed of its infirmities, it recovered the allegiance of multitudes. The Catholic Church, in the counter-reformation, revealed itself incapable of the death its enemies foretold. "And doomed to death though fated not to die," to quote John Dryden's classic line, the Catholic Church of that same sixteenth century, so far from being in mortal sickness, bore witness in its saints and martyrs to fresh vitality. The seeds of the Catholic counter-reformation sown in the evil time that preceded the Lutheran revolt were to bear fruit abundantly.

But the disaster for humanity remains unrepaired. And the loss to the Catholic Church of its German, Scandinavian, and British Christians with their descendants in America is also unrepaired.

II

Martin Luther — Augustinian Monk: 1505-1517

WHEN AT the age of twenty-two Martin Luther entered the monastery at Erfurt to become a novice in the order of the Augustinian Hermits he was already a graduate of the university in that town. On the threshold of what promised to be a successful career as an advocate, a safe and profitable career, the peasant lad, the son of a peasant — as he liked to describe himself in after years — turned from the world and from all that the world could offer to take the vows of chastity, poverty, and obedience and after a year of consideration to take them solemnly for life. No one persuaded him to this step, the call did not come from friend or neighbour; clerical influence cannot be alleged. His father utterly disapproved, and was long in being reconciled to what appeared a rash and headstrong decision.

Luther himself always maintained that his entrance into religion was the fulfilment of a vow taken in a moment of fear and terror; a vow he said he soon repented of, though he would not break it. Overtaken by a violent thunderstorm and believing himself in danger of death — a thunderbolt or an appalling flash of lightning made him fall to the ground — Luther called upon St. Anne to help him. With the invocation went the vow: "Help me and I will become a monk." He was alone when this crisis occurred and the "influence of an electric disturbance on the nervous system" is an accepted explanation of what Luther came to regard as a call from Heaven, a personal revelation of the divine will.

Emotional and nervous from childhood (his father, a stern man, his mother, at times violent in her correction of childish faults, imposed repression), subject to recurring fits of melancholy and moods of despair, liable to acute irritation when contradicted and to outbursts of verbal rage, Martin Luther was nevertheless for twelve years an active and useful monk of the Augustinian order; respected and trusted by his fellows in religion; greatly beloved by von Staupitz, the superior of the order in Germany. His exceptional abilities were recognised. He was plainly a coming man, an ornament to the Augustinians, a shining light. Dr. Staupitz sent him to Wittenberg, the new Catholic university founded by Frederick of Saxony, which was largely in the hands of the Augustinians, to lecture on philosophy. On receiving his doctor's degree, at an unusually early age, Luther became professor of Biblical studies — a permanent appointment. That Luther had the confidence of his fellow monks was proved by their sending him to Rome as their envoy at the time when the order was excited by internal questions of discipline. The Augustinians in Germany, like the Franciscans, were of two branches; the more strict being called Observantines, who followed the closer keeping of the rule of the order, while the remaining were non-Observantine priories and were considered relaxed. Staupitz endeavoured to unite the two branches and this was strenuously opposed by the Observantines. Erfurt was Observantine and Luther was chosen to carry an appeal to the General of the order in Rome. The appeal was ignored and Luther on his return to Wittenberg became a supporter of Staupitz.

Whatever the corruptions elsewhere, Luther nowhere suggests that the priory at Erfurt or indeed other houses of the Augustinians came short of the standard of the order. While for Staupitz, who never joined the revolt and died a Benedictine abbot at Salzburg, he retained a lasting affection.

On the journey to Rome and within the eternal city much that he heard and saw both depressed and distressed Luther, but there was also much that he enjoyed. Not the wonders of art — for Luther was always insensitive to art, music excepted — but the feeling that he was on holy ground moved him to enthusiasm. All that a pilgrim could do in his four weeks' stay was done by Martin Luther. Years later he could recall things he heard in talk with Germans resident in Rome of the low morals of the clergy and of the amazing immoralities at the papal court of Alexander VI; but nothing at the time even remotely suggests that Luther was stirred to revolt or given an inclination to break with ecclesiastical authority by his visit to Rome.

Not from without but from within came the urge that drove Luther far from Catholic unity, that set him travelling a road strange and new, a road that led him neither he nor his disciples could tell whither. To picture Luther as a man incited by the abuses he saw around him to become a reformer (and that is how he is depicted in the minds of millions) or to figure him aroused by monastic superstitions and clerical corruptions to proclaim a purer religion (and Luther is still so figured in more than one Protestant textbook) is to caricature the real Martin Luther and to mistake altogether the course of his life. It is the merest burlesque of the true story of this exceptionally nervous and introspective yet fiercely energetic monk of Wittenberg, Dr. Martin Luther, of the order of Augustinian Hermits, to see him as a good and learned man of peaceful disposition stirred from the quiet life of the cloisters by a divine inspiration that compelled him to arise and proclaim the gospel of Christ to a nation sunk in darkness. It is not a portrait of himself that Luther would recognise. The character, as we know from contemporaries and from Luther's own writings, was something vastly different. Turbulent and disquieted in mind, and therefore unhappy because of internal trouble, not because of external corruptions in the Church, Luther continued in this state till he believed he had found in certain epistles of St. Paul the healing his soul sought. With that supposed healing came the gradual discontent with Catholic practice and final revulsion from Catholic Faith. But there was no thought of future separation from the Catholic unity when Luther first found what was to him healing doctrine, no idea of cleaving to anything anti-Catholic when he felt he had the assurance of salvation he had so long wanted.

The trouble with Martin Luther was fear. He says so over and over again, describing how full of fear and trembling he was when he first said Mass, and his feelings of terror whenever he said Mass, and how he was "filled with unspeakable terror at the thought of the proximity of God" when he walked by the side of Staupitz at the procession of the Blessed Sacrament. Fear that he had offended God or that he might offend Him — that was the trouble. Staupitz and other monks at Erfurt helped him with wise and tender words, as Luther freely acknowledged, but could not effect a radical cure. He was for ever looking within, probing his motives and meditating on his unworthy self and the doubt of his eternal salvation. At times raised to the heights and satisfied that all was well, more frequently cast down to the depths at the thought of his own wretchedness.

(Dyspepsia added to nervous disorder may be inferred. Luther was irregular in his meals, now abstaining for long periods with fasts exceeding the prescribed fasts of the Church, and now eating rapidly. His gross habits at the table, heavy drinking and heavier eating, were very marked in later years.)

And then Luther was obsessed by thought of the devil;

self-projected images of the prince of darkness tormented him. So far was he from pantheism that often enough when he felt the devil's proximity he wrote as one who believed in pandiabolism. It was not current and popular superstitions in the Church that provoked Luther to criticism and outspoken condemnation. In his extravagant vituperation of witchcraft and sorcery he ranks himself with the worst of the persecutors, seeing the victims of the witch trials as the very minions of the devil.

Fearful of having incurred the wrath of God, horribly aware of the activities of the devil, self-tortured by scruples so that confession and absolution brought little comfort, how could he be sure he had made a full and complete confession? What if sins had been overlooked and left unconfessed? The assurance which he wanted must be an assurance of God's forgiveness absolute and unconditional. And this assurance he finally felt that he had found in the words of St. Paul.

But it would be a mistake to infer from all that Luther wrote of his temptations to despair, of his miseries at the thought of a possible predestination to hell, that he was regarded as a melancholic character, a gloomy and lugubrious monk in the years when he lectured at Wittenberg. There is abundant evidence that Luther was thoroughly popular with his pupils of the lecture room; that with the talent displayed in his lectures went fervent religious zeal, high imagination, and much amiability. It is certain that for Luther, as for Dr. Johnson's philosophic friend, "cheerfulness would break in." The humour, coarse enough at times, was always there, to find increasing outlet with the confidence of salvation; of unconditional forgiveness.

Everything in the Catholic doctrine of forgiveness of sins is conditional and this meant for Luther uncertainty. How could he or anyone be certain that his sins were forgiven, that he was justified before God and sure of eternal salvation when it was all so conditional? Forgiveness of sin depended on the sinner being truly sorry, on his humble confession of sin and on his making amendment, and on doing penance for wrong done. To be justified meant that man must aim all his life at pleasing God and doing the will of God, aided by the grace of God, and using the sacraments which God had ordained to help man on the path to Heaven. But all this was very conditional. The more so since salvation was dependent on man's perseverance to the end of his life. It was presumption, the Catholic Church taught, to be certain of dying in a state of grace and gaining heaven. The only certain thing was that every man who died in grace was saved, and to achieve that end all men must strive. Luther knowing himself to be a man of violent passions was at times distracted by the feeling that try as he might to be good there was always the possibility of falling from grace and coming short of heaven. It was an intolerable burden this feeling of uncertainty, this terrible doubt that the conditions required of him for his salvation and justification before God might be unfulfilled when he came to die.

Ruled by his feelings, longing for the assurance of God's favour, completely subjective in mental attitude, angered at a sense of frustration, Luther had at once the strength and the weakness of the egocentric. The strength, because once convinced that he had the truth there was no turning him, and all who opposed were but fools or knaves to be contemned and spat upon. The weakness, because there was no intellectual basis, no reasonable ground for the theological opinions, he developed. It was enough for Martin Luther that he *felt* things to be true. He turned impatiently in later years against fellow Protestants not possessed of these feelings. But all that was far ahead. In the Wittenberg days it was sufficient that he felt he had found the key to the spiritual problems that puzzled him. That the feelings are not to be trusted in the spiritual life and its adventures, and are no safe guide for the direction of conscience, Luther never learnt.

His theological reading fostered the subjective mind, encouraging Luther to dwell on the thought of complete surrender to God, of abandoning all to God's will, of becoming a passive instrument of divine providence rather than an active servant. For the scholastic writers of the middle ages Luther expressed nothing but open contempt. They gave him no help; threw no light on the difficulty of *feeling* saved. Of the work of the greatest of these writers he appears largely ignorant. Avowing that he would destroy the influence and authority of Aristotle, it was natural that Luther should know little and think less of St. Thomas Aquinas.

It was to St. Augustine Luther turned; for he discovered in some of the books of that mighty doctor of the Church much that was entirely congenial to his troubled mind. In fact Luther came to adopt Augustine and to write that "our theology and St. Augustine are making good progress and thanks be to God they prevail at our university," i.e., Wittenberg. Yet it is impossible to say how much of Augustine Luther had read. Nor can it be said that Luther either interpreted Augustine faithfully or that the Lutheran doctrine is identical with St. Augustine's teaching. The Pelagians, against whom Augustine wrote, belittled original sin and made out that man could of his own free will arise from sin and turn to God. Augustine replied man could do nothing of the sort without the grace of God. Yet man had his part to perform in the work of redemption. Luther went further than Augustine—Man could do nothing; God's grace did everything. (Hence Luther's denial of man's free will.) This was the exact opposite to the Pelagian standpoint, but it was not St. Augustine's. The probability is that Luther, feeling himself in sympathy with Augustine on the vital need of God's grace, passed over all that was not in accord as irrelevant, interpreting in his own favour other passages because he felt that was what St. Augustine must have meant.

But St. Augustine's theology is not easy reading and misunderstanding is explicable. The true and full Catholic doctrine on original sin, grace and justification was not clearly defined when Luther was professor of theology at Wittenberg, and a very wide range of opinion was allowed.

St. Augustine next to St. Paul is the author most quoted by Luther in support of his teaching. The influence of William of Ockham and the nominalist philosophy cannot be disregarded.[1] Two other sources — both entirely Catholic and orthodox — are named by Luther as eminently helpful to him in the years when he sought peace of mind. John Tauler, a Dominican preacher and writer of the fourteenth century, profound and mystical yet not really obscure, and another fourteenth-century priest, the anonymous author of a small book known familiarly to us as *Theologia germanica.*

The *Theologia germanica* won an immense enthusiasm from Luther. He ranked it next to Augustine and the Bible and edited it with a preface extolling its merits. This fourteenth-century book, which is a treatise on perfection, a call to unity with God through complete submission to the divine will, was the first work published by Luther.

Tauler also wrote of the working of God's grace and of the calmness of soul that was necessary for the complete absorption into God. In both writers the aim is perfection through contemplation; the process of union with God is not intellectual, it is mystical.

Luther read his own interpretations into these books, so abundantly full of consolation. Somehow the directly spiritual appeal of Tauler and the *Theologia germanica* stirred the impulse in Luther to discover within himself the presence of God and the assurance of salvation; to feel within

---

[1] The writings of William of Ockham, republished early in the sixteenth century, directly encouraged the state at the expense of the Church. It is quite probable, as Dr. Neville Figgis suggested, that Ockham was the source of Luther's knowledge of scholasticism.

himself God speaking plainly and audibly to the heart. The feeling that one was saved had become for Martin Luther the one thing needful. He was then just thirty. No monk of the Augustinian order in Germany was more strongly supported, more deeply trusted.

So deeply trusted, so strongly supported on fact was Luther that in addition to his professorial chair he was appointed visitor or rural vicar for three years, with the charge of supervising eleven monasteries, including Erfurt and Wittenberg. He was also expected to preach daily in the parish church of Wittenberg. Heavy responsibilities were thus laid upon Dr. Martin Luther by the superior of his order. The gifted and youthful monk was as powerful and effective in the pulpit as in the professor's chair at Wittenberg. An increasing self-confidence developed with the confidence given to him in the order. But religious practice suffered. Luther, describing his full days and his round of official duties in a letter to his friend John Lang, prior of Erfurt, mentions that he has "seldom time to say the divine office or celebrate Mass." To recite daily the Hours from the breviary, the divine office, was and is the obligation that every Catholic priest incurs. Grave causes, of course, release from the obligation, but else a cleric is bound to say his office unless dispensed by authority. To celebrate Mass is the privilege of the priest. If the numerous priests engaged in high official and political work in the sixteenth century—popes, cardinals, and bishops among them—did not avail themselves of this privilege very frequently, they for the most part were worldly minded ecclesiastics of relaxed morality, not clerics bubbling over in the excitement of a newly found theology as Luther was.

It is significant that this admission of neglecting his daily office and the saying of Mass was made in 1516, when Luther was already preaching the new theology of Justification by Faith alone, and the discouragement of good works. Quite early at Wittenberg, lecturing on the Psalms, Luther said many things that had the note of novelty. The emphasis is laid on Christ dying for all, as indeed the Church teaches, while denunciation of the idea that man can be justified before God by the help of good works is uttered. The Observantines within the order (i.e., the Augustinians who clung to their "Observantine practices") incurred similar denunciation. Bitter reproaches were hurled by the Wittenberg professor at the "little saints," as he called them, and their "self-righteousness." For that mastery of invective that Luther was to display the training had already begun.

With the lectures on St. Paul's epistles to the Romans and Galatians (1515–17) we have Luther's new doctrine first set out, the first public statement of the new theology of the Protestant Reformation. Man is not free, Luther insists, to do the thing that is good and pleasing to God. All that man does is tainted by original sin, all his efforts to win heaven are sinful. God alone is the cause of man's salvation. Christ has made atonement for sin, Christ alone fulfils the law. Man is saved by belief in his Saviour, man is justified before God by faith in Christ and by faith alone, through the merits of Christ being attributed to the sinner.[2]

With enunciation of the new theology went continual attacks on Aristotle and the scholastic philosophers, and urgent demand for the restoration of Augustine. "The only good law is the love of God" the *dilige et quod vis fac* of Augustine ("love and do what you will") becomes the golden rule. Luther's "only good law" was to lead many to anti-nomianism — as might have been foreseen.

Martin Luther being by far the most talented member of the Augustinian order and its greatest orator, the new theology at once gained adherents; enthusiastic disciples, for the most part, who acclaimed the words of the professor as the true gospel of Christ. Yet not all the Augustinians were

---

[2] Luther in after life dated his complete enlightenment concerning justification by faith to a sudden awakening of mind that came to him at the end of 1518.

persuaded. Hostile critics existed, and in considerable numbers among the more elderly monks, by no means willing to declare offhand that whatever Dr. Martin Luther said was true.

Luther for his part is positive that nothing in his teaching is contrary to true Catholic doctrine. There is not the faintest suggestion of breaking with the past, and a vehement condemnation of heretics for separating from the Church is expressed by him. The current theology is at fault, not the authority of the Church, is the text of Luther's repeated arguments. Authority, and the pope was named as that authority, could straighten out the errors of grace and justification that had crept into common usage, correct the abuses that were mixed up with church practices, and endorse the doctrine taught at Wittenberg. That was all Luther wanted in 1517.

In that year von Hutten and his humanist allies published their second series of scathing and scurrilous *Epistolae obscurorum virorum,* ridiculing the German clergy for their stupidity, gross ignorance, and credulity; a book of savage satire that was condemned at Rome as "the word of certain sons of iniquity, having no fear of God or man before their eyes, and impelled by wicked, damnable and temerarious loquacity."

The council of the Lateran was closed by Leo X in that same year. It had passed many excellent resolutions for the reform of abuses in the Church, besides affirming the immortality of the soul and endorsing the bull of Pope Boniface VIII declaring all Christians to be the subjects of the pope; but it left the papal curia, the centre of financial corruption in the Church, untouched.

In the previous year Leo X had concluded a concordat with the French king which gave that youthful monarch the right of nomination to all bishoprics, abbeys, and conventual priories. In return for this lasting hurt to the church in France, Francis I engaged to support the rule of the

Medici in Florence and gave a French princess in marriage to the pope's nephew Lorenzo. This alliance of the papacy with France disturbed and threatened the safety and peace of the Hapsburg dominions and estranged politically the empire from the papacy.

In that memorable year, 1517, the Dominican friar, John Tetzel, was appointed to preach in Saxony and the surrounding country the great indulgence for the rebuilding of St. Peter's at Rome and the reimbursement of the archbishop of Mainz.

A memorable year. No man could foresee the dangers ahead, no man foretell the coming catastrophe. Certainly not that genial tolerant lover of good literature and good living, the Medicean pope, Leo X, with his bull that enjoined peace on the sovereigns of Europe for five years. Certainly not the Augustinian monk, the fiercely energetic, emotional, passionate, and intolerant Dr. Martin Luther, professor of biblical studies in the Saxon university of Wittenberg.

III

The Ninety-Five Theses: 1517

THE BEGINNING of open conflict was the publication of the Ninety-Five Theses by Martin Luther at Wittenberg on the eve of All Saints, in the year 1517. History affirms this and it is true. Yet no evidence suggests that Luther either saw himself at the time committing any startling deed, or remotely supposed that he was starting an attack on the unity and authority of the Catholic Church. By accident not by design the issue of the Ninety-Five Theses marks the beginning of the Protestant Reformation, of that cleavage among the Christian people of God that exists unhealed to this day.

The reform that Luther really sought was a change of doctrine, a new theology; he wanted to proclaim the gospel of man's salvation and justification before God, through faith in Christ alone. Of course the change that Luther desired was revolutionary. He made the centre of authority internal. Not the conscience directed to obey an external authority, but the feelings within became supreme. The subjective mind was to rule, since objective truth depended on man's acceptance. Luther believed at the time this change was compatible with the Catholic Faith. The Ninety-Five

Theses said nothing about the new theology and did not advertise the reform. But they did advertise Dr. Luther, hitherto only a prominent figure in his order, and they advertised him as an opponent of the trade in indulgences, the spokesman of opinions held by a very considerable number of intelligent persons all over Germany.

The picture of a solitary monk challenging the pope and the organised forces of the Roman Catholic Church by posting up a true statement of the Protestant belief on the church door at Wittenberg is still cherished in remote places. It passed for history in textbooks of Protestant schools and colleges for many a generation, that, greatly daring, one Martin Luther had arrayed himself to do battle with the papacy by his proclamation at Wittenberg on the eve of All Saints. We know to-day that the real picture is something quite different from the romantic drawing entitled "Luther at Wittenberg."

The sale of indulgences or pardons in Germany had become a public scandal. Luther himself in 1516 had preached and given a very fair account of the teaching of the Church concerning indulgences, a teaching that did not countenance the methods of Tetzel. No doubt the new theology left little room for indulgences. No doubt Luther personally was already moving swiftly though unknowingly away from the whole body of Catholic doctrine that had been contained within the Church during the past fourteen hundred years and more. But there was nothing in the publication of the Ninety-Five Theses to astonish or distress the faithful in the manner that is so often represented, and there was much the faithful could entirely appreciate. Luther at the start gained a large body of support. He attacked an abuse that could not be defended, thereby making a name for himself throughout Germany; so that many were favourably inclined to hear him when he started preaching and writing on his own special dogmas. Others who were entirely in agreement with Luther in the attack on the abuse of indulgences withdrew from him when from indulgences Luther turned to attack the papacy and the doctrine of the Mass. But the first move on the whole was decidedly popular.

The issue of Luther's challenge on that eve of All Saints can be taken as the opening of the campaign only in the light of later events. All Saints was the castle church of the elector, but it was also the university chapel in Wittenberg. On its doors university notices were published. Dr. Martin Luther having resolved to make his protest against the tour of Tetzel, the well-known preacher of indulgences, did it in the proper academic way. In no less than ninety-five articles or theses the case against the present method of preaching and selling indulgences was stated or rather questioned, and of course in Latin. A few months earlier Carlstadt, a fellow professor at Wittenberg, had put out no less than 152 theses raising various theological points for discussion. Carlstadt was professor of theology and from having been a strong scholastic and devoted exponent of St. Thomas Aquinas had already lost his moorings under the Lutheran influence. But nobody responded to Carlstadt's challenge and the 152 theses were left neglected. Luther dealt with a vital grievance, and when the theologians at the universities of Leipzig, Frankfort, and Erfurt had received copies of the theses, a lively interest was aroused.

The doctrine of indulgences had grown up with the doctrine of penance in the Catholic Church. From the first it was part of the Christian teaching that repentance of sin must be accompanied by confession and that required satisfaction was to be made.[1] Transgression of the moral law in-

---

[1] The *Book of Common Prayer* of the Church of England contains in the introduction to the special Ash Wednesday Commination service a sentence that may be quoted: "In the primitive Church there was a godly discipline that at the beginning of Lent such persons as stood convicted of notorious sin were put to open penance and punished in this world that their souls might be saved in the day of the Lord."

volves the punishment of the transgressor. Christ and Christ alone has earned for all mankind the pardon of sins on due repentance. But this did not imply also the removal of all the consequences and temporal punishments of sins. Each one of us must do penance on full confession of sin. Absolution is the assurance that we are forgiven if we are truly contrite, but with the absolution a penance is enjoined on the penitent. The gravity of the sin confessed decides the gravity of the penance. Satisfaction is due to our neighbour if wrong has been done him. Not only in this world but in purgatory must we suffer by doing penance for sin if we are to enjoy the pardon Christ has won for us.

It is a natural feeling in man that he must, as far as he is able, make amendment for wrongdoing; that the more deeply he has sinned the more zealously must he make satisfaction and bring forth fruits of repentance. The temporal debt may be paid in part or even entirely here. In the early middle ages the penance of long and severe personal mortification, penances extending over years, gave way to good works which were arduous, and not seldom difficult and dangerous. To take the cross of the Crusader, to go on pilgrimage, to help in the building of a church, the construction of a necessary bridge — all these were good deeds, acceptable penances accounted equal to the mortifications that were spread over months or years. But since not all could perform the penance in person it became sufficient to pay money that others might perform the good deeds in question. (As to-day one might send a subscription to a good cause in lieu of more active support.)

The doctrine of indulgences (or pardons) developed with the doctrine of the communion of saints and the treasury of merits. The value of Christ's life and death was infinite; the merits of Christ's immaculate Mother and of the many holy men and women of heroic virtue and attested sanctity, were abundant and superabundant. Thus was provided a treasure of pardons that might be shared by all penitent souls. The guardian and dispenser of this treasure was the pope to whom as possessor of the keys of St. Peter it was granted to make available the richness of these merits, and to extend to souls in purgatory the benefits of an indulgence. The doctrine was not defined; it was left to theologians to explain its significance. But when it came, as come it did, that in outward appearance the money contribution for the specified good work was made the one conspicuously needful thing to gain the papal indulgence, then it is easy to see how the doctrine could be used for financial ends. Of course the faithful were told that the conditions of the papal indulgence required penitence and confession to a priest, and the instructions issued to those responsible for preaching the indulgence specifically provided that those who had no money and therefore were unable to give the appropriate offering could still win the pardon through prayer and fasting, "since the kingdom of heaven shall not stand more open to the rich than to the poor." But money was the thing that was wanted, money was the thing the indulgence procured.

The more so was this true when it came to be wrongly believed that the indulgence not only meant remission of the temporal punishment for sin previously committed, but pardon for the guilt of that sin itself. No man at this time was more successful as a preacher of an indulgence than John Tetzel, the Dominican.

Luther's sermon in July, 1516 (he returned to the subject on two occasions before the challenge of the Ninety-Five Theses), stated clearly that the papal indulgence did not remit the guilt of sin; it remitted the temporal punishment due to sin, whether as a penance set by the priest to the penitent or whether as a suffering that remained to be still expiated in purgatory for the sins committed. Warning his hearers at the same time that a plenary indulgence, that is, a full remission of all punishment, was not an assurance of salvation unless there was true contrition for sin and confession, Luther allowed that indulgences were to be valued because they were derived from the merits of Christ and His saints. Their usefulness was not to be denied and the pope had the power to issue them. Yet misgivings were expressed at the way indulgences were regarded.

The true doctrine, it is certain, was overshadowed by the financial gain. The elector Frederick of Saxony himself, Frederick, the Wise, was an industrious but undiscriminating collector of sacred relics — the faked were as numerous as the genuine — and Rome had granted enormous indulgences to all the pious and devout persons who paid reverence to these relics and gave an offering of money, if they could afford it. There was an annual exposure of the relics and this was a very profitable time for the Elector, since the pilgrims came in crowds to gain the indulgences.

The indulgence that Tetzel preached was resented by Frederick — who refused permission to Tetzel to enter his dominions — and by others because of the money it drained from the country. The scandal of the whole business provoked Luther's protest and his protest was heartily welcomed and warmly approved all over Germany.

The scandal was not a novelty, the abuse had grown with the recognition that a papal indulgence was a definite source of revenue. At first, with the great jubilee indulgence of Pope Boniface VIII in 1300, it was to be gained by pilgrims who actually visited Rome and performed the requisite devotions. Then it was extended to those who, unable to visit Rome in person, were willing to pay what the pilgrimage would have cost them.[2] Finally by 1500, with Alexander VI's jubilee indulgence and the indulgence proclaimed by Leo X in 1513, all who bought the papal letter, the *Ablassbrief,* from the accredited preacher of pardons, were promised forgiveness of sins or release from purgatory for them-

[2] The Papal indulgence of 1932 could be gained by all Catholics who unable to travel to Rome in person said the requisite prayers in their own parish churches.

selves or for parent or friend, with the understanding of course on the part of the Church that the necessary conditions of true supernatural sorrow for sin, confession, and all else had been complied with. An indulgence could not, of course, apply to sins to be committed in the future.

Chaucer has drawn in the *Canterbury Tales* the professional pardon-seller enjoying himself at the expense of simple folk. The author of *Piers Plowman* gives an equally unfavourable portrait. Erasmus in his *Encomium Moriae,* "Praise of Folly" (1511), the book dedicated to his friend St. Thomas More and found highly diverting by Pope Leo X, sketches a common view of what was called "the holy business":

> "What shall I say of those who flatter themselves so sweetly with counterfeit pardon for their crimes, who have measured out the duration of purgatory without a mistake, as though by a water-clock, so that a longer or shorter residence is assigned — ages, years, months and days like the multiplication table, according to the greater or lesser purchase of these paltry pardons? By this easy way of payment any tradesman, soldier or judge thinks he can by some small disbursement of his stolen property be washed clean of all his gross impieties; that all his perjuries, lusts, drunkenness, quarrels, murders, cheatings, treacheries and debaucheries are bought off, as though a bargain had been struck, all old scores paid off leaving him free to begin a new series of sins."

The indulgence that Tetzel was engaged to preach was the result of an arrangement between Pope Leo X and Albert of Brandenburg, Archbishop of Mainz, Primate of Germany, humanist and patron of men of letters. The latter at twenty held the bishoprics of Magdeburg and Halberstadt and when he was twenty-four had persuaded the chapter of Mainz to elect him archbishop by promising to defray all expenses incurred with the Roman Curia, including the cost of the pallium. To raise the necessary funds Albert had gone to the Fuggers of Augsburg, the great merchants and money-lenders of the age (Catholics and Christians, holding a similar place in the esteem of kings and princes in Europe to that held by the Rothschilds in the nineteenth century),[3] from whom he borrowed 30,000 golden ducats. To repay this loan he obtained a valuable concession from the pope. The indulgence that Leo X granted was to raise money for the rebuilding of St. Peter's and Germany was divided into three districts under different papal commissioners for the organisation of this indulgence. Archbishop Albert was the commissioner for the area covered by his dioceses and the mark of Brandenburg. The pope's concession gave Albert sole rights over the indulgences for eight years in these territories; in return Albert agreed to make an immediate payment of 10,000 ducats to Rome and to remit half the takings annually. At the same time the other half was to go to the Fuggers. It was all above board and without concealment, this agreement concerning *das heylig negotium,* "the holy business." (Erasmus corresponded freely with Archbishop Albert, and thought as well of him as he did of Pope Leo.) There was no pretence that money was not the object of the indulgence. The Fuggers had their clerks attached to the preachers of the indulgence in order to check the offerings paid by the faithful into the chests; Archbishop Albert had his clerks similarly employed; both were furnished with duplicate keys of the chests.

John Tetzel was engaged to preach the indulgence; no man more suitable could be found in all Germany for the purpose. Tetzel was an accredited and experienced preacher of indulgences; where his divinity was defective an exuberant rhetoric supplied the lack as far as popular audiences were concerned, making amends for theological shortcomings. His style it would appear, combined the eloquence of a cheap-jack at a country fair with the rhetorical powers of a

---

[3] The Fuggers lent the money required for the election of the Emperor Charles V.

revivalist preacher. It was certainly effective. No doubt many of the sayings attributed to Tetzel, like the anecdotes related of him, are not strictly true, for stories accumulate concerning the words and doings of popular preachers, and friends and foes alike are apt to concoct or at least exaggerate the pulpit utterances of notorious orators. There is no doubt at all that the gross libels so widely and freely published on Tetzel's private character during the controversy that followed are without justification. How, indeed, could historical accuracy preserve the open-air sermons preached by Tetzel on numerous fair grounds? No reporter attended to take down the words that brought so much money into the indulgence chest. All we do know is that it was the kind of preaching that moved crowds to buy, and buy eagerly, the pardons that Tetzel sold.

Rhetoric is rarely without an element of falsehood, and Tetzel was invariably rhetorical. Tradition makes him responsible for declaring that the indulgence cross erected in the churches and adorned with the papal arms was as powerful to save as the cross of Christ Himself; that he, Tetzel, with his pardons had saved more souls than St. Peter did by his preaching; that the moment money was paid into the chest a soul was released from purgatory: "when the coin in the casket rings the soul to heaven wings." If the couplet was not Tetzel's the doctrine apparently was his own—that the souls of the very parents or children amongst his hearers could be immediately freed from the pains of purgatory by some quite ridiculously small sum of money. Harrowing descriptions of the sufferings endured in purgatory was generally successful. Who could resist the appeal? If money could free the soul of the loved one from such pain who would grudge the payment? To make it easier, Tetzel, following the instructions of the Mainz authorities, taught that the dead were benefitted by the indulgence bought for them without it being necessary for the purchaser to be in a state of grace. In other words, the good deed of buying an indulgence was sufficient to release souls in purgatory without the usual accompaniment of confession of sin.

Tetzel was excluded from Wittenberg by the prohibition of the Elector Frederick, ruler of electoral Saxony, but he was not far away, and Luther was told of Tetzel's preaching and the unauthorised doctrine concerning the efficacy of indulgences for the dead. Luther must have heard other things attributed, no doubt unjustly, to the Dominican preacher,[4] for the arrival of an indulgence-seller in a German town was a great event, and on all the countryside it produced great excitement.

All this booming of indulgences by a Dominican friar, plainly ignorant of theology and of the authorised church teaching concerning indulgences, exasperated Dr. Martin Luther. Exasperating, too, he found it, that simple German peasants should be paying away money in this fashion. In his own mind Luther had no use for indulgences. Justification before God by the feeling that you were justified by faith in Christ alone made all good works useless — and the best that could be said for the purchase of an indulgence was that it was a good work. Nevertheless let the doctrine be clearly discussed and the truth declared. In the very church of All Saints at Wittenberg, the church of the Elector, friend and patron of the Augustinians, there would be crowds to gain the indulgences granted to the worshippers

---

[4] It was alleged that Tetzel said the indulgence he was selling availed for the pardon of sins not yet committed. Hence the story of the Leipzig man who asked Tetzel if he would sell him an indulgence for a sin he feared he might commit. Tetzel agreed to sell the indulgence paper for a fixed sum and the man from Leipzig departed with the assurance of God's pardon and forgiveness for the sin he feared he might commit. The sin was then actually committed. It was nothing less than the waylaying of Tetzel and the robbing him of all the money he was carrying. The robber before riding away explained that he was certain of God's forgiveness because Tetzel himself had guaranteed it. The story can hardly be true (Jortin, in his *Life of Erasmus,* quotes it from Seckendorff), but it is a specimen of the talk that was current at the time.

who visited the relics exhibited and made their offerings on All Saints' day.

The "holy business" of Tetzel had to be challenged, if possible, stopped. Dr. Martin Luther took the appropriate step. He composed his Ninety-Five Theses on the subject of Indulgences and duly fastened the composition on the university board, the door of All Saints' Church at Wittenberg. The document, in Latin and duly signed by Martin Luther, was naturally read by fellow monks and professors. It was not for popular consumption by the laity. When a former friend and fellow professor, Christopher Scheusl, wrote from Nuremberg expressing surprise at not receiving a copy, Luther answered that he had not thought of publishing the theses outside a very limited circle of friends and neighbours. The theses called for a consideration of a specific doctrine and assailed a practice that was a gross abuse. There was nothing to suggest that the challenge to a disputation on the subject of indulgences was the first step towards the break up of Christendom, the opening of a conflict that still endures. The gravity of the move could not be foreseen, nor the consequences foretold. To his own diocesan, Scultetus (Jerome Schultz), bishop of Brandenburg, for whom Luther expressed great regard, and to Albert, the Elector Archbishop of Mainz, in whose name the trade in indulgences was conducted, Luther sent his theses with covering letters. Scultetus replied sympathetically but advised that the subject might now be left alone. Archbishop Albert did not answer the letter but wrote to the chapters of Magdeburg and Halberstadt, who were responsible for the administration of those dioceses, that he had sent the papers to Rome. The archbishop also blamed the subcommissaries, the organisers of the "holy business," for unseemly speech and behaviour in the preaching of the indulgence and at the inns they frequented, and complained of deductions for the heavy expenses incurred by Tetzel and his assistants.

As for this historic document, the Ninety-Five Theses, it is neither a clear statement of theological belief nor a complete denial of the doctrine of indulgences. In no sense is it a manifesto or a program of reform. It contains repetitions, explains how grossly the doctrine was abused, points out the need for the teaching of the Church to be defined, and calls upon the pope to do right. There is no hint in the Ninety-Five Theses of Luther's dogma of justification by faith alone, no mention of an appeal to Holy Scripture.

At the start Luther insists that the repentance required by Christ is lifelong, that true penitence must needs show itself in external acts of penance, that humility demands confession, and that contrition of heart is the one and indispensable thing. In various ways the question of indulgences is examined and certain conclusions drawn. An indulgence can never remit the guilt of sin, nor the divine punishment for sin. Not even the pope can do either of these things, but only God. An indulgence is no more than release from canonical penalty imposed by the Church; what the Church has imposed, that can the Church remit. Therefore an indulgence cannot apply to souls in purgatory for the penances imposed refer to the living and not to the dead. The truly penitent sinner is already pardoned and in no want of an indulgence. The doctrine of the treasure of merits not having been properly defined cannot be properly understood by the people. The merits of Christ and the saints are effective without the papal intervention for "every true Christian living or dead has from God a full share of all the wealth of Christ and the Church even without letters of pardon." At the same time the remission by the pope of penalties is to be valued for it is the declared assurance of divine remission.

In several of the theses indulgences are contrasted unfavourably with good works. "Christians should be taught that it is not the will of the pope for men to believe that the purchase of pardons is to be compared with works of mercy." "Christians should be taught that to give to the poor or lend to the needy is a far better thing than to buy a pardon," because "a man does not become better, by the pardon he is only freed from punishment, whereas by performing works of charity his charity is increased." Again "Christians should be taught that anyone who passes by a poor man and then goes and buys a pardon gains no indulgence for himself from the pope but rather the indignation of God."

Two theses warn that "the buying of pardons must be free and not ordered" and that "the papal pardons are good and useful so long as people do not put their trust in them; they are hurtful if they result in the loss of the fear of God."

Other theses remonstrate with the pope directly: "Christians should be taught that if the pope knew how the preachers of indulgences made their exactions he would rather the basilica of St. Peter should lie in ashes than be erected out of the flesh and skin and bones of his sheep."

"Why, if the pope can release souls from purgatory on payment of money, does he not for very charity and for their necessity empty that place of cleansing fire?" And "why since the pope is wealthier than the wealthiest Croesus does he not build the basilica of St. Peter out of his own money rather than with the money of the poor?"

Elsewhere in these theses Luther insists on the "due reverence to be paid by bishops and priests who receive the commissioners of the papal indulgence," and is certain that "if sermons were preached setting forth the mind and intention of the pope the objections of the laity to the almsgiving system of the indulgences would be refuted and dissolved." So far is he from repudiation of indulgences or papal authority that he declares "let him who contradicts the truth of the papal indulgence be anathema and accursed."

The whole document is full of confused utterance; certainty that Tetzel's methods are wrong and hurtful to the Christian conscience; uncertainty as to what the true doctrine of indulgence really is; impatience with the pope for authorising such shady methods of raising money; confident assurance that the pope will respond and put an end to the iniquities now that Luther has called attention to them; determination that the doctrine of indulgences shall be carefully examined and defined, to the total discomfiture of Tetzel and all his subordinates.

The materials for an exciting controversy were supplied. The challenge could not be ignored. The financial supplies of Archbishop Albert and recognised sources of papal revenue were openly threatened. The methods of John Tetzel, the Dominican preacher, were held up to contempt. By the end of the year Luther's criticism of indulgences had won sympathetic attention all over Germany, his invitation to debate had set various clerics sharpening their wits to reply.

An exceedingly brisk discussion with much lively exchange of uncomplimentary epithet was expected. The vital issue was still hidden from men's eyes at the close of 1517, that memorable year of the Ninety-Five Theses.

IV

Luther and the Papacy: 1518-1519

THE ACRIMONIOUS dispute on the whole subject of indulgences that followed Luther's hostile criticisms of the work of Tetzel was taken at Rome to be no more than a display of ill will between Dominicans and Augustinians. If Pope Leo did not at the outset dismiss the subject as "a quarrel between monks" — evidence for the statement is quite inconclusive — he might very easily have done so. The fundamental issue was really the authority for the declaration of indulgences, the prerogatives of the Holy See, and this was not perceptible in the first year of the dispute. Gradually Luther turned from the pope; then with increasing violence flouted the papal power; finally he poured contempt on papal claims. Luther was so sure of his own case, so entirely self-persuaded that the pope would be on his side, that Leo's inability to look favourably on the Ninety-Five Theses, to define the true doctrine of indulgences or promise any reform of the prevailing abuses, angered the monk of Wittenberg. In wrathful disappointment all former loyalty to the pope yielded to bitter irritation. Time allowed the anger to mature, the sense of injury to fester, till explosion was inevitable.

It is nearly three years from the posting up of the theses at Wittenberg to the bull of Leo X that gave judgment and required submission. Three years of gathering storm and impending separations; storms and separations that will affect not only Germany but all Europe for the centuries to come; and beyond Europe to the uttermost ends of the earth. In those three years what seemed originally a quarrel of monks—a friction between two religious orders, such as Catholic churchmen had known before and might know again, a matter of no vital consequence—developed into mortal feud and enlarged into the ferocious controversy that was to rack the souls of nations and shatter the peace of Christendom.

Not till the end of three years was it made plain to Pope Leo that the recalcitrant Augustinian, Dr. Martin Luther, mistakenly regarded as a rebellious, probably heretical, person of no particular importance, a mere unruly monk defying authority and needing to be corrected, was an exceedingly popular figure, favoured by princes, encouraged by the humanists at the universities, highly admired within his own order, and enthusiastically applauded by peasants and townsmen in all parts of Germany.

Pope Leo was far from enjoying theological controversy; entirely remote from him was the desire to suppress ill-considered opinions. His tastes were not theological, were hardly ecclesiastical. At the same time discipline must be maintained, and it was utterly irregular for a subordinate member of a religious order to declare the customary method of raising funds by a papal indulgence a practice to be condemned. Since the attention of His Holiness had been called to Dr. Martin Luther's proceedings, let the superiors of his order deal with the matter. The Augustinian general in Rome sent word that Luther must attend the next general chapter of his province to be held at Heidelberg in April, 1518.

Pope Leo might dismiss the problem of Luther and think

it solved. Not so readily could he dispose of the political problem, the safety of the papal states. If the Hapsburg emperor held both Milan and Naples, then at any time war with the empire meant encirclement of Rome; unless France was strong enough to defend the northern passes. In any case the emperor had the best troops; trained veterans, German *landsknechts,* Spanish infantry, and the Swiss mercenaries; though the latter were often engaged by the popes.

Apart from the fact that this German monk, Dr. Martin Luther, gravely threatened a valuable source of revenue there was no reason why Pope Leo should be disturbed. Roman theologians would examine and report on these Ninety-Five Theses and there the matter would end. Severity would be untimely since the University of Wittenberg was the foundation of the good Catholic elector of Saxony, a probable successor according to report of the elderly Maximilian on that emperor's decease. Elector Frederick must be conciliated and deference paid to his wishes. Pope Leo could return to the more congenial studies of classical literature and the fine arts without neglecting that ever-present problem of the political safety of his dominions, the problem of Italy.

So Luther was summoned to attend the spring chapter of the Augustinian hermits at Heidelberg, and duly went, but not till there had been a brisk discharge of pamphlets on the indulgences. Tetzel had something to say both in self-defence and on behalf of the papacy, and the Dominicans were not for letting Dr. Luther have it all his own way. Two other priests, Andrew Carlstadt, Luther's colleague at Wittenberg, and Dr. John Eck, professor at Ingoldstadt, joined in the argument, both of them eager disputants, destined to play larger parts in the tragedy of the reformation in Germany and directly to influence Luther's movements.

With that natural caution that guided Luther's steps, that instinct of self-preservation that kept him, a peasant and the son of a peasant, from all avoidable personal risks, Luther obtained from the Elector Frederick a written safeguard and an armed escort for his journey to and from Heidelberg before setting out. Opposition he knew was aroused. The "holy business," it was said had been hurt beyond recovery. Luther had no intention then or later of falling into the hands of his enemies, of being silenced or imprisoned by the Dominicans and the Inquisition. At Heidelberg Luther's reception was altogether cordial. Instead of condemnation that had been expected by the general of the order in Rome there was an unmistakable majority on Luther's side and no hint of censure. So, far from disapproval, a great public disputation was arranged in the Augustinian monastery in order that Luther might expound his new theology and invite all comers to debate the theses propounded.

Luther's forty theses, theological and philosophical, of this occasion contained no reference to indulgences but assailed the teaching of Aristotle and claimed the authority of St. Paul and St. Augustine for the new doctrine of salvation by faith alone and man's utter impotence to justify himself before God. There might be shaking of heads among the older monks, the younger men were entirely on Luther's side and the chapter at Heidelberg gave Luther the first taste of popularity outside his own order. Among the young men drawn to the new theology at that Heidelberg disputation was Martin Butzer (Bucer) a gifted Dominican student at Heidelberg university.

Luther returned to Wittenberg rejoicing as well he might at his success, and prepared to win further recognition. He appealed to the pope. The Heidelberg theses with a number of explanatory "Resolutions" were forwarded to Rome through Staupitz, and Luther dedicated the writings to Leo in a preface full of expressions of loyalty to the Holy See and of devotion to its present occupant. Luther was torn between feelings of confidence in his new theology and feelings of misery that at times approached despair. An abject humility is the note in the address to the pope, while at the same time the "Resolutions" contain several articles that conflicted with traditional Catholic doctrine.

Luther long afterwards recalled his mental agony in the first years of revolt, of the distress of conscience, the intense suffering felt at the thought of being cut off from God. All the soul of this highly emotional and nervous man cried out for sympathy. The feeling that one was saved and justified before God by faith in Christ was, it seemed to him, overborne by diabolical insinuations of terror and dread.

Craving for the sympathy of his fellows, anxiety not to be cast out as a heretic, unconcealed hope that Pope Leo will be moved favourably by the suppliant tone of the writer, all these are natural expressions of a character such as Luther's. They are as much part of a nature in whom simplicity and complexity were strangely blended, as the superb pride that would tell the whole Christian Church where it erred and point to Martin Luther as the prophet raised up by God to lead the German people into all truth.

When Luther wrote to Pope Leo X: "Most Holy Father, prostrate I offer myself at the feet of your holiness with all that I am and all that I possess. Do as thou wilt to me. Be it life or death. Call or recall, approval or reproof. I will acknowledge your voice as the voice of Christ, reigning and speaking in you. If I have deserved death I shall not refuse to die"—the exalted and exaggerated note of self-abasement reveals the mood that hungered for support and confirmation.

Pope Leo was unresponsive; such a display of sentiment left him cold; it was not thus that Cicero spoke. Let Dr. Martin Luther of Wittenberg amend his theological errors and cease to trouble the peace of the Church. Pope Leo, no heresy hunter, asked for that decent compliance with the decrees of authority which the Church has always the right to demand of its clergy.

Luther also wrote in modest tone to his bishop, Schultz of Brandenburg, that his theses were matters for disputation not to be taken as final expressions of opinion: "among them are items of which I doubt and of which I am in ignorance. Other items I deny, and none I positively assert, but all is submitted to holy Church and its judgment."

To Spalatin, Elector Frederick's chaplain, Luther is equally restrained: "Though I may err in argument never will I be a heretic. I desire to define nothing but still less do I desire to be led captive by the opinions of men."

Protest his moderation as he might, Luther was urged by internal forces to abide by no contradiction from without. If the pope were on Luther's side all would be well. If the pope were otherwise then it was not Luther's fault if trouble came. Already, while pouring out his absolute submission to the pope, Luther is feeling uncertain about the papal claims to the obedience he so effusively promised. While Rome considered the reply to be sent to the "Resolutions" Luther published a sermon on the "Force of Excommunication" to prove that bishops had too often abused the powers of excommunication and that therefore an unjust excommunication did not really cut off anyone from the soul of the Church.

The theologians at Rome to whom the pope committed the examination — one of them a Dominican, Sylvester Prierias, an official censor and inquisitor — found heresy in Luther's theses and according to the usual procedure Luther was cited to appear at Rome to answer the indictment.

At once Luther appealed to his patron, the Elector Frederick, and the latter who was attending the diet of the empire at Augsburg stoutly refused to allow his Augustinian professor at Wittenberg to be deported. Wittenberg was the elector's pride, it was the university he had founded and Dr. Martin Luther was its most distinguished professor; Cardinal Cajetan being present at the diet as papal legate the pope agreed that Luther should be excused attendance at

Rome and — his personal safety again guaranteed — answer to the legate for his heretical propositions.

Cardinal Cajetan, who was also a Dominican, remained at Augsburg after the diet was closed. He was instructed not to offend the Elector Frederick, since much depended on the good will of that prince of the empire if the campaign against the Turks desired by pope and emperor was to be advanced.

The discussions between Cajetan and Luther — the proceedings did not resemble a trial for heresy — came to nothing. The legate was patient enough with this very difficult and troublesome German professor from Wittenberg, and Luther went so far as to acknowledge in writing that he had been wanting in respect to the Holy See and that he would keep silence in future about indulgences if his adversaries also kept silence. But the legate insisted on Luther's formal retractation of two at least of the Ninety-Five Theses: (1) the denial of the treasury of the merits of Christ and the Saints, the fundamental doctrine of indulgences; (2) that faith alone made the reception of the sacraments effective. On neither point would Luther budge.

In vain did Cajetan set out that the authority of the Church and of the pope was of God, in vain quote the arguments from St. Thomas Aquinas. Luther fell back upon Holy Scripture, protesting that he was not conscious of having said anything contrary to the Fathers of the Church, the decretals of the pope, or right reason. "For all I have said seems to me to be sound, true, and Catholic."

What should have been the recantation of heresy was turned into a prolonged discussion. When Luther suggested an appeal to the imperial universities of Basel, Freiburg, and Louvain, or even to the University of Paris for judgment on his theses, and offered to debate publicly or in writing on the objections to certain theses, the legate explained that he was not there to contend but as the pope's representative to listen and advise. Luther must recant. On that Luther replied that he would appeal from the legate to the pope, from His Holiness Pope Leo X ill informed to His Holiness more correctly informed.

The "trial" was at an end. Luther returned to Wittenberg. On the day of his arrival a year had elapsed since the posting of the Ninety-Five Theses. At Wittenberg he was among friends and enthusiastic disciples, the youthful Melanchthon being already among the foremost of these and the most trusted lieutenant.

Cardinal Cajetan took the only course open to him. He sent a formal condemnation of Luther's errors to the Elector Frederick with the request that since Luther refused to retract he should be banished from Wittenberg and from the elector's territories; alternately the elector was asked to send Luther to Rome. The elector was prepared neither to banish his most popular professor from Wittenberg nor to send him to Rome. He excused himself to Cajetan on the ground that after all Luther's doctrine had not yet been found to be heresy.

Luther himself publicly declared that he appealed from the pope to a general council. Which of course aggravated his offence, since if any priest censured for theological error can summon the bishops of the Catholic Church all over the world to a council to discuss and pronounce judgment on the truth or falsehood of the error, the turmoil would be intolerable. The suggestion at the time Luther made it was negatived by canon law. Yet though he persisted that he had a right to appeal from the pope to a general council, in the event of condemnation by the former, and confessed his uncertainty concerning the prerogatives of the pope, Luther by this time was not even firmly convinced of the powers of general councils. For within a few months of announcing his appeal to a general council Luther had to admit that general councils themselves might err. In fact, as confidence in the authority of pope and council waned, the stronger grew the conviction that Martin Luther's doctrine of justification by faith alone was the truth, the whole truth, and nothing but the truth. Truth revealed by God, manifestly asserted in the writings of St. Paul and confirmed by St. Augustine. Therefore all who denied this dogma, be they bishop or pope or general council, were ignorant of the true faith of a Catholic and a Christian. To oppose Luther was to oppose God — to that conclusion Luther was fast being persuaded.

Natural aversion from extreme measures and political considerations kept Pope Leo from any hasty step. It was of first importance that the Elector Frederick should remain well disposed to the papacy. Yet by some means Dr. Martin Luther must be compelled to cease from troubling. Therefore Leo sent Miltitz, a Saxon nobleman in minor orders, employed at Rome as papal chamberlain and agent for the courts of Saxony, with the Golden Rose for the elector. The pope was accustomed to pay this compliment of a gift of the Golden Rose every year to the prince whom he desired to honour. It was a conciliatory gesture, and so far from helping to influence the elector, entirely futile.

Miltitz, who is described as an "incompetent man and a seeker after benefices," found on his arrival in Germany a state of affairs vastly unlike what was pictured in Rome. Luther was a man full of vigour and, it appeared, had three supporters where the pope had one. In Saxony Tetzel, utterly discredited and living in retirement, his occupation gone, his health shattered, was interviewed by Miltitz, who heaped reproaches upon the unhappy Dominican for the scandal he had caused. In a few months Tetzel was dead. Then Miltitz had several conversations with Luther and very amicable relations were established. The papal envoy went so far as to promise that if Luther would refrain from controversy nothing should be said on the other side. Miltitz also promised to report to the pope on the conditions in

Germany and to arrange for Luther's case to be examined by some German bishop chosen by Luther himself. Luther on his part promised that he would willingly recant if convicted of error and that he would "no further impugn the honour and power of the holy Roman Church."

The proposals of Miltitz, made entirely on his own authority, were responsible for Luther's last professions of orthodoxy and of obedience to Rome. In his *Unterricht,* "Instructions," Luther affirmed belief in the invocation of saints (though it is better to ask them for spiritual help than physical); in purgatory (though we do not know whether it affects amendment as well as satisfaction); in indulgences (as pardons from the penances for actual sin); in the observance of the commands of the Church (though these must not be confused with the commands of God); in good works (because we do not become holy by doing good works but because it is only those made holy by the grace of God who can perform good works); in the holy Roman Church (because it is honoured by God above all others and even if things are not as they should be in Rome that is no reason for separating). The exact powers and prerogatives of the Holy See, he held, may be left for the decision of theologians, for the sake of unity papal injunctions should be obeyed and the command of the Holy See followed.

Luther followed this *Unterricht* with a letter to Pope Leo, sent in March, 1519. In the main this letter was both a personal apology and an attack on his enemies. The latter, Luther complains, have brought infamy upon the holy Roman Church in Germany by their avarice; they have done evil in the name of His Holiness and cast suspicions upon Luther for his endeavour to protect the honour of the pope. Emphatically Luther denies any thought of infringing on the prerogatives of the Church or the pope, and professes that he will say no more about indulgences if only his adversaries will also be silent. His one and only object, he declares, has been to preserve the purity of the holy Roman Church and the deliverance of the faithful from the error of thinking that indulgences are greater than charity.

Miltitz wrote with complacency of the success of his mission, and the pope, anxious to do nothing that might draw Elector Frederick into an anti-papal attitude, for the death of Maximilian left the succession to the empire uncertain, waited till the end of the month before issuing a brief calling Luther to Rome. The brief was not harshly worded but it mentioned that Luther must abandon erroneous notions and be personally instructed. As for Miltitz his efforts and undertakings in the cause of peace were repudiated by the Roman authorities.

Luther, safe in Saxony, relying upon the good will of the elector, did not ignore the brief. It never reached him nor was he told of it. The elector on receipt of the papal brief simply suppressed it.

The time had now come when Luther, like many another who clings outwardly to a position already abandoned intellectually, could no longer hope for the pope's approval. It set him examining the claims of the papacy more closely and his doubts increased the more he pondered the origin of the pope's supremacy. Strong in the self-assurance that he possessed the truth, Luther noted that the pope had shown no favour to his teaching; rather had indicated through his official delegates that Luther was wrong. But Luther was sure that he was right. Therefore it was plain the pope must be wrong; and if wrong so gravely wrong that no spark of right was visible—so profoundly wrong that it would soon appear the pope was no better than anti-Christ, or at least the representative of anti-Christ. Not for a minute would Luther tolerate the notion that the pope might have right on his side. The pope had failed to meet Luther in agreement; the pope was utterly and irretrievably damned, the papal claims a fraud. With a command of invective rich in an age when invective was commonly full-flavoured, Luther expressed his disappointment.[1]

The year 1519 was a decisive year for Luther; a year busy with fresh contentions and a considerable literary output. The printing press, a comparatively recent invention, was available for the distribution of his writings and no man in that century used the press more effectively for the gaining of converts and the angering of opponents.

They were not directly controversial, these publications of 1519, and included sermons, a plain exposition of the Lord's Prayer, a commentary on the Psalms, and the first edition of his commentary on the Epistle to the Galatians. The *Exposition of the Lord's Prayer for Simple Laymen* was in German as well as in Latin, and was read all over Germany. (Duke George of Saxony complained that simple laymen were saying that if they followed Dr. Luther he would make them spend four days over a single paternoster — but the popularity of the treatise is certain, and translations were made into Italian and into Bohemian). Luther's talent for forceful, homely German that all could read and understand, aided by the printing press, brought adherents and won supporters to the new theology. In controversy of the pen Luther then acknowledged no master. The humanists were frankly on his side in the first few years, so that we find Erasmus in 1519 writing of the many in England, and men of highest standing, who held Luther's writings in great esteem. At the same time Erasmus, while declining to be identified with Luther's theological innovations, writes to the archbishop of Mainz of Luther's moderation. And in that year we have probably the first use of the word "Lutheran" in *The Reply of the Ignorant Lutheran Canons,* the

[1] In a few years time an English king — Henry VIII — in similar fashion to Luther became convinced that the pope was the enemy of true religion. When the pope (Clement VII) could not agree with Henry that the marriage of the latter with Katherine should be annulled, Henry decided that the pope's supremacy in the Church must be abolished.

answer of Oecolampadius to John Eck, who had publicly contemned the "ignorance" of Luther's disciples. Oecolampadius, a Briggetine monk and a professor at Augsburg, passed from Luther's influence to become a colleague of Zwingli in Switzerland, and to incur Luther's undisguised ill will.

Dr. John Eck of Ingoldstadt brought matters to a climax at the debate of Leipzig.

Carlstadt and Eck had issued written challenges to dispute a number of theological propositions; the question of papal supremacy included. Carlstadt denied and Eck undertook to affirm the true doctrine of the pope's headship of the Church. Luther, for all his promises to Miltitz and his professions of loyalty to the pope, knew himself to be the man really challenged by Eck and eagerly rushed into the fray. The bishop of Merseburg, Leipzig being in his diocese, formally forbade under pain of excommunication the public disputation; but nobody took any notice of the episcopal prohibition. Leipzig was a Catholic centre and many were curious to see and hear this Dr. Martin Luther. Eck's debate with Carlstadt was chiefly on the question of divine grace and man's free will. It was with Luther, Eck disputed on the primacy of the pope, and it was Eck who drew from Luther the definite opinion that decisions of general councils were no more infallible than papal decisions. The Council of Constance might have erred in its condemnation of Huss as a heretic, Luther admitted, and it might have erred on the question of the primacy of the pope.

The disputation went on for several days and Luther's opinion of the proceedings is summed up in the words "a loss of time, not an inquiry into truth." The Leipzig divines were not impressed by the eloquence of Wittenberg while the Wittenberg contingent thought nothing of Eck. Duke George, who attended with great regularity, was strongly set against Luther. Luther might say what he liked about the papal claims and the papal supremacy, "human right or divine right, the pope is the pope and remains the pope," was the conclusion of Duke George. The plain man could not grasp the notion of a Catholic Church without a pope.

Luther had appealed from pope and general council to the Sacred Scriptures at this Leipzig disputation; hence its significance. He returned to Wittenberg to inaugurate his campaign against the papacy. John Eck went to Rome with the proofs of Luther's heresy. The battle was set.

How Luther appeared to his contemporaries may be learnt from the letter of a Saxon humanist, Mosselanus, who was present at the Leipzig disputation:

"A man of middle height, so lean of body and spare through study and anxiety that one can almost count his bones, but with vigour undiminished and in the prime of life (Luther was then 36). His voice, Mosselanus noted, was high and clear, and his knowledge of Sacred Scripture admirable, so that it covered a readiness to give chapter and verse for his quotations. An easy man in private life at Leipzig, Luther showed himself; nothing of the stoic about him and nothing supercilious, invariably manly in social intercourse. Festive, too, and jocular and brisk, entirely unmoved by the terrible threats of his opponents." The portrait is the impression of a friendly critic, so much so that Mosselanus wonders whether Luther is not helped by divine assistance. Nevertheless unpleasing qualities are discerned. Luther is too aggressive in giving blame, too savage in speech; his methods are rash for one introducing new articles of religion and indecorous at a theological disputation.

John Eck, the same critic found, to be the more skilful debater, and a man of larger frame and bigger voice. Otherwise the personal preference is for Luther.

The year closed with Lutheran controversy disseminated throughout Germany, universities censuring the new theology, humanists rallying to the Wittenberg professor, simple people reading Luther's writings, and the supporters of Charles and Francis busily bribing the electors of the emperor. For Maximilian was dead and Charles V not yet elected.

Memories of Huss revived; the whole system of Catholic theology with its sanctions of faith and morals was questioned; doubts concerning the validity of the pope's supremacy were raised; admiration for Luther was countered by denunciation; hostility to Rome for its excessive financial demands on the German people was expressed in towns and cities; among the peasants were mutterings of the storm that was brewing against nobles and high ecclesiastics who kept their tenants in wretched serfdom.

Miltitz still sought to engage Luther in futile efforts at compromise, but the fire had spread too fiercely to be quenched by control of bishops or subordinates, and neither Luther nor his compatriots who stood by the papacy and the old paths could mend matters. For at the end of that critical year Dr. John Eck was on his way to Rome with further documentary evidence of the heresies of Dr. Martin Luther, professor of Biblical studies at Wittenberg.

V

Excommunication and Retaliation: 1520

IN 1520 John Eck returned to Germany with the papal bull that declared Martin Luther excommunicate.

In the same year Luther published three short and highly popular treatises, and at Wittenberg in December publicly burnt not only a copy of the papal bull but also the volumes of canon law.

The formal condemnation of Luther could not be hurried; partly because neither the head of his own religious order nor any bishop in Germany had pronounced against him. On the contrary the Augustinians were by this time prepared to give Luther very general support. At their provincial chapter, where Staupitz retired from office, his elected successor was Link, an early friend of Luther and already an advocate of the new Lutheran theology. As for the bishops, Luther made a last appeal to the archbishop of Mainz and the bishop of Merseberg to read and consider fairly his writings and to instruct him if there was error. From these prelates came no formal condemnation, merely reproof for the vehemence and violence of his language.

But the bishop of Meissen, on the advice of his cathedral chapter, stirred by a sermon published by Luther on the

Blessed Sacrament, did issue a decree on January 24 ordering this sermon to be prohibited on the ground that its doctrine was contrary to the teaching of the Church, since it directly opposed what had been laid down at the fifth Lateran council. This was the first episcopal censure.

In the sermon censured Luther had stated, with other criticism of Catholic doctrine and practice, that it would be a good and becoming thing to give the sacrament to Christians in both forms of bread and wine. Since this giving of the cup to the laity was one of the distinctive grounds for separation by the Bohemians and by the disciples of Huss, it brought Luther sympathetic attention from the Hussite groups in Germany. On the other hand it kindled hostility where memories of Huss and of the Hussite wars still lingered.

The bishop's censure drove Luther to a further outbreak. He now declared that not only was the use of the chalice a question that might well be decided by the next general council, but such a council might also find it well to allow parish priests to marry. The Greek clergy had wives; why not allow a similar liberty to the German clergy?

The Elector Frederick, while he sought through his chaplain, Spalatin, to restrain him, still protected Luther. He still urged, in reply to criticism, that Luther's doctrine had not been refuted "by solid arguments and clear witness of Scripture" and pointed out that this doctrine "had already so rooted itself everywhere both in Germany and elsewhere" that to suppress it by the terror of ecclesiastical power would only result in horrible tumults, "whence no good could come to our most holy lord, the pope, or to anyone else."

True, the universities of Cologne and Louvain, through their theological faculties, condemned Luther's printed works, but this only drew from Luther a characteristic reply pouring scorn on the universities for setting themselves up as theological censors.

Meanwhile Rome at last was moving. The mission of

John Eck strengthened the Dominican insistence on the urgency of dealing sharply with Luther before the revolt spread beyond the power of Church and state to subdue it. The growing number of Catholics in Germany that regarded Luther's teaching as an open question and favoured his standpoint made definite action a necessity. Ignorance of theology, for the very low standard of theological studies amongst the clergy left the laity quite ill instructed, is a primary explanation of the ready acceptance encountered by Luther's doctrines.

But Rome never moves hastily. It took six months for consistories and committees, Cardinals Cajetan and Accolti (the latter is usually known as Aconitanus) conspicuously assisting, to reach the conclusions to be promulgated by Pope Leo X in the bull *Exsurge, Domine, et judica causam tuam*. In this historic document forty-one theses of the ninety-five issued by Luther at Wittenberg are pronounced heretical; in addition all the rest of Luther's published works are condemned publicly to be burnt, their circulation prohibited, and their author forbidden to preach. Luther himself is called upon officially to retract or to present himself personally in Rome, there to make his recantation. Otherwise he will fall automatically under the greater excommunication; to be arrested by the spiritual and secular authorities, and deported to Rome. Sixty days from the publication of the bull in Rome and in the cathedral churches of Brandenburg, Meissen, and Merseberg were allowed for submission, and if at the end of that time Luther and six of his adherents, including Carlstadt, had not made their submission, they must be judged to be heretics.

The bull *Exsurge, Domine,* was drafted in the traditional manner of the medieval Roman curia, the condemnations pronounced on certain of the propositions belong exclusively to the time. These are, of course, in no way to be regarded as papal utterances of divine inspiration. For instance, Luther's thirty-third thesis — that to burn heretics is against the will of the Holy Ghost (*Haeriticos comburi est contra voluntatem Spiritus*) — is censured as heresy, because in the sixteenth century the death penalty by fire was still regarded as necessary and appropriate; nor was it abandoned by Protestants till nearly a hundred years later. Luther's proposition was treated then, by civil and ecclesiastical authority, as public opinion in most lands to-day treats the statement that murderers ought not to be executed.

Again, Luther's thirty-fourth proposition declared that "to go to war against the Turks is to resist God, who punishes our iniquities through them," and this was condemned as heresy. We should to-day perhaps prefer to describe such an opinion as treason. So it was regarded then. Treason to the commonwealth of Christian nations.

Long before the bull was published Luther was made aware that the choice before him was submission, complete withdrawal from the position he had taken, unconditional surrender to that authority at Rome he so heartily hated and despised, or excommunication which meant the ban of the empire and outlawry.

The surrender asked for was not made.

For Luther such a surrender involved the denial of the doctrine of justification by faith alone, and that was for him the saving doctrine, the very essence of the Christian teaching, the one thing needful for all true believers. The original dispute over indulgences was no longer the issue. The battle, as Luther saw it, was between anti-Christ — for there was no doubt now in Luther's mind that the pope was anti-Christ — and Martin Luther; Martin Luther called by God to proclaim the gospel and enlighten the darkness throughout the world and more especially in his native Germany.

This was no time for surrender, no time for yielding; but rather a call to attack; to rally all Lutheran forces against a common enemy. Within his own Augustinian order, at the universities of Erfurt and Wittenberg, at Leipzig, Augsburg, Neuremberg, Luther could count disciples, name friends and allies. The protection of the Elector Frederick was at least for the time sufficiently assured. There was no immediate personal danger. If there had been, Luther might have accepted the protection offered by von Hutten's friend, the knight von Sickingen, that violent champion of the lesser nobles and accepted leader of the robber chiefs, and by the Franconian noble von Schaumberg. Hutten, violently nationalist and anti-papal, cared nothing for Luther's new theology but hailed the monk of Wittenberg as the deliverer from priest and pope, seeing in Luther a power that would destroy the moral restraints of Catholicism and the penal discipline of the Catholic Church, and abolish once and for all the authority lodged in ignorant clergy by virtue of the sacrament of Orders.

Luther without undervaluing the support of von Hutten and Sickingen preferred the surer and more respectable safety of Wittenberg.

From that safety he set forward his attack. Before the bull could be published Luther had printed three startling manifestoes to the German people: (1) the *Address to the German Nobility;* (2) the *Babylonian Captivity of the Church;* (3) the *Freedom of a Christian Man.* The second was written in Latin and speedily translated. Luther carried his dispute with Rome beyond the universities and appealed to princes and nobles and the common people. And not in vain. It was a declaration of war, not a set of theses for academic discussion, that Luther issued while Rome gravely prepared its ultimatum.

The *Address to the Christian Nobility of the German Nation* — to give the title in full — had a large sale and was immensely effective. It was received as a trumpet call to war by Lange, Luther's supporter at Erfurt. The high emotional appeal — and the emotional element that belongs to all great religious changes, for better, for worse, is a predominant element in Luther's character — combined with an invective of surpassing richness, assertion of recognisable grievances, and practical proposals for reform, made this tract or pamphlet highly exciting reading. Here, as in the other books of that critical year, the author portrays himself as the Man of Destiny, raised up by God for the deliverance of the Christian Israel of Germany from the tyranny of the anti-Christ of Rome. Addressed to the laity it is in the main a direct assault on the papal authority without pretence of theological argument. The civil or temporal power must be exalted above the spiritual, Luther contends, while the notion that the pope has the right to interpret the Sacred Scriptures and summon general councils must be destroyed; since to all baptised believers is given the priesthood and a truly free council could well be summoned by the civil authority.

The priesthood of the baptised laity is the call that Luther sounds for the overthrow of popes, bishops, and clergy generally. Temporal rulers are appointed for the correction of sinners. Evildoers, however highly seated in church or state, must be punished by the temporal authority. The sufferings of the German people and indeed of all Christendom under the tyrannical yoke of papal supremacy are set out by Luther in this *Address to the Nobility* as an intolerable injury. The cure proposed is the total subordination of the Church to the state. To the several princes of the Empire, accustomed to an absolute sovereignty over their subjects in temporal matters, this novel proposal came in time to be seen as a sensible and not unprofitable arrangement. Many who were not aware that they groaned under any papal tyranny came to believe it; as men will under instigation come to believe in injuries not hitherto perceived. But the young emperor, the newly elected Charles V, though he might later find in the pope a political enemy, never at any time saw himself in the role of Charlemagne or as the head of the Church in Germany, with the pope deposed in his favour. First and last he was a Hapsburg and the head of the Hapsburgs.

Nobles were addressed, but the call was sounded to all laymen and to all who laboured under irksome obligations. Even the clergy were invited to join the attack on existing institutions and break the bonds of canon law. Monasteries, described as prisons, might be turned into free dwelling places, Luther suggested, with no one compelled to stay in them longer than he pleased. The secular clergy, too, should be allowed to marry, for this celibacy that constrained them was nothing but a device of the devil whose agent was the pope.

Judged at the time, and to this day so judged, as Luther's most masterly piece of polemical writing, the *Address to the Nobility* was a challenge to ecclesiastical authority and a summons to battle that won immediate response. At the same time, in that very year, 1520, Luther writes calmly and respectfully to the Emperor Charles and for the last time to the pope. With Luther all moderation is discarded, all restraint thrown to the winds when the prophetic vein is upon him, and he feels himself another St. Paul; but, in quieter moments the desire is still uppermost for the approval of the authorities he flouted, the favour of sovereigns whose sovereignty he disdained, and the more polite and prudent note is sounded. The complexities of Luther's character are never finally untangled.

To the emperor Luther appeals for protection against enemies, as Athanasius appealed to the Roman emperors in ancient times. He describes himself as dragged all unwillingly into public controversy when his own longing is for the hidden life of the religious and the service of truth. He has done nothing but proclaim evangelical truths in opposition to superstitious opinions; and because of that he has, for nearly three years, been pursued by anger, contempt, and all the hurt his enemies can devise. Vainly has he pleaded for forgiveness, vainly offered to keep silence, vainly proposed conditions of peace, vainly asked to be better instructed. Preparations are being made for his extinction and for the extinction of all evangelical truth. Let him not be condemned unheard but let his doctrine be examined before sentence is passed. All he asks of the emperor, as the "king of kings," is that he, Martin Luther, may be better instructed and if in error convinced of his error. Not as a heretic, not as an impious man does he ask for protection.

The emperor ignored the letter, and, it is said, tore it up at the Diet of Worms.

Luther's last letter to the pope was sent after the bull of excommunication had actually been promulgated in Rome. Miltitz, still busying himself to no purpose in Saxony over plans for peace between the pope and Luther, advised the dispatch of this letter. He also advised the writer to antedate the letter so that it should appear to have been composed before excommunication had been pronounced.

Once more in this letter Luther protests that he is innocent of all personal attacks on the pope. It is only the wickedness and corruptions of Rome and the papal court that are attacked. Luther's enemies, especially Eck, are the enemies of the pope, and it is Luther who has earned the favour and gratitude of Rome by exposing the villainies of Eck. Let Pope Leo, who is no better than a sheep among wolves, a Daniel among lions, not be deceived by the flatterers and fawners by whom he is surrounded, by those flatterers who babble to him of his overlordship of the world, of his supremacy above councils and of his sole right to interpret the Sacred Scriptures. Rather let Pope Leo listen to those who humble him and not to those who exalt him, since God hath put down the mighty from their seat and exalted them of low degree. But the pope must not expect Luther to retract anything he has written, because the "Word of God which teaches all liberty must not be bound."

Luther finished the letter — and what Leo X thought of it or indeed whether he even read it we are not told — with a request for the pope's attention to the treatise he enclosed:

On the Freedom of a Christian Man; the third and smallest of the three books issued in that decisive year. To the pope Luther wrote, of course, in Latin, but the letter and the *Freedom* treatise were immediately published in German and enjoyed enormous sales. The *freedom* of the writer's mind is the treasure contained in faith and complete trust in God. By virtue of his faith the Christian man is both the lord of all things and subject to none, and at the same time the servant of all things and subject to everybody. The spiritual man is free in his inner life; in his outer life, in his bodily works, he is in servitude. By faith his sins are forgiven and he is justified and at peace, with all the commandments fulfilled and free of all things. (The derivation seems plainly from the mystical works of Tauler, the fourteenth-century Dominican.) Interior freedom, the writer insists, is entirely compatible with service due to one's fellows in a Christian society. Good works done to one's neighbour must spring from faith and love of God. They are in no way meritorious in themselves and do not lead to salvation. A Christian does not become devout by doing good works; it is because he is devout that he performs them.

Luther's bitter, controversial note is remarkably absent from this treatise. Its fervour and the vague yet comforting description of Christian liberty were sufficient to win disciples repelled by violent polemics.

As for the third treatise, *On the Babylonian Captivity* of the Church, which preceded the *Freedom of the Christian Man,* it is an uncompromising attack on the papacy, the bishops, and the sacramental teaching of the Catholic Church. Here Luther is not the tender shepherd of simple souls, but the theological professor, the doctor of Wittenberg, laying down the law on current papal falsehoods and on Lutheran truths. In substance the book is destructive; for apart from his doctrine of man's justification by faith alone Luther had not the synthetic mind and his theology is fluid and mobile. (To the last he remained antipathetic to positive dogmatic statement, venting his furious hate against the Swiss schools of Protestantism and their cut and dried systems of theology with the vigour with which he assailed all papal dogma.) Under the shadow of impending excommunication Luther asserts the sacred right of the individual, of the baptised believer, to acquire all truth and knowledge without external compulsion. The Christian Church is in captivity to the papacy, and the papacy is the empire of Babylon. Under this Babylonian captivity the doctrines of the Church have been twisted into falsehoods, and the sacraments of the Church enslaved. The writer by means of the Word of God offers deliverance from falsehood and proposes to free the sacraments from their chains. In Luther's mind the sacraments are in bondage because they have been increased to seven, whereas he is quite certain there are only three — Baptism, Penance, and the Eucharist. By faith, and by faith alone, are these sacraments efficacious.

With the seven sacraments of the church reduced to three, the next thing is to show the doctrine of the Mass a falsehood. The doctrine of Transubstantiation is repudiated, though Christ is certainly present in the consecrated bread and wine (for the chalice must not be withheld from the laity), and the Mass is in no sense a sacrifice.

All commandments of the Church hamper the freedom of the Christian man and vows of celibacy are particularly obnoxious. The fundamental dogma in Luther's *Babylonian Captivity* is the freedom of the individual, the baptised individual, in whom faith is born through careful reading of the Bible. No one, neither pope nor bishop, has any right to dictate to the individual Christian what he shall or shall not believe. There is really no need for Church authority, for the Bible is sufficient for the believer to gain a certain knowledge of the truth. The writer gained this certainty of true belief through study of the Sacred Scriptures and all who will allow themselves to be so guided will come to agree with him. That they didn't arrive at his conclusions after making a study of the Bible was one of the things that puzzled and outraged Luther when the Protestant sectaries multiplied. It was for him inexplicable and abominable that Christians delivered from the "despotism" and "superstition" of the Papal Babylon should differ from their deliverer.

Aware of the immediate promulgation of the bull, Luther styles this *Babylonian Captivity* treatise a Prelude, threatens a sequel against the papacy of greater and more astonishing force, and finishes with the declaration that this treatise may be read as part of the retractation he has been called upon to make.

Then after the final letters to Charles and the pope and the issue of the tract on the *Freedom of a Christian Man* there was nothing more to be done but await the bull of excommunication. Luther had consolidated his forces, he had delivered attacks upon the papacy and the whole Catholic system that had been but feebly met, he counted his supporters throughout Germany and relied upon the protection of the Elector Frederick for safety in Wittenberg. The main contentions in these writings of 1520 won increasing acceptance. On the religious side justification by faith alone, the priesthood of the believer, and the freedom of baptism — doctrines that made each one independent of ecclesiastical authority — by their very novelty and assurance won assent among numbers of the laity, ill informed in the Catholic faith of their fathers and alienated from the Catholic Church by the worldlings of the episcopacy and by the unspiritual lives of clerics, religious and secular.

Again, among the clergy this unspirituality was a fertile ground for a doctrine that repudiated celibacy and denied the vow of chastity to be of God.

On the political side Luther's argument for the civil supremacy over the ecclesiastical and for the extinction of money payments to Rome had a peculiar attraction for nobles and princes and for the self-governing municipalities of Germany.

The reception of the bull was not encouraging for those who stood by the old paths, who feared and hated Luther and his new theology, men and women in whom allegiance to the Holy See was an ineradicable loyalty and the sacrifice of the Mass, the central act of worship.

Dr. Eck was delegated by Rome to promulgate the bull in Germany. On his arrival in September with copies of the papal condemnation of Luther, it was an ill welcome that greeted him. For Eck himself was not a popular figure. His prominence as the pope's messenger was resented, his return disliked as untimely, and the excommunication he brought regarded unfavourably by the German episcopate. The bishops trusted that Luther and his agitation would die a natural death if let alone, they were jealous of external interference, and Eck and his papal bull simply brought matters to a crisis and ended all hopes of peace. Besides who was Dr. John Eck that he should go about Germany giving instructions to bishops concerning papal bulls? While some of the bishops pretended to doubt the genuineness of the bull and hinted at forgery others ignored the receipt of their copy and delayed publication till the following year.

In fact the bishops and universities by their procrastination and by their displeasure at the mission of Dr. Eck thwarted the policy of Rome and diminished the force of the sentence pronounced by the pope. Luther gained time to develop his campaign, and win more recruits to his standard of revolt.

Eck's own diocesan, the bishop of Eichstadt, though he gave orders to the University of Ingoldstadt to publish the bull—which the university did very halfheartedly—himself delayed official publication till the following January. The bishop of Augsburg only yielded on December 30, after two notices from Eck. The archbishops of Salzburg and Mainz, the bishops of South Germany, of Meissen and

Merseberg, of Ratisbon and Passau, all by their masterly inactivity helped to discredit Dr. Eck, to reduce the pope's authority, and thus indirectly to encourage Luther.

Nor were the universities any more favourable to Eck and the bull he brought. Erfurt, after questioning the form of the bull, openly opposed its publication, and the students riotously tore up all copies of the bull that could be found in the booksellers' shops. The University of Vienna refused to carry out the requirements of the bull in spite of the decision of its theological faculty. Leipzig, on the advice of Duke George, took no steps in the matter for months. Nowhere could Eck find any enthusiasm for the papal condemnation of Luther.

The emperor alone stood conspicuously by the pope. Crowned at Aix-la-Chappelle, on October 28, he at once agreed to the requests of the papal legates at his coronation and ordered Luther's books to be burnt in the imperial territory at the universities of Louvain and Cologne. And this was done. Frederick, the elector, anxious for the welfare of his University of Wittenberg, refused to be drawn into direct conflict with Rome or to withdraw his protection from Luther. He would neither promulgate the bull in his own dominions nor deny the papal supremacy in the Church. Like the meddling, incompetent Miltitz, the Elector sought an accommodation, and Luther at his command published a careful defence of his forty-one condemned propositions.

But Luther was busy over other matters than the exposition of theses already three years old. Against Eck his wrath is poured out. Eck with his "Bulls and Lies," for Luther refuses to believe that the bull is authentic and the pope responsible for its issue. It is all an "Eckian Lie" and an "infamous blasphemy."

A second pamphlet followed, *Against the Bull of Anti-Christ,* and in this Luther accepts the genuineness of the papal document, and denouncing Leo X as "an unjust judge, an obstinate heretic and schismatic, an enemy and oppressor of Holy Scripture" declares that he once more appeals from the pope to a free and general Christian council.

Finally, since his own works had been publicly burnt at Louvain and Cologne, Luther resolved to retaliate and burn the whole collection of papal decrees known as the body of canon law. It was not by any means a new idea or a sudden and unpremeditated action, the bonfire at Wittenberg on December 10. Five months earlier, while yet writing civilly to pope and emperor, Luther had announced that he "despised alike the favour and fury of Rome, and wished neither to be reconciled with her nor to hold any communication with her." As far as he was concerned Rome might condemn and burn his books, in return he will burn "the whole pontifical law, that breeding place of heresies."

Now the hour had come for that threat to be fulfilled. Melanchthon nailed on the door of the church at Wittenberg the notice inviting all "pious and studious young men" to assemble on the morning of December 10 outside the Elster Gate and there witness the "pious and religious spectacle" of a holocaust of papal decrees and scholastic theology. They duly assembled — students, lecturers, professors, doctors — at the funeral pyre, and when the fire with its books of canon law and other volumes had been kindled, to the accompaniment of songs and cheers, and was well alight, Luther dramatically stepped forward and threw a printed copy of the bull of excommunication on the flames saying at the same time *"Quia tu conturbasti Sanctum Domini, ideoque te conturbet ignis eternus"* ("Because thou hast destroyed the Holy One of God [i.e., the Truth of God, Christ] so let eternal fire destroy thee").

It was a great occasion for the university students of Wittenberg, December 10, 1520. Luther retired to his Augustinian monastery while the bonfire blazed and smouldered, but the undergraduates made a day of it, as undergraduates will, stirring up the fire from time to time, some singing a *Te Deum,* others some ribald chorus; and then in the afternoon, attired in fancy dress, roystering through the town with a cart that held a ridiculous figure representing the papal bull. So till dusk they kept up the boisterous fun, demonstrating their approval of a favourite professor, all cheerfully unaware of the gravity of events. How could they, these lively youths, foresee the consequences of this gesture of Dr. Martin Luther? What was it to a mob of high-spirited undergraduates that the parting of the ways had come? That nevermore in Germany and elsewhere would Christian men and women worship at the same altars? "If youth but knew!" But they didn't know, these boys of Wittenberg, and how could they know when there had been none to tell them?—that Dr. Luther's act signified a fundamental change in religion, a revolution in doctrine and in public worship; that a new theology, placing man's private judgment in the seat of authority and promising assurance of personal salvation, was inaugurated? The riotous buffoonery on that December day at Wittenberg was sufficient for the students who took part in it. It is not probable that they were seriously concerned with the nature of Dr. Martin Luther's quarrel with the pope. The pope was nothing to them; their Dr. Martin Luther was a popular professor, a great man. The pope was an Italian and a long way off. Dr. Martin Luther was German as they all were. In any quarrel of Dr. Luther's his students, indulging the hero worship that youth is prone to, could be trusted to rally round their favourite.

Luther could attract young men; he had the gift of drawing youth to his side. His lecture room was thronged with increasing numbers in the next year. Only one other lecturer at Wittenberg, Philip Melanchthon, professor of Greek, had a larger attendance, and Melanchthon was Luther's surest, sanest, and most trusted disciple. In the University of Wittenberg whatever Luther and Melanchthon said carried the day. In fact throughout Germany, Wittenberg meant Luther and Melanchthon. But why Luther had been condemned by the pope, or what the bull that condemned him contained, few could have told.

In the years that followed that fateful burning of papal laws and decrees the hundreds of students that crowded Luther's and Melanchthon's lecture rooms would become a solid body of support for the new theology, stalwarts in the war against the pope.

Luther lost no time in explaining to Wittenberg students and to all Germany his position. The day after the bonfire he spoke in his lecture room of the iniquities of the papal see; declaring it was the anti-Christ of Rome that should have been burnt rather than a mere volume of canon law. As they looked for salvation all who heard him must depart from obedience to the rule of the pope.

Rome had excommunicated Luther, Luther's reply was to excommunicate Rome. What the pope had done, he, Martin Luther, could do. Against the authority of the supreme pontiff Luther set up the authority of the individual believer, once more making himself the spokesman of all who put personal and private conviction before the accredited creeds of the Church. Through the printing press he told all Germany "Why the Books of the Pope and His Disciples have been Burned by Dr. Martin Luther." It is an apologia of abounding confidence in the author's righteousness, setting forth the self-justification for censures on the Church of the papacy.

To Staupitz, the but recently retired Augustinian provincial, Luther wrote exultingly of the strife and rejoicing in the tumult he had created. But Staupitz for all that he felt the winning powers of the younger man, and was happy in his friendship with Luther, hoped for reform within the Church. Disappointed in his hope, Staupitz left the already disintegrated Augustinian order and retired to Salzburg, where his friend, the archbishop, made him abbot of the

Benedictine monastery. There, as abbot, Staupitz died a few years later. By that time the forces of disruption he had done nothing to control, had swept over the land and the new theology he had vaguely encouraged had captured the hearts of many.

The startling manifesto in which Luther gave his reasons for the bonfire at Wittenberg was as forceful as most of Luther's writings and as plain for all folks to read. Again, it is the pope and the officials at Rome who are to blame, and he, Martin Luther, a simple baptised Christian but also a Doctor of Holy Scripture, is entirely in the right in denouncing the false doctrine while others neglect their duty. Bad books ought to be burnt, and the books burnt at Wittenberg were decidedly bad; but when they burnt his, Martin Luther's books, great injury was done to the unlearned because these books were truthful. God has prompted him to prefer his own judgment above the authority of the Church, for the system of that Church throughout the middle ages is unchristian, immoral, and dangerous to the salvation of souls. As for what may happen now that he has raised the standard of revolt — that, Luther declares, he cannot foretell. It is enough for him that he has uttered the truth.

In this spirit of proud confidence, conscious of the headway he had made in Germany, conscious also of the poor defence put up by the supporters of the old religion (the Dominicans and Franciscans alone, with the indefatigable Eck, attempted any serious answer to Luther's writings in that grave time) aware of dangers ahead, but glorying in his liberty now that he had thrown off utterly and for ever all allegiance to Rome, broken away from the discipline and authority of the Church he affected to despise, and exchanged the Catholic sacramental system, the ordinances and observances, and above all the sacrifice of the Mass, for the personal assurance of salvation through faith that justified, Martin Luther awaited the diet of the empire that was to meet at Worms early in 1521. Excommunicated by Rome, it was for the emperor to pronounce sentence of outlawry, and place the excommunicated heretic of Wittenberg under the ban of the empire.

VI

Edict of Worms and the Wartburg: 1521-1522

THE EMPEROR Charles V was not yet twenty-one when the diet of the Holy Roman Empire assembled in the city of Worms, early in 1521. The several states had been summoned primarily to settle questions of foreign policy and internal administration. The affair of Martin Luther was of lesser interest. The condemnation of the heretical monk of Wittenberg was an episode in the proceedings. Imperial interests other than theological were of first importance. The separation of the Austrian and Spanish dominions of the house of Hapsburg — the former being resigned to Ferdinand who subsequently came to rule over Hungary and Bohemia as well, while Charles retained Spain with its territories in the Netherlands, Naples, Burgundy, and the new world beyond the Atlantic — was made known to the diet. The danger of war with France, that danger never to be escaped from, compelled imperial demands for levies of troops; compelled also agreement with the pope that would avert a Franco-papal alliance. That an internal danger had been provoked by Luther's attacks on authority was but dimly perceptible till the diet closed.

Many, of course, at the diet were curious to see the recalcitrant monk of Wittenberg, the notorious cleric who wrote in so bold a strain and dared defy the pope himself; many, too, who sympathised with the heretic's denunciation of heavy financial payments to Rome were there; many whose discontent with the state of the Church in Germany was voiced by this Dr. Martin Luther. Not that Luther had any following in the diet for his new and revolutionary theology. Apart from Philip, the landgrave of Hesse — a younger man than the emperor — and Frederick of Saxony, who never became a complete Lutheran, few princes, nobles, knights, and representatives of the free cities were at that stage prepared to adopt a change of religion. But the diet, politically anti-papal and largely anti-clerical, was determined to hear what Luther had to say.

The emperor desired that Luther should be declared an outlaw by the diet, since the pope had pronounced sentence of excommunication; the papal nuncios, Cardinals Aleander and Caraccioli, who were attending the diet urged this course. But the estates of the diet strongly opposed this simple method of procedure. They insisted that Luther should be summoned to Worms to retract and that only on his refusal to retract should he be placed under the ban of the empire. Charles yielded. No other decision was possible. He was not yet twenty-one and but too recently elected to antagonise national feeling in Germany. For Luther's appearance at Worms the diet is responsible. All that the emperor could do was to summon Luther to attend and to send the written safeguard without which Luther would hardly have ventured to present himself.

Aleander, a man of learning and in earnest for Catholic reform, a former friend of Erasmus and the humanists, the reputed author, on no very sure evidence, of the saying "Luther hatched the egg that Erasmus laid," wrote of the youthful Emperor Charles V at this time: "He seemed to me well endowed with sense and with prudence far beyond his years; to have much more, however, at the back of his head than he carries on his face." Aleander also noted when the estates were assembled at the diet and Worms was full to overflowing with clergy, notaries, secular and clerical, and the multitude of retainers brought by princes and nobles "that all the lawyers and canonists were pro-Luther and the majority of monks, friars and lesser clergy — save only the parochial rectors." As for the uproar and commotion in Germany, "nine out of every ten cry 'long live Luther!' while the tenth cries 'death to the Church of Rome!' even if it doesn't care what Luther says." Everywhere people "were shrieking for 'a Council, a Council' and would have it to be held in Germany."

The dispatches of Aleander, who left Worms on Luther's arrival, have been fully preserved. The nuncio did not minimise the discontent at the abuses in the Church nor the gravity of the occasion. He placed his hope in the emperor, confident that "Caesar has the best inclination of any man born these thousand years past," and satisfied that "if he perseveres as he has begun will carry everything according to our wishes and will give peace to the Church."

The imperial herald brought Luther his safeguard and preceded him on the journey from Wittenberg to Worms; that triumphant journey with its cheering crowds and enthusiastic receptions at Leipzig, Naumberg, and above all at Erfurt. Not as a criminal did Luther appear, an excommunicated heretic, under sentence and journeying to hear his doom, when the people greeted him with such applause. It was rather as a successful conqueror or at least as a popular hero that Luther travelled the road. Warned by his friends that there might be danger in Worms, since the safeguard for his journey expired on the day of his arrival, Luther, at one hour full of boisterous high spirits, and in the next fearful and depressed, wrote in reply that he would go to Worms "though the devils in that town be as numerous as the tiles upon the roofs."

A hundred knights escorted him into the city when Luther entered Worms, on April 16, and thousands thronged the streets and accompanied him to his lodgings; crowds also followed him the next day when he made his first appearance before the emperor and the estates of the diet. There was a certain irony about the business that made everybody want to see Dr. Martin Luther. That a priest, and an Augustinian monk at that, should be excommunicated for denouncing the pope, and for printing all manner of things against the Church, was peculiarly intriguing. And now this Dr. Martin Luther was to answer the diet and the emperor himself as to what it all meant—unless, of course, Dr. Luther thought it better to withdraw all the nasty things he had said and written against the pope; and with so many on his side that was not likely. Besides, after all, everybody knew he was right in standing up for his own people, knew that it was a scandal that so much good money should go out of Germany to the pope, when the pope was no friend to the German people. This Luther, too, was saying that we could all go to heaven without so much church-going; that Christ could save us without the help of priests—and why not? Luther it seemed was for less taxes to Rome and less money to priests.

When Luther came before the diet on the day after his arrival, and for the first time in his life confronted the emperor and all the great ones of the empire, his appearance made no favourable impression on the assembly. Shyness and hesitation fell upon him as he listened to the titles of the books he had written, read out by the speaker of the diet, John Eck, chief officer of the archbishop of Trier (not to be confounded with Luther's earlier opponent, Dr. Eck). Called upon first to admit authorship and then asked if he would retract what he had written, authorship Luther did not deny, but he wanted time, he said, to consider the question of retracting. He pleaded respectfully for opportunity for deliberation, so that he might give answer to the question of recanting without imperilling his soul or opposing the Word of God.

It was pointed out that he knew quite well why he had been summoned to the diet, and that he had had ample time to consider and prepare his answer. Nevertheless he should be granted twenty-four hours' delay since he had requested further time. More evasion it seemed to some, this postponement; and the emperor who looked coldly upon Luther remarked on his departure "this man will never make a heretic of me." Aleander, to whom the proceedings were reported, wrote that some thought Luther mad, others that he was possessed, while others regarded him as a man filled with the spirit of God.

Luther, surrounded by his friends, was quite determined to retract nothing.

It was already dusk the next day, April 17, when in a larger hall and before a still more crowded audience Luther began his reply to the question of retracting all or any part of what he had written. He spoke forcibly and effectively, first submitting that his purely religious and evangelical writings could not be offensive, then detailing at length his writings against the papacy, dwelling on the wrongs suffered by the German nation at the hands of the popes—fully assured on that point of the sympathy of many princes and nobles—and asking how he could withdraw words that attacked the doctrines and practices of the court of Rome without giving assistance to tyranny and impiety? For a peroration he warned princes and rulers of the fate that overtook the kings in the Old Testament who resisted the will of God, spoke of "my Germany" and appealed to emperor and nobles not to suffer him to be brought into ill repute by the efforts of his enemies.

He was listened to without interruption and only when he had finished did Eck point out that his erroneous doctrines were the repetitions of heresies long ago condemned by the councils of the Church and that it was incredible the Church had erred. He pressed for a plain answer, would Luther retract his errors or not? To this Luther replied that unless he was convinced by Holy Scripture or plain Christian teaching that he was wrong he could not retract anything, for popes and councils had often erred and contradicted themselves. To do otherwise would be to act against his conscience. He finished with the common formula, "God help me. Amen."

Romantic writers of a later age depicted a solemn audience hushed to silence while the bold and heroic figure of Dr. Martin Luther concluded his address with the words "Here I stand, I can no other, God help me. Amen." (*Hier steh' ich: ich kann nicht anders, Gott helf mir. Amen.*) The words have been handed down and passed on from pulpit to pulpit, and from teacher to pupil, in countless classrooms and lecture halls. But the familiar peroration is quite unhistorical, and it would be difficult to name an accredited scholar to-day who would maintain its accuracy. The usual formula, "God help me, Amen," was the plain finish. Neither was there an impressive silence, but far otherwise. For it was dark and torches had been brought in before Luther finished and the place was in an uproar with Eck still trying to press for a plain "yes" or "no"; many were trying to make their way out, and others were declaiming furiously against Luther for saying that general councils had erred. The emperor declared the assembly adjourned, and Luther left with his escort, calling out, and repeating, in high spirits that he was "through," and that he had succeeded.

For a few days more Luther remained in his lodgings in Worms, but he was not to meet the Emperor Charles again. Efforts were renewed to arrange some sort of reconciliation and the archbishop of Trier was particularly busy in trying to effect an accommodation. Luther with supreme self-assurance refused submission to emperor or pope, to diet or general council, unless it could be proved that his teaching was contrary to the New Testament. To the archbishop, pointing out that his doctrines had been condemned by the Council of Constance, Luther could only reply that the council by so doing had condemned the Word of God. Never was Luther more confident that he was utterly right and all who differed from him incurably wrong than in those last days at Worms. Confident, too, that he was the true Catholic and that the pope and all who held by the papacy and the old paths in religion were servants of anti-Christ. In this mood of exalted confidence in a prophetic mission, strengthened by many signs of a considerable popularity. Luther would yield nothing to bishops and electors.

Bishops and electors on their part found it too hard a thing to believe that God, after allowing the Catholic Church to go astray for a thousand years, had now set apart this young Augustinian monk, Dr. Martin Luther, to ride roughshod over all authority and teach the whole Church its duty. Too hard a thing to believe this new theology of Luther's — that believing you were saved was enough; that the Mass and the regular means of grace must be put down to a much lesser place than Catholic life and practice had hitherto ordered. Besides Luther also insisted that every doctrine must be proved by the New Testament and how could this be done? German bishops and nobles had plenty of grievances against the court of Rome and if Luther had not mixed up these grievances with heretical notions and anti-Catholic opinions concerning the Mass, favouring the revival of the old heresies of Huss that had plunged the land into an appalling war, he might have won a more immediate and a larger body of support. Others he alienated by discrediting general councils, for hopes of reform rested in the calling of a council to correct abuses. But there were signs of revolutionary support, ill omens of peace in the Church. A placard posted at night on the town hall of Worms announced that 400 knights declared war on the

"Romanists." No signatures were attached but the word *Bundschuh* appeared three times at the end, after a threat that 6,000 were ready for war. A sinister word *Bundschuh,* implying that members of the secret society which had for its device a shoe, with long leather straps, as worn by peasants, were prepared to rise against all who interfered with Luther.[1] The emperor's safe conduct made Luther secure. Had this been violated a popular rising would have occurred.

On the other hand the emperor was convinced that had Luther been acquitted civil war would have broken out.

When it was plain to the archbishop of Trier and all who talked with Luther in the days that followed the adjournment of the diet that negotiations were futile, since Luther would yield nothing, nor would he withdraw from the position taken up, no further obstacle remained but to warn Luther that the date of his safe conduct would soon expire and pronounce sentence of outlawry.

On April 26 Luther departed and the imperial herald went with him as far as Friedburg. There Luther wrote to the emperor and to the estates protesting his personal loyalty to the former and his willingness to submit his doctrines to the test of the Word of God. He cannot, he pleads, deviate from the Gospel of Christ. The assumption here as elsewhere being that the writer has interpreted the Word of God in the only way it should be interpreted.

The Elector Frederick always avoided meeting Luther, yet was determined to protect his Wittenberg professor from the attacks of his enemies. Therefore, knowing that sentence of outlawry was about to be pronounced, he arranged for Luther to disappear on his homeward journey. So it hap-

[1] This "union shoe" society had its scattered branches and members throughout Alsace, and that part of Germany now called Baden. It was anti-clerical; its program included the secularisation of church property. Though often suppressed it reappeared, and for thirty years preceding the Peasant War of 1525 kept the spirit of revolt alive.

pened that near Eisenach Luther's carriage was stopped by a party of armed men, his two companions driven off, and Luther himself taken on horseback to Wartburg Castle, a property of the Elector Frederick, who having left the selection of a place of safety to his counsellors wanted to know nothing save that Luther was hidden somewhere out of danger.

The sentence of outlawry, called the edict of the Diet of Worms, was dated the eighth of May, though not actually published till May 26 when the members of the diet had dispersed. It was composed by Aleander and was issued by the emperor with an introductory statement concerning the imperial responsibility for the suppression of heresy. His predecessors, Charles declared, the most Christian emperors of the German race, archdukes of Austria and dukes of Burgundy, were until death the protectors of religion and the defenders of the Faith. They left behind them a Catholic heritage and in the Catholic Faith he would live and die. What his forefathers had established at Constance and other councils of the Church it was his privilege to uphold.

The edict set out the heresies of Martin Luther and in the official language of ecclesiastical authority declared the heretic an outlaw throughout the empire. It is not only forbidden to provide him with shelter, with food or drink, it was ordered that he is to be seized wherever found and handed over to the imperial authority. Disobedience to the edict brought the penalty of high treason, and all who disobeyed were themselves to be treated as outlaws. All protectors and adherents of the heretic were to be arrested and their property surrendered to those who proceed against them.

As for Luther's writings, without exception they must all be burnt, and the plague of books against the pope, against bishops and princes must be exterminated. No books must henceforth be printed without episcopal approval and all books concerned with matters of faith must be submitted to the bishop's censor or to the nearest university theological faculty. This wide censorship, fully in accord with a decree passed at Pope Leo X's Fifth Lateran Council of 1515, was powerless to check the flood of pamphlets that were now being published; even as the Lateran decree had been largely ignored in the preceding years both by Luther and by his opponents. At the time of the very Diet of Worms anti-clerical and revolutionary pamphlets were printed and sold in the city, with other publications deriding the papal nuncio, Aleander, glorifying Luther as saint and hero, and explaining the new Lutheran doctrine.

The edict was issued, thundering condemnation by Church and state. But nothing happened. Save that in the emperor's dominions of Burgundy, and in France by order of the parliament of Paris, and in London, there were bonfires of Luther's books.

While Luther remained in safe quarters, the secret of his hiding place well kept, the Lutheran doctrines were rapidly spread by his disciples. In that same July of the year of the ban, the archbishop of Mainz wrote to the pope that day by day in spite of bull and edict the forces of the Lutherans increased; not only were there very few laymen openly well disposed to the clergy, but a large proportion of the clergy were on Luther's side, and most were ashamed to stand up for the Roman Church, so hated were papal decrees, so great the scorn with which they were rejected by the men of Wittenberg and by others.

Beyond the borders of Saxony, beyond the frontiers of the empire, in Switzerland — particularly in Zurich and Geneva — in France, in Italy itself, and in England, and as far north as Scotland was Luther's printed word carried; to provoke attention, dispute, and controversy; always to win a sympathetic attention in some minds, always to repel others. Accepted or rejected they were read, these writings of Martin Luther, read and discussed while their author lived his hidden life in the Wartburg. Excommunication and sentence of outlawry neither quenched the spirit of revolt in Martin Luther nor shook the strong conviction that he was raised up by God to destroy the papacy and preach the gospel of salvation through faith alone. Excommunication, sentence of outlawry and prohibition of Luther's books neither hindered the sale and circulation nor stopped the printing press.

And while Lutheranism spread, to the dismay of all lovers of the old order in religion, to the anger of the few who discerned the seeds of strife and anarchy, to the satisfaction of souls comforted by the assurance of personal salvation, and to the open rejoicing of anti-clericals who welcomed this vigorous onslaught on ecclesiastical authority, Pope Leo X, exulting in the victory of his new ally the Emperor Charles over the French King Francis, died suddenly in Rome. The death of Leo was in November. Next year the conclave elected the emperor's old tutor, Adrian VI, cardinal of Utrecht, to the papal throne.

For less than a year Luther remained in retreat in the outbuildings of the castle at Wartburg. Structural alterations of a later date have improved the room Luther occupied while legend has been busy adding decorative details to the life of the occupant in those ten months of retirement. Neither from Luther himself, nor from his contemporary disciples, for instance, is the story of the inkstand thrown at the devil derived. Years afterwards Luther spoke of the torments he suffered at the Wartburg from diabolical visitations and from ghosts and other intangible appearances.[2] Yielding to internal imaginings his mind projected visions of good and evil that affected him profoundly. The solitude brought experiences painfully hard to bear, for Luther was eminently a social person, depending on sympathetic companions for the happiness he enjoyed and tor-

[2] Quite possibly he was the victim of *Poltergeist*—a word used by Luther himself.

tured by melancholy in his loneliness. Valiant in the face of opposition, combative when antagonised by disapproval, he had a craving, common to men of such character, for the praise of friends, to hear the spoken expressions of good will.

But whatever the psychic experiences and tumult of brain storms that Luther suffered in his exile — his Patmos as he loved to describe his retirement at the Wartburg, seeing himself and anxious that others should see him as another St. John, the evangelist — the outstanding wonder is the amount of writing done during that time. By far the greatest piece of work accomplished is the New Testament turned from Greek into a German that all could read and enjoy, so that Luther's New Testament has had as profound an influence among his compatriots as the English translation of the Bible, the authorised version as we call it, has had among the British people throughout the world. It remains an amazing performance, carried out by a single man in a few short months without external aid.

The immediate popularity of Luther's New Testament was no doubt assisted by the illustrations, wood blocks that pictured Babylon of the Apocalypse as papal Rome; while at the same time these illustrations and various anti-papal emendations in the text, helped the Lutheran campaign against the pope's authority. But nothing can detract from the greatness of Luther's literary achievement and time has not depreciated the service to the German language rendered by this version of the New Testament. German translations existed before Luther and were there for all who wanted them in the year of the Wartburg retirement. But these existing translations were dull and lifeless, literal translations from the Vulgate, unilluminated by a spark of genius. Luther was not content to turn the Vulgate into the language of contemporary use, he translated from earlier texts and did not hesitate to paraphrase freely as he went. A few years later and the whole Bible was turned into German, but in the ten months at Wartburg was the start made with the New Testament; the first instalment of Luther's most influential, because most enduring, literary work.

With fierce rapidity Luther drove his pen in that solitary time, and certain friends at Wittenberg, sharing the secret of the hiding place, arranged for printing and publication. Fresh attacks on the papacy and the Mass; commentaries on the psalms and the *Magnificat*—the latter richly devotional; lengthy treatises denying the validity of monastic vows; a book on Confession setting out to disprove that a layman was bound to confess to a priest—all in addition to the New Testament; besides long letters to Melanchthon[3] and Spalatin.

The book on Confession was written and dedicated to Luther's turbulent friend and patron, Count von Sickingen, leader and captain of the free knights who lived by war and plunder. In that same year, 1522, Sickingen, to his undoing, made war on the archbishop of Treves. For the princes, allying themselves with the archbishop, were too strong for the old freebooter and Sickingen died of his wounds. His death delivered Germany from one frequent source of disorder. The free knights and their military forays were finished.

Luther looking back on the Wartburg period saw it not as a season of intense literary activity, but as a time of strife with the devil, of struggle with the unseen hosts of hell; yet not always unseen, he believed, for Luther was convinced of the reality of his hallucinations. Then, as throughout his life, it is the hero in the drama enacted that Luther depicts,

---

[3] In a letter to Melanchthon, August, 1521, Luther uses the famous phrase: "Be a sinner and sin boldly but believe more boldly still" (*Esto peccator et pecca fortiter sed fortius fide*). This was not an encouragement to sin, but a reassurance to Melanchthon who was troubled by fear of sinning. Sin was inevitable. Let it be frankly recognised. Only trust the more in the pardon earned by the Lamb of God. Defy the devil. Let the devil do his worst. Believe you are saved, and believe the more fervently.

and that hero is inevitably himself. A hero beset by gross temptations but emerging the conqueror of the tempter; Luther must always win because he is always right. To make his victory the more wonderful, the conqueror the more heroic, the tempter must be represented as an evil being of extraordinary powers. The note of exaggeration is discerned when Luther recalls the defeats he inflicts on his enemies, visible and invisible.

There is no doubt that it was a stormy time in the intervals of hard literary work, that ten months of residence in the Wartburg. Nervous disorders, grave depressions occasioned by physical troubles — Luther suffered, he tells us, from terrible constipation—plunged him into gloom. Study of the book of the prophet Daniel brought conviction that the end of the world was at hand and that Rome bore all the marks of anti-Christ. In letters to Melanchthon Luther mentions temptations of the flesh that made it hard to pray. At another time he writes to the same correspondent of idle days and heavy meals. He no longer dressed as a monk — though he returned to the monastic habit when he went back to Wittenberg — but fancied himself a cavalier; and to complete the picture he grew a beard and long hair. "Squire George" was the name Luther was known by at the Wartburg; occasionally in the character of a country gentleman he would join the chase. No one in the castle knew him for Dr. Martin Luther, the heretical monk of Wittenberg. For his part Luther did nothing to invite exposure; carefully avoiding the chaplain who came to say Mass in the castle; refraining from all practice of his priestly office.

A stormy time and a critical time for Martin Luther that ten months in the Wartburg. His personal safety was never in danger from without; but his sanity was threatened. In one of his writings, in especial in his criticisms of the universities, the theological faculty of Paris, and the pope's

Maundy Thursday bull, the foulness of Luther's invective reveals the monstrous images of a disordered mind. Years were to bring increasing indulgence of this liking for the coarsest, and often grossly indecent, figures of speech in denunciation of enemies.

But the close application, the concentration on his literary work, stop the obvious suggestion of madness. All we can say is that the reactions from spells of labour brought violent license of speech and free abandonment to shocking language.

It was also a critical time for the followers of the new Lutheran theology. While Luther wrote and fought with devils in his solitude, disciples at Wittenberg and Erfurt put the new theology into action. The German reformation was initiated. Archbishops and abbots did nothing to counter the spread of Lutheranism, but confessed a sheer inability to withstand the revolutionary movement. Princes remained indifferent onlookers.

The reports of startling, and by no means approved, developments of the new theology at Wittenberg and elsewhere brought Luther from retirement. He saw the great movement he had started changing into something neither contemplated nor desired. Irresponsible agents were directing the forces of revolt. It was time to take charge and check vagaries.

VII

Spread of the New Evangel: 1523-1524

DISINTEGRATION within the Augustinian priories of Erfurt and Wittenberg, which was to spread rapidly in Germany throughout the order and threaten the peace of all houses of religion, confusion of mind among the laity; tumults, riots, disturbances — thus was the Reformation initiated among the Catholic population in the dominion of the Elector Frederick of Saxony, Frederick of the Ernestine line. Duke George, of the Albertine line, the elector's cousin, ruled his own part of Saxony without concessions to the new movement, but the disintegration went on. Disintegration of the Catholic unity and disintegration of those already separated from that unity. Feeling usurped the place of thought, private judgment came to be raised above all decisions of pope and council, so that quite suddenly, as in a night while men slept, new creeds and new beliefs cropped up and demanded public expression. Since every man was now assured by his reading of Luther's works that with good will and a knowledge of the Sacred Scriptures he could arrive at the truth of revealed religion without external guidance or instruction from priest, confusion was inevitable. Disorder accompanied the confusion when the repudiators of the old faith of the German people forced their new forms of public worship on the townfolk of Erfurt and Wittenberg. Having got rid of the papal authority, the sacrifice of the Mass was abolished and the whole Catholic doctrine of the priesthood cast overboard, for now it was discovered that all true believers of the male sex were priests and kings before God. Destruction of statues and images in the churches followed — graven images being forbidden by the Commandments of God recorded in the Old Testament — and at the same time to invoke our Lady and the Saints or to pray for the dead were condemned as futile performances dishonouring to God. Man was saved by believing that he was saved and all else was vanity. So Dr. Martin Luther had taught, and no matter how widely Christian men and women might differ from the rest of Dr. Martin Luther's teaching, on this point they were agreed.

Carlstadt, professor of theology, who as exponent of Aquinas and the scholastic philosophy had at an earlier time been highly critical of Luther's new theology, now took the lead in the revolutionary movement in Wittenberg, repudiating his priesthood, trampling on his religious vows by taking a wife and then declaring that all clergy must marry, all nuns be set free from their convents. The uprooting of chastity involved the abolition of religious orders, and this destruction of monasteries and convents became an essential article of belief for Lutherans and for all the Protestant churches that emerged from Lutheranism. Abolition of papal supremacy, repudiation of the Mass, contemptuous disregard of vows of chastity — these are distinctive signs of the reformed churches. Student mobs rioted in the churches where Mass was still celebrated. Gabriel Zwilling, a young Augustinian monk, became immensely popular as a preacher of the new religion, and won an enthusiastic body of admirers when he led his particular disciples on an image-breaking campaign throughout the country round Wittenberg. Catholics, loyal to the faith of their fathers, to whom all these things were abhorrent, watched, as though paralysed, the work of destruction; unorganised and unready, they were incapable it seemed of active resistance; bishops and priests, officially the spiritual guides of the laity, either consenting to the desecrations or keeping silence.

And all the time Luther was under the ban of the empire, an excommunicated heretic, to be arrested and handed over to the imperial power by the first good citizen who found him. Carlstadt, too, had been named in the bull brought by Eck from Rome as another heretic under sentence of excommunication.

The ecclesiastical anarchy in Wittenberg troubled the Elector Frederick.

Melanchthon, whose power was persuasive in the lecture hall but of no account with men moved strongly by passion and self-will, contributed a volume called *Loci Communes* to the body of Lutheran divinity (1521). The book maintained that theology must be restated, insisted amongst other matters that all things happened of necessity, in accordance with the predestination of divine law and denied that man enjoyed free will; it was highly approved by Luther and went through many editions. (Melanchthon subsequently withdrew his denial of free will and was vexed that Luther would not also change his mind on that point.) As a restraining influence in that year of Luther's absence in the Wartburg, Melanchthon was useless. He was respected in Wittenberg, esteemed as a scholar and admired as a public speaker. The private character, too, of this least forcible of men was found singularly attractive. Then by his marriage with Catherine Krapp, the daughter of the burgomaster of Wittenberg, Melanchthon had entered into the social life of the city. A naturally tolerant mind, anxious to exercise the spirit of forbearance, to reconcile rather than separate, Melanchthon was always favourable to efforts at ecclesiastical compromise. His own efforts never had any success. That critical year of Luther's absence was no time for compromise.

The disintegration of religion, the disorders that accompanied it, were increased by the coming of Taborites, Christian communists and strange sectaries from beyond the frontiers of Bohemia; and by the arrival of two "prophets" from Zwickau, Nicholas Storch and Mark Stubner, cloth weavers by trade and Anabaptist preachers by vocation; men with apocalyptic visions of the speedy destruction of the ungodly, zealous missionaries of a creed that forbad infant baptism.[1]

Luther hearing of these strange and disturbing elements at work in his own city of Wittenberg was at once indignant and impatient to return. Melanchthon instead of repudiating the unauthorised "prophets" had taken kindly to their impassioned oratory. Carlstadt and the iconoclasts felt no compelling restraint that might lead to moderation. It was as evident to Luther in the security of the Wartburg as it was to the Elector Frederick that the reform movement was carrying its adherents no man could tell whither. In the absence of their leader and master the disciples of Luther had got out of hand and the whole of the "evangelical" campaign would end in anarchy unless something was done, and that promptly, to restore order and discipline. Private

---

[1] Men and women akin to these prophets of Zwickau have appeared over and over again; especially in Protestant lands and English-speaking countries. St. Thomas More, as a young man of twenty-five, had poked fun at such self-appointed doctors in his verse concerning the *Merry Jest:*

> When a hatter will go smatter in philosophy
> or a pedlar wax a meddler in theology,
> all that ensue such crafts new
> they drive so far a cast,
> that evermore they do therefore
> beshrew themselves at last.

Charles Dickens three hundred years later recognised the type and portrayed it in the preacher at Little Bethel in the *Old Curiosity Shop*—"by trade a shoemaker, by calling a divine."

Storch settled in Thuringia, helped Thomas Münzer to draw up a program of communism for the peasants, and died in Munich in the year of the Peasant War.

judgment was right enough when it coincided with Luther's judgment. It was nothing but an imposition of the devil when it was contrary to the Lutheran program. As for the claims of the Zwickau "prophets" to a supernatural guidance and special revelation, Luther would have none of them. So he wrote to Melanchthon bidding him tell the "prophets" that not even raptures that transported men into the third heaven proved a divine commission. Let them work miracles if they would have their claims justified; let them experience as he, Luther, had experienced, the depths and height of spiritual darkness and light if they would have their message accepted as true.

Unless he returned to Wittenberg to direct the movement Luther saw nothing but disaster ahead, the collapse of the "gospel" he had so successfully declared. Personal safety at the Wartburg was of small account if the work that made security necessary was destroyed.

Luther took the step that brought him back to the command. He wrote to the elector announcing his return to Wittenberg. The elector replied that Luther knew best what should be done.

Courage was needed for the step taken. Luther was still under the ban of the empire, an outlaw and excommunicate, his life threatened by Duke George of Saxony. To reappear at Wittenberg was to defy the emperor and the imperial authority. The risk was considerable. On the other hand, the emperor had no power in the elector's dominions and Duke George at Leipzig would not wage war on his cousin Frederick for the sake of getting Luther arrested.

In an historic letter to Frederick announcing his departure from the Wartburg, sent by Luther when he had reached Borna, the writer insists that the devil is causing the trouble at Wittenberg and that it behooves him as one who has received his Gospel from heaven and not from man, not to give way to the devil. God was his protector, and under this protection he was safe from the threats of Duke

George and did not even need the protection of the elector. It was rather the elector who needed Luther as a protector than Luther the elector. For the writer's faith was strong while the elector's faith was weak. Should he be taken or murdered he would not have the elector oppose the imperial authority, for that authority came from God and to oppose it would be to oppose the will of God. The emperor can hardly expect the elector to become Luther's gaoler. The letter ended in a note of exaltation. The writer having faith had the vision of God, the elector not having faith was without that vision.

In the strong conviction of a man called by God, and in the garb of "Squire George," Luther went back to Wittenberg early in March, 1522. He returned triumphantly escorted by a company of knights who had met him on the way.

Fast and furious was the pace of the movement in the next few years. In Wittenberg, throughout electoral Saxony and the free cities of the empire and the northern regions, the new Lutheran religion spread rapidly, and the old Catholic order crumbled. The energy of Luther and the strength of his convictions checked the vagaries and extravagances of the "prophets" and drove out the discordant elements from Wittenberg.

The time had not yet come for the open revolt of the Anabaptists and Carlstadt withdrew to seek and preach another gospel than Luther's, to travel far from the Church of his priesthood. There remained no one to dispute Luther's authority as the apostle of the new evangel — though Münzer, the Anabaptist and communist leader, continually challenged and criticised the Lutheran position — and Luther used that authority with singular effectiveness to consolidate his disciples and increase their number.

Not that Luther was by any means an able organiser or a man of iron discipline. His fluid mind favoured an easy forbearance when agreement was given on what to him were the essentials of belief. Seeing these essentials as entirely reasonable and absolutely true no one according to Luther but the utterly perverse could refuse assent. It was all so simple to Martin Luther in those years of building up the evangelical church in electoral Saxony. That the pope was anti-Christ, that the sacrifice of the Mass was a grievous idolatry, and that all who had taken vows of chastity, priests and nuns in especial, should be released and marry; that the only test of true doctrine was the New Testament as interpreted by Martin Luther, and the only doctrine that really mattered was consciousness of personal salvation by faith in Christ crucified — these items summed up the creed of Dr. Martin Luther. Why could not all good Christians hold the same creed and live in charity with one another without troubling over matters that would right themselves in time? Images in churches, the chalice at holy communion, the apparel of ministers at public worship — what did these things of quite secondary importance matter? Love God and hate the pope were the two commandments. (They have remained the two commandments of certain Protestant bodies to this day; the second in particular.) At the same time the wandering Anabaptists, chiefly from Bohemia, with their doctrines of communism and the coming reign of Christ on earth, were utterly anathema to Luther. For Luther believed in the sinfulness of man and his salvation through faith in a Saviour, while the Anabaptists preached man's perfectibility and the extermination of the ungodly.

The Lutheran reforms were threatened, as Luther saw, by the iconoclasts and by the social revolutionary "prophets." Neither from the pope nor from the emperor could the check on Luther's influence be effected. After the short reign of Adrian — no politician, anxious for unity to be restored in Germany and for Christendom to be made safe from the Turk — came the election of the Medicean Pope Clement VII. Once more political considerations were of absorbing interest to the papacy, and were ultimately to result in war with the emperor and the sack of Rome by the constable of France and his German troops. The emperor himself was in Spain in the years of Luther's re-establishment at Wittenberg. The council of state for the empire, the *Reichsregiment* established at Nürnberg, had no resources to meet the Lutheranism, now growing and spreading in Germany.

It was not only the clergy, regular and secular — the latter including several bishops — who inclined to Luther's side and soon openly abandoned the old faith of Germany for the new evangel, the laity in electoral Saxony and in the free cities and in the dominion of Philip, landgrave of Hesse, accepted in increasing numbers the ministrations of the Lutheran divines. What else might well be expected to happen? Lutheran pastors were the clergy who had administered to them as Catholic priests and only by degrees was the order of public worship changed and the Mass perceptibly abolished. In Wittenberg, when Luther had reasserted his authority, the Mass was no longer the Mass because the officiating priest deliberately left out all the words of the canon and all the prayers that made it the sacrifice. But the clergy were advised by Luther to continue wearing the old vestments, to elevate the Sacred Host at the consecration, and to retain the choral singing and the Latin hymns, lest the worshippers should be driven away by unfamiliar and unliked changes in public worship.

Luther relied on the sermon and on propaganda by the printed word for the complete overthrow of the old religion. In the pulpit and with the pen his energy was terrific. Others, hitherto Catholic priests, now on Luther's return became active lieutenants of the new evangel. Notably Dr. Justus Jonas and John Bugenhagen, the latter to be known as the trusted organiser of Lutheranism in Denmark and the Scandinavian countries. Luther himself was the power that conquered so much of Germany for Lutheranism. Not always, in the pulpit, in the study, or in social intercourse was he the sharp controversialist and bitter enemy of the papacy. In that period of consolidation, the years immediately following the return from the Wartburg, Luther was often enough the preacher of morals, of neighbourly duties, and of common Christian practice in everyday life. Much of his writing was directed to assist Christian people in their daily prayers and conduct. The writer was in touch with the people to whom he preached and for whom he wrote. Luther never forgot that he was the peasant's son. He could handle his audience, as we say. The foulness of speech, the coarseness of expression that revolted many of the humanists favourable at the beginning, were no stumbling block to ordinary laymen, since in all ranks of masculine society coarseness and foul speech are familiar to the ears. Against the hatred for men in opposition to him Luther balanced as strong an affection for his disciples and for students and simple people seeking help. The pride that set Dr. Martin Luther up above popes and kings who withstood his message, had its counterpart in the genial unaffected friendliness displayed to intimates. No pride of place, no dignified reserve of manner marked the person of Luther in his circle of friends, in the intercourse with younger men. Nor did his marriage with Catherine Bora, the Cistercian nun, for all her high descent, bring social exclusiveness within the family circle.

Then, too, Luther was a poor man in those years at Wittenberg. The Augustinian monasteries, now for the most part anti-papal centres of the new teaching, were in poverty. Lutheranism having no room for monks or nuns, the *raison d'être* for the Augustinian priory no longer existed.

The agitation for a married clergy with the repudiation of all vows of chastity was successful in drawing secular priests to matrimony, and also in reducing the numbers of both men and women in religion. Many of the latter, it is certain, as willingly as monks and friars, came back to the world and married because they never had any desire and never any vocation for the religious life. The reforms effected by St. Theresa disclosed the easy conditions in the Carmelite order in Spain. In Germany the conditions were even more relaxed and the nunnery was at times but little different from a ladies' club in the twentieth century. Perhaps a women's hostel or college would present a closer resemblance. Unfortunately the sixteenth-century German nunnery was not infrequently the home proposed for young women of respectable and often of the noble family to serve for a place of life-long residence, as the only alternative to marriage; and on no other ground. The result was that many inmates wearied of the routine of religion. Though by no means shut out from the world or deprived of worldly interests — since visitors were freely admitted in the convents of relaxed observance and the fullest opportunities for talk were allowed — yet the spiritual life, which had been sparsely tended at the best, was frustrated and the whole aim of the religious order and the high purpose of its vows forgotten. When therefore the news spread that Augustinian priests were declaring that all nuns should be let loose from their convents; when it was told that priests, including monks, were publicly getting married, it was inevitable that women disaffected from the religious life, should become restless. Remaining under its discipline only because no alternative presented itself, they may never have really recognised it as a vocation. As the pressure to leave the convent increased and no particular tie to remain was strengthened, nuns broke away from their environment to marry the priests who sought them.

Luther's energy, impatient of local opposition, found fresh means of assisting the spread of his evangel in Germany. He encouraged the forcible suppression of the Mass when the populace backed such suppression, imposed silence on priests who still believed in the Mass in Wittenberg and neighbouring towns, incited independent princes to place themselves at the head of the reformed churches in their territories, and drew up a new order of public worship and a collection of German hymns.

The most famous and the most popular of all Luther's hymns *Ein feste Burg* ("A safe stronghold our God is still") is of later composition, but the collection published in 1524 represented Luther's happiest efforts as an adapter of the old Latin hymns and the maker of what may be called religious folk-songs. In making these spiritual songs a feature of public worship Luther ministered to the instinctive desires of his fellow-countrymen, fostered the pleasurable emotion that a music-loving people feels in choral singing, and reconciled many to the changes that were taking place.

That the Reformation in Germany was practically forced on the laity by the clergy in electoral Saxony in the first place, and that only on its development was it imposed by the secular lay government — the prince or city council — on the subject people, is implied in the answers of two provosts and the Augustinian prior at Nürnberg to the list of questions sent out by their diocesan, the bishop of Bamberg in 1524.

To the enquiry as to the due administration of the Holy Eucharist and the other sacraments of the Church the reply was that the chalice was given at Holy Communion to all recipients; that no one was exhorted to auricular confession "but we allow our assistants to give a Christian exhortation before the reception of the sacrament"; not only the gospel and epistle were read in German at the Mass but the whole Mass was said in German "so that the bystanders may understand"; children were baptised "in our own tongue"; unction for the sick was ignored "neither enjoined nor forbidden."

As to prayers for the departed: "We have given up both the watching and the masses for the dead, and if any person desires such service we decline to allow them."

The answers to four other questions indicate how far the Lutheran teaching now possessed the Nürnberg clergy:

1. Were the hours of prayer and feasts of the Church observed according to the order of the bishop of Bamberg? "We do not pray according to episcopal ordinances but according to the devotion of our heart. Fast days and saints' days are announced but not enjoined."

2. Was the obligation to obey the general councils of the Church recognised? "Where an entire council has decreed anything relating to the Christian faith according to the tenour of the simple and pure work of God we hold that we are bound to be more obedient to the word of God than to men. Where, however, councils decree anything contrary to holy Scripture one is under no obligation to obey."

3. Were they ordained to the priesthood according to the order of the Church? "Alas! yes, and God have mercy on us."

4. Do they admit themselves to be under the bishop's jurisdiction? "We have no Lord but God alone; for His sake we submit ourselves to all creatures. We confessed that at our ordination we promised to obey your grace but we call the word of God to witness that we are bidden and commanded to do otherwise.

"Before making any change we did approach your grace, and your grace replied that we must make no change till the coming general council had been held. But since the council is still unheld and is probably postponed for a considerable time we have changed the ancient customs of the Church and ordered them after the word of God, since we are bound to obey God rather than man."

The city fathers of Nürnberg and Augsburg passed swiftly to Lutheranism. When the imperial diet met in Nürnberg in that same year, 1524, the letters of Friar Paolo Ziani who was in attendance on the papal legate, Cardinal Campeggio, revealed the hostility to the old order. The legate had to enter the city "like a mere horseman." "Some of the nobles and the mass of merchants are all tainted; nay they are obstinate and not to be converted, so that at present neither the authority of the legate nor the will of the princes can stem so strong a current." Diets, the writer judged, "profit little, because the free towns that really are not subject to anyone cannot be curbed; and these free towns abet Lutheranism and are asylums for all converts."

Nothing was accomplished at that Diet of Nürnberg. The legate's demand that the decree of the Diet of Worms against Luther should be put into operation was met by the expression of a pious opinion: the edict should be executed "as well as they were able and as far as was possible." The estates of the Holy Roman Empire represented at the diet could say no more than that. No effort was made either to arrest Luther — for that could only be done by first deposing the Elector Frederick — or to stop the propaganda of his disciples.

Catholic members of the diet, though in a very big majority, were more concerned with the neglect of German interests at Rome than anxious for the suppression of Luther. (Pope Adrian VI had admitted through Chieregati his nuncio but a year before that grave abuses existed in Rome and that Luther was not to be blamed for calling attention to these abuses. But now Luther's heresies threatened destruction; of all law and order no less than of property.) The diet called for a general council, or failing that, a national synod in order to settle the various points that divided Lutherans from Catholics.

The first signs of the coming division of the empire into Catholic and Protestant states may be detected, shortly after the Diet of Nürnberg, in the assembly that Campeggio convoked at Ratisbon, an assembly of Catholic princes; and in the counter gatherings of the cities and nobles favourable to Luther at Spier and at Ulm.

The beginnings of Protestant diversity are also notable. No less notable is the complete withdrawal of the humanists from alliance with the advocates of the new evangel; made manifest to all Europe in a special way through the repudiation by Erasmus of Luther's denial of free will.

The division between Erasmus and Luther, widened and deepened by the latter's vituperative reply to the defence of free will, was not to be mended. At the same time the clergy who rallied to the new evangel and became accredited preachers of Lutheranism included several men of influence. In addition to Melanchthon, always to be ranked as the first of Luther's captains, may be mentioned Justus Jonas, rich in social gifts, a companion highly congenial to Luther in hours of relaxation, and no mean Latin scholar; John Bugenhagen, indispensable for composing rules and regulations for the Lutheran church and the stout defender of Luther's doctrine of the Eucharist against the negative Swiss opinions; Nicholas von Amsdorf, who went from Wittenberg to superintend the new church at Magdeburg and was always aggressively Lutheran besides being personally sympathetic; and two more elderly clerics, Jerome Schurf, senior of the jurists at Wittenberg and Luther's legal adviser at the Diet of Worms, and Wenceslaus Link, once vicar-general of the Augustinians in Germany. The Augustinian monks generally embraced the new evangel, but few Franciscans and fewer still Dominicans — the notable exception among the latter being Martin Bucer — were persuaded to renounce their vows. Oecolampadius the Brigettine monk, and Osiander, a secular priest, stand out among the foremost antagonists of the Faith in which they had grown up. But the former attached himself to Zwingli and the Swiss school; the latter earned the reputation of a prolific writer of controversial divinity.

These are but names — Oecolampadius, Osiander, Schurf, Amsdorf, Jonas, and the rest — footnotes to the pages of the history of the German reformation. Their utterances and voluminous contributions to Lutheran theology are heavy reading. To revive an interest in their proceedings is a hard matter.

It is not so with Martin Luther. The energy and passionate vitality of the man, whose flashing eyes were noted by all who came in contact with him, have left enduring marks. The disruption he wrought is maintained. The homely wit, the foul invective, the utterly unspeakable abuse of enemies, the praise of friends, astonishing in its lyrical enthusiasm, are remembered. His very moods, deep melancholy that at times verged on despair and the high spirits of supreme confidence when all seemed well with him; demonstrations of human affection alternating with expressions of fiercest hate; avowed abandonment of restraint when self-will pointed the way; contempt for clear thinking and scientific theory—these qualities endeared Luther to many of his contemporaries and still attract where feeling is ranked above intellect. The same quality made no appeal to the unemotional—to the Emperor Charles V, for instance—and left Duke George of Saxony quite unfavourably impressed. Lutheranism has exhibited many varieties of belief since the time of its founder. Its hold on German and Scandinavian people—no other Protestant nations adopted Lutheranism—is inseparable from the attachment to its founder.

In that year, 1524, Luther was the mouthpiece of what may justly be called a popular movement; pre-eminently the peasant's son, the avowed foe of tyranny, of the tyranny he ascribed to the pope of Rome in especial; the champion of harshly used labouring folk; the preacher of a free evangel to respectable townsmen. So far his movement had not depended on political patronage for the success achieved. Outside the dominions of the Elector Frederick and Philip of Hesse, and the precincts of certain cities, the new evangel had not been protected by the authority of princes or supported by civic government.

Catholic layfolk had acquiesced in varying degrees of satisfaction and dissatisfaction in the changes in public worship and in the doctrines preached by their clergy. What else could they do? There is no reason to suppose that either in town or country the laity in any considerable number particularly resented the changes in religion forced upon them by Lutheran divines and by Swiss reformers. Nor is there evidence that such changes were generally welcomed. The laity stood by the old paths where any lead was given them. Without leaders, since few priests even when hostile to Luther were capable of shepherding the faithful at a crisis, the laity succumbed. They thus came to embrace the new evangel or the more drastic reforms of Zwingli—already favoured in southwest Germany—to follow the strange, mystical, and entirely subversive teaching of Anabaptist prophets and other revolutionary preachers of communism.

Luther, then, the spokesman of a movement to be described as popular had, though he knew it not, reached the crossroads in that year 1524. On the eve of the Peasant War he was the avowed champion of the most oppressed class in Germany. Before the war ended Luther had allied himself with the princes against the rebel peasants. Anabaptist communism, professed by the latter, made this inevitable. Lutheranism henceforth was political; its success depended on the adoption of its tenets by rulers of states. The Peasant War marks the change.

VIII

The Year of the Peasant War: 1525

FOR MORE than seven years Luther was at once the driving force in the anti-papal movement we call the Reformation in Germany and its recognised leader. By tongue and pen he had persuaded many that his message was true, and so withdrawing them from obedience to the old religion had brought clergy and laity, monks and nuns, to proclaim themselves free to follow where Luther led; in some cases to pursue a path that was by no means of Luther's choice. For seven years then, whatever might be happening in Switzerland, it was true to say that in Germany the reformation was Luther and Luther was the reformation.

After 1525, the year of the Peasant War, Luther is no longer seen as of supreme importance in the establishment of Lutheranism and its evangelical church. Influence he still exercised. Power with the pen and command of violent language were not diminished in the twenty years of life that remained. But the Peasant War marks the change of direction. Henceforth the control is not chiefly in Luther's hands.

Luther himself cannot justly be held responsible for the revolt of the peasants against intolerable conditions, for the war waged in the spring of 1525; still less for the destruction wrought. Spasmodic agrarian revolt occurs in the thirty years preceding; the once formidable organisation of the *Bundschuh* was never totally extinct. It is the immense number involved in the Peasant War, the revolutionary program of its ablest leaders, the utter ferocity displayed, that distinguish this struggle for independence and for mastery from the earlier and lesser revolts; as a general strike for revolutionary ends may be distinguished from a local or trade strike to secure improved industrial conditions.

Luther never contemplated social revolution when he urged princes to treat more considerately the demands of long-suffering peasants for the mitigation of ills; when he pleaded with the nobles to treat sympathetically requests of overburdened men for relief. By his very nature and upbringing Luther could feel for the miseries of the peasants, could desire in all sincerity that their wretchedness should be diminished. Yet he was far from wishing to see peasants supplant princes when the latter favoured the Lutheran evangel. He was furiously angered when the peasants waged war against all who withstood them, and, while professing articles of evangelical faith, made arson, robbery, and murder the signs of their warfare. It was disaster to the whole anti-papal and evangelical movement if the program and practice of rebellious warring peasants were to be identified with Lutheran doctrine.

At the same time Luther's own revolt from ecclesiastical authority, his doctrine of the priesthood of the laity and uselessness of a hierarchy, and no less his lavish abuse of opponents in high estate, favoured social and moral discontent. Many a familiar landmark in the round of church service had been removed since Luther began his campaign against Tetzel, and however distasteful to Luther the social upheaval of the peasant revolt it is true that he had encouraged a spirit of insubordination, had released forces hostile to all duly constituted law and order.

As for the peasant leaders any opinion of religion they expressed showed them nearer to the hated Anabaptists than to Luther. In the main the opinions expressed in their Twelve Articles, composed and circulated before the actual rising, were moderate enough though the note of a Christian communism is apparent.

The charge that the peasants by assembling together were exhibiting the "fruit of the new teaching" as a lawless conspiracy to overturn all authority in church and state is answered in the introduction to the Twelve Articles. So far from the Gospel being the "cause of revolt and disorder" it is set forth as the message of Christ "teaching only peace, patience and concord." The reader is advised to study the Twelve Articles and judge for himself how far the reproach against the evangel is deserved.

The Twelve Articles disclose a reasonableness in social matters that won no response from princes or nobles, a reasonableness utterly disregarded on both sides when the peasants took up arms. In brief the demands of the Articles were:

1. Each community to choose and appoint its own pastor and have the right to depose an unworthy minister. The pastor thus chosen is to "teach the Gospel pure and simple, without any addition, doctrine or ordinance of man." (The peasants, of course, were here implying the Lutheran conditions.)

2. Each parish to pay a fair tithe of grain; from this tithe the pastor is to be paid "a decent and sufficient wage" for himself and his family; what remains is to be given to the poor. Other tithes and taxes to be abolished.

3. All serfs to be set free; obedience is to be rendered to elected authorities.

4. Right to fish in rivers is to be extended to peasants.

5. Denial of woodcutting in the forest to peasants except under heavy payment to be abolished; every member of the community to be free to help himself to such firewood as

he needs in his home. Forests to belong to the community.

6. Excessive services at present demanded from the peasants, and daily being increased, to be reduced.

7. Further oppression of the peasants to cease and agreements to be drawn up defining the landlord's powers; peasants to be paid for their services.

8. Just rents to be fixed for holdings since the high rents exacted bring ruin on the tenant.

9. The constant making of new laws and unfair administration of justice to be checked by return to the "old written law." Each case to be decided on its merits and impartially.

10. Enclosure of common lands and appropriation by private persons to be remedied by restoration of all such lands to the community. When such enclosed land has been purchased some "brotherly arrangement to be made according to circumstances."

11. Death duties (*Todfall,* in England *heriot*) to be wholly stopped. Widows and orphans no longer to be thus shamefully robbed.

12. Any article here set out if proved to be contrary to Scripture to be given up. Further complaints of offences committed if found to be justly formulated according to Scripture will however be added to the articles.

All through the late summer and autumn of 1524 the peasants in the Black Forest and upper Suabian regions were refusing to pay tithes, perform serf duties, or make serf payments. They were enrolled in a union that covered all that was later called Baden. The articles drawn up by the union leaders are very similar to the Twelve Articles and as moderate. The chief points are the abolition of serf labour, of excessive taxes, of the game laws that gave the nobles hunting rights and other exclusive privileges, protection against arbitrary arrest and unfair magistrates.

To gain time the nobles promised consideration. Both sides prepared for war. And on Passion Sunday (1525) the war began.

The whole countryside of southwest Germany from the frontiers of Switzerland to Thuringia and Saxony rose in arms against princes and nobles, and destroyed castles and monasteries. Upper and lower Alsace, Wurtemberg, all Suabia, Hesse, Franconia, the Austrian provinces of Styria, Carinthia and Carniola with the city of Salzburg were filled with armies of peasants and men from the mines. Middle-class citizens opened town gates to the invading hosts, choosing a conciliatory part rather than perish in the fury that distinguished the progress of revolt. Many attached themselves to the uprisen peasants in rural parts, as many citizens did, from sheer fright; intimidated as men in all ages are by the fear of the herd, unable to withstand the pressure of "public opinion," shrinking from resistance to the majority. Outlaws and robbers, the criminal element that attaches itself to every revolutionary movement, flocked to the peasant standard, to become prominent when murder and plunder were afoot. Yet in spite of their vast numbers and the fact that the professional soldiers of the empire had not returned from the campaign that ended at the battle of Pavia leaving Charles victorious and Francis a prisoner, the peasant armies were overthrown in that springtime of 1525 and their leaders everywhere slain. Internal jealousies made success hopeless from the start; the armies of the peasants coming from different parts would not, perhaps could not, coalesce under a common command, were unable to adopt any strategy that promised military victory. Divided from one another by mutual suspicions army after army of these desperate but untrained country folk was beguiled to an armistice or persuaded to make peace before being slaughtered.

The enthusiasm of visionary communists setting out to battle with the feeling that they were as the Israelites of old waging war "with the sword of the Lord and of Gideon" against enemies doomed to perish, prevailed among certain of the leaders, and for that vision they died. It was not shared by the bulk of the peasants, whose demands were simple enough, and who were now exasperated to savagery by the disregard of all their petitions. The ablest of the revolutionary peasant leaders, Thomas Münzer, an ex-priest, quite without military experience and quite the most resolute of the Anabaptist preachers, saw in the uprising the revolution that was to end all social tyranny and usher in the day of communism and universal brotherhood. Only it was necessary to kill those who withstood the revolution before peace could be assured.

Münzer did not share the illusions of other Anabaptists who declared that the millenium was at hand and that the reign of Christ on earth was about to begin. Münzer, moving further and further away from all doctrinal belief in Christianity to a materialist nationalism — and contending furiously with Luther in the course of that movement, berating Luther as the friend and flatterer of princes — was the itinerant preacher of revolutionary Anabaptist communism throughout Thuringia, Suabia, Alsace, and northern Switzerland. He was prepared to enforce his communism by violence since no other way seemed open. Even before the peasant revolt became general Münzer and his disciple Pfeifer had established a communist dictatorship at Muhlhausen with Münzer as the recognised prophet of the revolution and its executioner. Defeat and utter rout came in May and Münzer was beheaded. A month later and the whole war was over.

The Anabaptist propaganda survived Münzer's death, to trouble Lutherans and Catholics, to emerge finally from revolutionary surroundings and become the germ of modern Baptist churches throughout the world. But after the Peasant War the Anabaptist was regarded as the anarchist came to be regarded in the late nineteenth century and as the communist or bolshevik in our own days. No distinction was made between the revolutionary Anabaptist, avowedly intolerant of all Christian beliefs, and the entirely pacific

Anabaptist whose ideal was brotherhood with all who shared his faith, whose notion of happiness was family life extended to converted neighbours. The colonies of Protestant separatist sects that flourished in America, the Owenite and Tolstoyian colonies in England, and the Moravian groups were composed of persons much of the same type as the quiet nonresisting Anabaptists of the sixteenth century. As all communists to-day — bolshevik or pacific — are suspected of revolutionary aims and penalised in many lands as enemies of society so all Anabaptists came to be feared and hated by civil authority in the sixteenth century as conspirators against law and order. Zwingli at Zurich was not satisfied till the Anabaptist preachers who entered the city and refused to give up their beliefs were imprisoned and then drowned.

But few of the German peasants who engaged in that destructive and savage war in the spring of 1525 shared in the visions of a millenium; neither did they, any more than did the townsmen and citizens who openly joined the revolt, profess the communism of the Anabaptists. The strength of immense numbers gave confidence to the peasants at the beginning, and conscious of their power they took vengeance on their traditional enemies, the large landowners, making no distinction between the lay nobles in their castles and abbots who held the vast estates of the larger monasteries. The occupants of castle and monastery were driven out, the buildings fired and the wealth of treasure carried off or burnt. The peasants had their crowded victorious hour and left ruined castles and smouldering monasteries to mark their triumphant course. It was a short hour and the vengeance taken was repaid with terrible interest when princes and nobles once more employed professional soldiers set free for home duties after the battle of Pavia.

So far from urging pity Luther called on the princes to show no mercy to the defeated and fugitive peasants. In speech and in writing he denounced the baseness and

wickedness of the rebels with a fury that matched the
of the peasants and the vengeance of the nobles, finding
them too vile to be allowed to live. All the violence he could command went into these denunciations—and it was an exceedingly extensive command of invective that Luther possessed. Such encouragement to repression was superfluous. With the peasant armies scattered or annihilated, princes and nobles could take swift measure of revenge on the surviving remnants, could prove themselves as savage as the peasants themselves. Only the fear that there would be none left to work for them if all peasants and miners were put to death stopped the work of hangmen and torturers.

Luther's violent condemnation of the peasants and his injunctions for their heavy punishment naturally put an end to his career as a popular leader. The leadership was lost beyond recovery when from Dr. Martin Luther, the peasant's son and one-time advocate of justice for the peasants, came the bitterest and loudest cry for vengeance on rebels. At the same time it was not only rebellion and social revolution that aroused Luther's hatred. On all sides he saw varieties of belief and extravagances in religion that, if not suppressed, would prove fatal to the success of his evangel.

To compensate for the loss of popularity Luther's relations with the princes, with bishops and abbots, became far more friendly after his frantic appeals for the exercise of authority. His position was regarded less unfavourably, since it was plainly hostile to conspirators and the social revolution. Definitely he was on the side of "law and order." Luther, it now appeared, for all his rebellion against the pope was no rebel against the rulers of Germany; rather he enlarged the powers of princes and would have them rule over the church as well as over the state.

Catholics who had suffered in the Peasant War looked to the arm of the civil authority for protection against fresh outbreak and relied on the princes to save them from the terror of social revolution, from the ruthless proletarian multitude that hated monks and the religion of monks.[1]

Lutherans now simply made the prince who was sympathetic to the new evangel the head of their church. Philip of Hesse and John, the successor of Frederick, Elector of Saxony, were in their respective dominions supreme in the church no less than in state. In both lands the religious houses, with their vast estates, passed into possession of the state, abbots and priors offering no resistance.

Thus Philip made himself master of the famous abbey of Fulda — Fulda with historic associations that went back to the days of St. Boniface, for Boniface himself had been given the lands of Fulda by Duke Carloman and in the lifetime of the apostle of the Germans four hundred monks were settled there. The purpose of this donation had been to make the abbey, subject to no authority save that of Rome, a centre of civilisation in that dark period of the eighth century.

Now, eight hundred years later, the abbey of Fulda, independent but no longer a centre of civilisation, no more a place of learning than a house of devotion, its abbot living as other great nobles lived, with few monks but more than four hundred serfs to labour on the rich and highly fruitful lands, passed into the hands of the state. A long chapter in the religious history of Germany closed when Fulda became the secularised property of Philip, landgrave of Hesse, as many a similar chapter closed in England a few years later when Henry VIII dissolved the monasteries. With Fulda securely annexed other religious houses were easily appropriated.

Luther, whose flexible mind had for a while favoured a

[1] For a study of the reaction of the religious orders — the Carthusians in especial — to the increased powers of the State after the Peasant War see *The Reformation and the Contemplative Life,* by David Matthew and Gervase Matthew, London, 1934.

federation of free congregational churches as the ideal for his disciples, now accepted the principle of the state church.

He had no choice.

Lutheranism, to exist at all as the creed of an organised church, must rely on the protection of the state. Otherwise it was bound to crumble, dissected by private judgment, the prey of every wild and fanatical preacher, the victim of ignorant and lawless mobs. Having rejected the authority of Christ's Vicar, Luther decided that, henceforth, the state must be the constituted ruler of the new church. Moreover, only in those lands and free cities where the civil authority adopted and enforced the new evangel was Lutheranism successful. In the end Lutheranism was to emerge as the creed of the evangelical state church of Prussia, to survive as the official religion of the nineteenth-century imperial Germany. The year 1525 saw the beginning of that emergence.

The practical advantages for the princes in the new Lutheranism over the old papal Catholicism had for some time been obvious to others in high estate besides Philip of Hesse and John of Saxony; notably to Albert, grand master of the knights of the Teutonic Order; also to members of the hierarchy, George von Polentz, bishop of Samland and Eberhard von Queiss, bishop of Pomerania, the first of the German episcopate to proclaim their preference for Lutheranism. Both these Prussian bishops were under the authority of the grand master, and he raised no objection to their remaining in office after renunciation of the old religion. His own passage to Lutheranism was already accomplished. On the repudiation by Albert of all knightly vows, followed by his marriage, the two bishops promptly took wives in like fashion.

Lutheranism in Prussia, established by these bishops with the full encouragement of Albert, required a drastic uprooting of Catholic order, Catholic customs, and Catholic piety. It declared that two sacraments only were henceforth to be allowed, baptism and the Lord's supper. Auricular confession to priests was directly abolished, the daily mass forbidden as an "abomination." Abolished also and prohibited were pilgrimages and religious processions, masses for the dead, and prayers for the dead, the ceremonial use of holy water, salt, the Ash Wednesday ashes, the Palm Sunday palms, the Candlemas tapers, and the "greenery" used for the decoration of churches. All religious orders were dissolved, bishops were only retained as superintendents and not for the ordination of clergy. Priests, monks, and nuns had full liberty to marry. All the old Catholic holydays—save Christmas, Easter, Whitsun and Sundays—were summarily dismissed as "sheer nonsense and fables," and since they kept men from their daily work must no more be observed. No feast, no fast—the observance of fast days was no longer required. At the time of Communion the consecrated bread must be taken as God's Body, but it must not be reserved nor so taken at other times.

In Prussia the new evangel even pursued Catholic piety within the home and forbad candles to be lit before sacred pictures.

As for the funds of brotherhoods and guilds, these must no longer be spent on masses for deceased members, but must be devoted to the poor and "other pious uses."

Luther could write with exuberant confidence to Bishop Polentz in that spring of 1525, "See the miracle! How rapid the stride of the Gospel to Prussia, with what full sails it is hastened!"

To bishops, backed by the grand master of the Teutonic Knights, who dared offer contradiction? Whatever lingering affection for the old religion existed—and the Faith was not utterly moribund—no vital opposition to the new Lutheran order of public worship is recorded in Prussia.

The immediate financial advantages of Lutheranism over the Faith of the holy Roman Church were self evident. Payments to Rome, fees and initial expenses on appointments to benefices or bishoprics, ceased. No more collections for "Peter's Pence." No further drain of good German money to an anti-German and pro-French pope by the purchase of indulgences. Freedom to marry, the legal marriage of clerics superseding illicit unions — children formerly illegitimate henceforth born in wedlock. Freedom, too, from old rules of fasting and other irksome mortifications of the flesh, which however ill-kept were a source of physical discomfort. Complete freedom from foreign spiritual overlordship signified to minds, covetous of sovereignty, an alluring prospect.

The practical advantages of turning Lutheran were obvious. The reasons for remaining loyal to the obedience of the holy Roman Church were inconspicuous to men of high estate, lay or clerical, when faith was diminished and charity grown cold.

In the case of Albert Hohenzollern, grand master of the order of the Teutonic Knights — once famous as crusaders but long fallen on evil days and become a wealthy community chiefly engaged in trade — personal inclination favoured change as far as observance of religious rule was concerned; neither from within nor from without could pressure or persuasion urge loyalty to the old religion.

Albert of Brandenburg-Ansbach, last grand master of the Teutonic Knights, is presented in history and may be studied as a type of high ecclesiastic in northern Germany who so far from opposing Luther readily welcomed the new evangel. One of the many sons of Frederick, the Margrave, brought up in courts and camps, untaught in theology and without education in letters, Albert was elected grand master on the advice of Duke George of Saxony in 1511. The Teutonic Order with large estates in Poland and Prussia had wealth, but the occupation of the knights was gone. Riches, joined with unemployment, naturally brought corruption. Commercial activities left no room for high spirituality. No pretence of keeping the vow of chastity was exhibited by the clergy or knights of the order. The alternative to reform was dissolution. Reform was hardly feasible when the knights had nothing to do except look after trading profits, and the original purpose of the order long obscured was largely forgotten. It had been founded to combat the advancing Turks in Hungary, a task not in itself attractive, which now appeared a servile submission to the Emperor Charles, and as such earned Luther's veto. With these reasons in mind the grand master decided on dissolution. For some years past he had been drawn to Luther's anti-papal teaching and after a visit to Wittenberg had directly encouraged Lutheran preachers in the territories of the Order. Again Luther's positive commendation of marriage was not disagreeably received by the grand master. To dissolve the Teutonic Knights and marry, and at the same time remain master of the property of the order, was Albert's policy and he carried it out skilfully, provoking no active opposition.

Intermittent warfare between the Teutonic Order and the king of Poland was brought to an end by Albert making peace on terms entirely agreeable to the latter. All the lands of the Order in Prussia were made over to the king of Poland who in return gave them to Albert on condition that Albert acknowledged the suzerainty of Poland. This done the late grand master proclaimed himself duke of Prussia, the black eagle displaced the old black cross of the Teutonic Knights. Lutheranism was swiftly established as the official religion. Heavy penalties, at the same time, were imposed on all clergy who stuck to the old Faith or did not loyally carry out the changes in public worship enjoined by authority. Albert's marriage with a daughter of the king of Denmark strengthened the power, as it enlarged the political importance of the duke of Prussia.

While Lutheranism spread, the influence of its founder

was seen to wane. Approved by princes Luther might be, and indubitably was, for his denunciations of peasants. But this approval, extended to Luther's new evangel, contained no strong element of respect.

Luther's own marriage in that same year of the Peasant War certainly provoked uncomplimentary remarks. Men accustomed to Luther's bitter denunciation of celibacy shook their heads disapprovingly: were somehow shocked at Luther himself, the Augustinian monk, taking to wife a Cistercian nun, Catherine von Bora. Melanchthon wrote privately expressing his regret.

Martin Luther was now forty-two. A dangerous age for men of strong passions. Glorying in the matrimonial adventure, Luther wrote with his accustomed coarseness of the marriage bed. But a popular hero, a national leader engaged in preaching the righteousness of a cause and the necessity for overthrowing all enemies, can hardly turn aside in the midst of conflict to get married without losing some measure of the admiration and esteem that flow from disciples. The choice of bride is criticised by many. Others take it for a sign of weakness, of the common frailty of lesser men, this craving for the indulgence of human love and its carnal gratification. Unworthy somehow of Dr. Martin Luther, who had led them out of the papal house of bondage into the land of free gospel, this avowal, that he was, after all, as other men, in the lusts of the flesh. In Wittenberg itself canon lawyers doubted the legal propriety of a marriage between a monk and a nun.

Luther and his Catherine went their way. The Elector Frederick, to whom Luther presented the Augustinian monastery at Wittenberg, had returned it to his favourite theologian; so the house of monks was turned into a dwelling place for Dr. and Mrs. Luther. Five children were born of the marriage. The pleasures of domestic life brought mental and bodily relaxation to Martin Luther. Music comforted him and brought harmony to his conflicting passions.

In music Luther found the harmony that was not to be found without him or within. But the direction and control of the movement he had initiated escaped him.

Not only could princes and free cities order the new religion after their own desire, without consulting its founder, but the advance from Switzerland of the doctrines of Zwingli threatened, and in several areas superseded, the Lutheran faith in southern Germany. At Strassburg Martin Bucer, the ex-Dominican, already dispensed from his order by papal authority, evolved for his congregation a confession of faith that was taken to be somewhere midway between the opposing creeds and catechisms of Wittenberg and Zurich.

Bucer was given considerable importance in England, and as Cranmer's friend and divinity professor at Cambridge, had his part in drawing up the Book of Common Prayer. In Germany the struggle between Luther and Zwingli for supremacy in the new churches was not greatly affected by Bucerian propositions.

These two, Luther and Zwingli, were antipathetic; agreed only in hatred of the papacy and in the fundamental Lutheran dogma of salvation by faith alone. For Zwingli, a secular priest, educated in the renaissance, with none of Luther's high emotionalism or morbid introspection, but with a zest and capacity for politics that Luther never had, the time and the place alike were eminently favourable for revolution in the church. Zurich in 1510 had been made, by agreement with Rome, a free city. Its council, exempt from the jurisdiction of the bishop (whose seat far away at Constance was rarely left for visits to Zurich), possessed authority over the regulation of monasteries and the guardianship of public morals. Zurich a great centre for the recruiting of Swiss troops for the papal armies must needs be conciliated by Rome, but the liberties granted brought the extirpation of Catholicism within the territories of the city — and far beyond.

Zwingli was not alone in opposing the enlistment of the finest youth of Switzerland for the mercenaries of the pope; in hating the drain of life from his native land for foreign service, the service of an alien monarch. Laws were passed and continually broken to stop the emigration of young men for military enterprise. Bribery on a large scale was required for the success of the nefarious trade. Then, too, the lure of military service in a famous regiment won many a Swiss to the papal armies. But the letters of Zwingli reveal how fiercely this priest at Zurich detested the engagement of Swiss mercenaries for the endless campaigns of the popes.

Zurich, enjoying political independence, found it an easy matter to achieve ecclesiastical independence, to discard totally every allegiance to pope and absentee bishop. Compromise was not in Zwingli's nature. The principle that governed Zwingli and the city fathers of Zurich who carried out his church policy, was a return to what was supposed to be "primitive Christianity." Hence in the Zurich churches it was not enough to abolish the Mass and the Catholic ritual, to destroy all images and statues, pull down every altar; even the very organs must be broken up lest the familiar music should recall the medieval worship.

Luther's love of music had been far too deep to sanction any such course in Germany. Neither could Luther tolerate the radical doctrines of Zwingli concerning the sacrament of the Lord's Supper. With faith in the Mass gone Zwingli's practical mind and matter-of-fact intelligence would not allow the sacrament to be anything but a sign and memorial of Christ's death. The Lutheran dogma of consubstantiation — the substance of the bread joined with the presence of Christ — he utterly rejected as less worthy of credence than the old Catholic dogma of Transubstantiation.

In that year, 1525, evidence that Luther's influence in southern Germany was gravely checked by the spread of Zwinglian doctrine is manifest. To the favourable attention given to the Swiss invasion, by Philip of Hesse and other independent rulers, was added a sympathetic audience to Zwinglian preachers.

Luther might rejoice over the conquest of Prussia to the new evangel, he could but vainly rage when a doctrine other than that of Wittenberg, a doctrine more austere, with a starker discipline, from Switzerland, penetrated his Germany, capturing the hearts of many, withdrawing many souls from the true Lutheran faith.

Till his death Luther was never reconciled to the exercise of a private judgment in religion that brought departure from Lutheranism, or involved separation from the true believers of the evangelical church. It remained inexplicable, an insoluble mystery, that men and women could read the Bible and not discern the meaning of the Sacred Scriptures as Martin Luther discerned it.

Anabaptists and Zwinglians, Luther concluded, must be led by the devil in their resistance to the gospel revealed by Martin Luther. God had appointed him, Luther said more than once, to preach the gospel; therefore that any man should preach another gospel was an intrusion of the devil.

Anabaptists and Zwinglians simply stuck to their private judgments, denied Luther's claims, and continued to win disciples from Lutheranism and from Catholicism. Caspar Schwenkfeld, prominent as an ecclesiastical layman and effective as a preacher of Luther's evangel among his fellow nobles in Silesia, also came to a denial of the Lutheran dogma, and to carry his followers with him in the establishment of a fresh and independent evangelical church, vague and mystical in creed, in south Germany. In vain Luther fulminated against the desertion of one of his earliest disciples.

IX

Attempts at Reconciliation: 1525-1534

DEPRESSION rested on the Catholic laity in the years that followed the Peasant War. Lutheranism might be distracted by preachers of radical Zwinglianism and by the wilder prophets of Anabaptist communism whom no persecution could extinguish, but for Catholics who clung to the old Faith there was scanty comfort in the spread of religious anarchy, in the displacement of unity by cities of confusion. Unshepherded, unprotected, distracted, the Catholic laity in whole territories and important cities of Germany were left to accommodate themselves as best they could to alien theology, to become as strangers in their native land, to see their children grow up in what their parents had been taught was heresy.

Where could help be sought, or found? Emperor Charles and his brother Ferdinand had no liking for Lutheranism or any other kind of heresy, but Charles was rarely in Germany and Ferdinand was chiefly concerned with the government of his Austrian dominions and the pressing need of defence against the Turks. Both men tended carefully the fortunes of the house of Hapsburg.

Besides for Charles there was always the threat of invasion from France to be guarded against, the struggle to maintain the Hapsburg supremacy in Italy not neglected. Princes and prince-bishops professing the Catholic Faith were not enthusiastic for action in support of imperial policy. Jealous of encroachment on their territorial sovereignty, the Turk might reach the walls of Vienna, for all these princes cared, rather than that they should suffer the emperor to extend his powers. Yet for mutual aid the Catholic princes of the empire, lay and clerical, were driven to unite in a League — the League of Dessau — after the Peasant War. Men for political ends will fight for the Faith, while neglecting to practice their religion. Here and there in Catholic dominions heretics were burnt as enemies of the State, as Lutheran princes executed Anabaptist heretics and put witches — poor, friendless, and elderly women mostly — to death. Revival of Christian charity, deepening of spiritual life, instruction of the faithful in the truths of their religion, renewal of sacred promises, none of these things being contemplated by the worldlings who held bishoprics and abbeys as their own or reigned as secular princes, the consequence was that the laity sank into indifference. In apathy and in despair they passively accepted what Lutherans, Zwinglians, or Anabaptists told them.

As for the pope, the Medicean Pope Clement VII, he was far too absorbed in the political problem of papal independence to give attentive hearing to news from barbarous Germans in revolt against the Holy See. Clement's concern was the overwhelming power of the emperor and the danger this signified to the papal states. In Pope Clement's view the Catholic emperor menaced the welfare of the papacy far more than the heretical Wittenberg monk, or the Swiss rebels at Zurich. The emperor had armies and commanded the Spanish infantry. He held Naples and could encircle the papal states of the church unless defeated. With the pope's ally, Francis of France, routed and taken prisoner at the battle of Pavia, the safety of the papal states was unassured.

Unless fresh allies could be found the pope would be left at the emperor's mercy. Therefore, in 1526, Clement joined the new league of Cognac, and together with Henry of England; with Francis of France, now self released from captivity by the violation of his word, and with the republic of Venice, he combined against the overweening power of the emperor. The unexpected result was that Bourbon, constable of France, deserting to Charles, led a victorious and unpaid mutinous army, including thousands of Lutherans, into Italy and into Rome itself. The fate of the Eternal City, taken and given over to horrible massacre and unchecked outrage in 1527, with the pope first a prisoner in Rome, then a fugitive, marks the end of the Italian renaissance. The sack of Rome was the harvest of Clement's fatal policy, and this appalling and shocking thing was the work of the troops of the Catholic emperor, Charles V. Not that Charles had contemplated so terrible a vengeance on the pope or desired that the city should be the prey of ill-paid soldiery. Luther took the sack of Rome for a sign that Christ was on his side. "The emperor is compelled by Christ to destroy the pope for Luther's sake," he wrote when the news reached Germany.

More and more it was questioned in Germany why the German people should remain loyal to the pope when the pope was at war with the emperor. Answer there was none, and when peace was made at Cambrai, and three years later as a sign of reconciliation Pope Clement crowned the emperor at Bologna, in 1530, it was still industriously taught that the pope was no friend to Germany, that patriotic Germans had no need of any pope to order their religious beliefs. Princes and prince-bishops, largely sharing this point of view while retaining their traditional Catholicism, had no zealous inclination to coerce Lutherans.

One fact stands out in these years of the Catholic depression, as it stood out in the earlier years of Luther's revolt — the number of ex-Catholic priests who busied themselves in the establishment of the new evangel and in the work of withdrawing the laity from their old obedience.

Then, too, Catholic Germany was without a leader; for Duke George of Saxony, steadfast himself in the old Faith and in loyalty to the emperor, hating Lutheranism as a disruptive element in church and state, had none of the qualities of a crusader. Neither ambition nor the spirit of adventure urged him to action outside Saxony. Circumstances favoured the party that attacked. Lutherans, Zwinglians, Anabaptists were far more interested in upsetting the existing ecclesiastical order, in bringing in their own particular doctrines and forms of public worship, than were Catholics in the exclusion of heresy. Indifferently instructed, in many places scandalized by the lives of their prelates, Catholics at the best stood on the defensive, anxious only to be left alone in the practice of their religion. Unprepared to withstand the violence of the attacking forces, they felt secure merely because of the protection their rulers accorded them. When princes turned Lutheran, their subjects generally followed their rulers and dutifully became Lutheran.

As for controversy, no Catholic writer could be found in Germany to match Martin Luther in his popular appeal. In sheer force of invective alone he surpassed all contemporaries. He could overwhelm his adversaries with a string of pointed epithets and delight readers with the variety of his ludicrous comparisons and the fullness of his vituperation. With satire and abuse went homeliness of illustration. Luther could be sure of readers; his writings were well printed and their sales were successfully organised. Dominicans and Franciscans wrote zealously in defence of the Catholic position — to find themselves ridiculed and misrepresented when Luther replied. Secular priests can also be named among the apologists for the Catholic Faith, temperate writers for the most part, yet ready enough often in flinging back scurrilous epithets intended to damage the reputation of the heretic at Wittenberg. But when it came to the selection of personal epithets for opponents Luther had a far wider range at his command, a far greater skill in affixing the damaging word. Luther's writings were "good sellers," anti-Luther literature found comparatively few purchasers.

If Luther ridiculed and misrepresented his enemies, there were plenty of libels circulated on the anti-Lutheran side. Drunkenness was one libel; a charge based on the fact that Luther, gross enough himself at the table, made light of much of the heavy drinking that was common. The answer to this charge, apart from the lack of evidence, is Luther's literary industry and the number of sermons preached; a drunkard could not have fulfilled these tasks. It is also admitted that no man ever saw Martin Luther drunk. Equally without foundation was the libel that Luther was the father of illegitimate children. Here again Luther's free talk on sex, disclosing obsession with the carnal needs of man, and the gratification of the flesh — is partially responsible for the falsehoods circulated; falsehoods recognised as such in Luther's lifetime.

The direction of the anti-papal movement had passed from Luther's hands to be assumed by the secular princes of the Empire. But Luther remained the unrivalled champion of the movement, its great exponent, a European figure challenging Catholic Christendom. His writings for years to come poured across national frontiers. Earlier, Henry VIII, King of England, had been provoked to write *contra* Luther in defence of the Seven Sacraments and was rewarded by the pope for this good work with the title "Defender of the Faith" for himself, and all future kings and queens of England. Luther, not to be put down by emperor or German sovereign, still less by any king of England, replied to Henry with customary truculence. This brought in St. Thomas More and St. John Fisher as apologists for the old Faith, the former not disdaining to return invective for invective, since no other means seemed appropriate or serviceable in dealing with so foul-mouthed a controversialist; the latter replying with his sober and scholarly "Defence of the Priesthood." In Great Britain as elsewhere Luther's printed works, however much prohibited, trickled through forbidden channels to purchasers and readers. With the changed outlook on the relations of Church and state, the emphasis of the writer on obedience to the civil authority and loyalty to the ruling prince, won naturally from kings and ministers, already committed to absolute rule, a less hostile reading.

Luther, never by nature a revolutionary, now long persuaded that the obedience claimed by the pope and the doctrines and devotions developed and associated with the dogma of papal supremacy must be discarded as innovations, accepted a situation that on the whole offered success through state patronage alone. He was satisfied that his new and pure evangel should thus everywhere be preached and believed.

Obedience to authority became the first and great commandment in Lutheran teaching. (Yet Luther is always wavering on the question of duty of submission to the emperor, the power of the emperor being strictly limited and circumscribed.) In the meanwhile certain original items of the Lutheran confession disappeared. The priesthood of the individual believer, absolute liberty of conscience, freedom of the church from state supervision, election of clergy by the Christian people of God, all these fundamental tenets of the new theology of Wittenberg were of necessity discarded or ignored when the ruler within his own dominions was acclaimed by Luther as the guardian of church doctrine, the font of ecclesiastical justice, the steward of the revenues of the church, the patron of church benefices.

That streak of hard common sense, which Luther for all his moods of violent mental disturbance never entirely lost, joined with a contempt for logic and consistent thinking, made it impossible for him to trust the mass of lay people, already falling out among themselves and embarking on the wildest and most subversive social schemes. There was no alternative but the rule of the state, the absolutism of the territorial sovereign. For their part princes, Catholic and Lutheran alike, approved the argument for new and wider powers, and acted on the teaching. No man more so than Philip, landgrave of Hesse, an autocrat complete within his own dominions.

The Catholic princes of the empire could produce no such leader as the landgrave. Small of stature was Philip of Hesse, restless, highly strung, large hearted. Contemporaries found him persuasive and, when he liked, pleasant. (They noted also the passionate indulgence of carnal desires.) Supple and versatile in politics, ready to dismiss prejudices as mere scruples, Philip cared nothing for the welfare of the empire. When imperial interests clashed with the interests of sovereigns within the empire, the emperor must be opposed. Philip's liking for the Lutheran evangel succumbed to a preference for the starker doctrines of Zwingli, but political needs made him strive for reconciliation of the rival systems of new theology as earnestly as he sought to bring the two leaders into some sort of agreement.

But compromise was impossible for Zwingli while Luther, always anxious to keep on good terms with the landgrave, could not accommodate his sacramental beliefs to the austerity of Zurich.

The inclination to Zwinglianism gave Philip keener enmity to the Catholic emperor and the imperial house of Hapsburg. That Ferdinand should succeed his brother Charles would never be if the landgrave of Hesse could prevent it. Philip prepared for the diet of the empire to meet at Spires, 1526, by organising the league of Torgau, in alliance with John of Saxony. Successor of Frederick, the latter was Luther's old protector, an avowed Lutheran.

The Catholic electors of the empire had their defensive

league, set up at Dessau, but Philip's league was a far more militant affair. When the diet of the empire met at Spires (1526), and a message from the emperor urged the enforcement of the edict against Luther, the Lutherans were strong enough to defeat all proposals for enforcing the sentence of outlawry and to carry their own resolution — the *recess* — declaring that the execution of the sentence against Luther must be left to the discretion of individual rulers. This decision introduced a new state of things for hitherto the empire had been, at least officially, one in its religious faith.

For Charles at war with the pope, for Ferdinand watching the advance of the Turks in Hungary, it was no time for enforcing decrees against Luther, with half the empire apparently on Luther's side.

Three years later, when the diet was again summoned to meet at Spires, the Catholics were the better organized party. Zwinglians and Lutherans were then outvoted and the imperial authority reasserted. Against the proceedings of this diet came the protest of the minority, and those who signed the historic protest and their adherents earned the name "Protestant" — a convenient name, all-inclusive of opponents of the Catholic order. Lutheran, Zwinglian, Anabaptist, and in years to come Calvinist, Anglican, Methodist, Unitarian, would all enroll themselves under the Protestant banner, and "protestantism" become the generally accepted term for the religion of Christians separated from the Catholic unity at the time of the reformation.

Of course it must not be inferred that the five princes of the empire (Landgrave Philip of Hesse, Elector John of Saxony, Margrave George of Brandenburg, Duke Ernest of Brunswick-Luneberg, Prince Wolfgang of Anhalt) or the governing councillors of the fourteen free cities of the empire (Strassburg, Ulm, Nuremberg, Constance, Lindau, Meiningen, Kempten, Nordlingen, Heilbronn, Reutlingen, Isny, St. Gall, Weissenberg, Windsheim), who signed the protest, were aware that they had brought a new and most serviceable word into the history of the Christian Church.[1] The majority at the diet rescinded the *recess* of 1526, affirming that the edict of Worms must stand until a general council was assembled, declaring further that the "innovations" in religion should not be allowed in Catholic territories, while in the Lutheran states there must be no prohibition of Catholic worship. The religious peace of the empire proclaimed at Worms with its sentence of outlawry on Luther must continue. Anabaptists and Zwinglians were to be penalised as inciters to rebellion.

While Luther and Melanchthon were uneasy at the apparent readiness of the Zwinglians to break up the empire and bring in the radical doctrine of Zurich to the displacement of the more conservative creed of Wittenberg, Philip of Hesse, vitally concerned with smashing the Hapsburg power, sought to federate all anti-Catholic forces into one communion. The "protest" united for the moment the elements, opposed and fundamentally irreconcilable, of Wittenberg and Zurich. Philip of Hesse judged shrewdly that enmity between Zwinglians and Lutherans was fatal to the Protestant anti-imperial federation of his plans. Acting on this judgment, he decided that Zwingli and Luther must be brought together. Agreement once established between the leaders, their followers would naturally coalesce. Zwingli frankly anti-imperial, contemptuous of Luther's reluctance to accept the radical Protestantism of Zurich and pursue the argument of revolt to its logical conclusions, agreed willingly enough to Philip's proposal for a conference, a theological disputation on the doctrine of the Eucharist. Luther

[1] "Of such slender dimensions was the original Protestant church; small as it was, it was only held together by the negative character of its Protest; dissensions between its two sections increased the conflict of creeds and parties which rent the whole of Germany for the following twenty-five years." *Cambridge Modern History,* Vol. II, Chap. VI. Professor A. F. Pollard on "Social Revolution and Catholic Reaction in Germany."

and Melanchthon also agreed, but less willingly. They had misgivings.

In the end Philip brought together in his castle at Marburg the ablest leaders of the schools of Wittenberg, Zurich, and Strassburg. Luther and Melanchthon led the Wittenberg contingent, which included Jonas, Myconius, Cruciger, and Menius. Zwingli brought Oecolampadius with him from Zurich. Bucer had two companions, Hedio and Jacob Sturm. For the three days various conferences were held — with little result. The famous public debate between Zwingli and Oecolampadius on the one hand and Luther on the other, when the latter chalked on the table the words of Christ *Hoc est Corpus* lest he should stray from the ground of his belief — Christ present in the sacrament though the bread remains bread — brought no change of mind to either side.

Zwingli, at the prompting of Philip, pressed for a union of hearts, since Luther would not budge from his eucharistic doctrine of consubstantiation. Zwingli, as a practical politician, did not regard the disagreement as a matter grave enough to hinder a common working alliance for Protestant ends. Luther, distrusting himself, fearful of being drawn into Zwingli's rationalism, was with difficulty persuaded to promise fraternal union.

The political union directed against the emperor, which Philip and Zwingli had hoped for, was not consummated. Zwinglianism made some progress in the cities of the Rhine lands, while Lutheranism was more favoured by territorial rulers. Wherever the Zurich creed was adopted altars and images in the churches were destroyed and a temper hostile to the imperial policy exhibited.

Luther's fifteen articles of Marburg were accepted by Zwingli and Bucer in the interests of "fraternal union"; but this was not a hard matter since Luther admitted in the article on the sacrament that differences of opinion existed concerning the Presence of Christ and that "Christian charity should be mutually extended as far as each man's conscience can allow on both sides."

The disputants left Marburg unconvinced, and efforts made by Luther himself to reconcile the separate groups of Protestants were as fruitless as the Marburg conference. Zwingli, while professing personal good will to Luther, could yet hope "to isolate Wittenberg" and thus leave the field clear for the Zurich program.

Luther, afflicted at that time, before and after the visit to Marburg, with mental distress that made him self-persuaded he was the victim of a vast conspiracy for his overthrow, suffered from strain of overwork. Pope and emperor, princes and bishops, attack him, he cries piteously. Erasmus and the Swiss sacramentarians, "nay the whole world," is ranged against him. The severe depression with its moods of bitter despondency, the excited rages against the devil, the wild notes of exaggeration, all the signs of nervous exhaustion, must be put down to overwork.

Distracted by the decay of morals on all sides, and no less by the spectacle of people abandoning the old religion without making any general submission to the new, Luther drew up his Catechisms — the Little Catechism "for children and simple folk" and the Large Catechism for the preachers and pastors of the evangel of Wittenberg.

These two catechisms, admirably effective for the instruction of ministers and laity, express the official Lutheran doctrine. Enjoined as textbooks to be studied and taught in dominions ruled by Lutheran princes, they became part of the library of Lutheran theology. Luther's intimate knowledge of the people for whom he wrote, his capacity to persuade and convince the indifferent, are manifest in these catechisms. No invective nor violent abuse of the pope, the Mass, or the old religion of Germany distract the reader or arouse ill will to the author. Luther, writing for people still nominally Catholic but largely ignorant of Catholic Faith and doctrine, avoids creating prejudice against his evangel.

He intrudes no comments liable to hostile interpretation. The old Catholic rule, long obscured through the neglect of bishops and parish priests, is followed in the Little Catechism and the Ten Commandments, the Creed, and the Lord's Prayer are made of first importance in the religious education of lay people. The sacraments of baptism and the Lord's Supper are also expounded. But the essentially Lutheran doctrine of justification by faith alone is not unduly stressed, and no suggestion is made of the right of private judgment for readers of the Bible; neither is it suggested that the articles of the creed of the church may be subject to private judgment. As for Luther's once passionately directed attacks on free will and his strongly avowed dogma of man's predestination to heaven or hell — on such controversial matters the catechisms are silent. Luther's purpose was to establish a lively and reasonable Christian faith among people growing up in doubt and extreme perplexity — the old order being apparently overthrown, a new order not plainly set up — and to check the flood of paganism that threatened to submerge all Christian belief and the very existence of all moral law.

When Luther wrote he rarely wrote in vain. The catechisms did achieve very largely the purpose of their author. Thousands lost to the Catholic Church were saved from utter unbelief by these documents.

Though the course of the Protestant Reformation was no longer directed by Martin Luther, for political and economic interests rather than zeal for the new evangel animated the princes and governing bodies of the cities, he still exercised power through his pen. That prolific pen was rarely at rest in those years when the political forces, Protestant and imperial, were gathering in opposition. Acute nervous prostration that brought feelings of misery and despair, beclouding his mind in terrible gloom, was the result.

Catechisms, treatises on the administration of baptism and the marriage ceremony, lengthy writings against Anabaptist and Zwinglians are not the full tale of Luther's literary work in those exacting years. He was steadily proceeding with his translation of the Old Testament, a work not finally completed till 1534.

Luther did his work, suffering mental torture in the process; Philip of Hesse and the princes of the empire did theirs. Emperor Charles, at peace for the time with the pope and with Francis, turned his attention once more to the religious question in Germany.

The imperial diet was summoned to meet in the Bavarian city of Augsburg in June, 1530, and thither at the time appointed came princes, Catholic and Protestant, lay and clerical, with official theologians, Cardinal Campeggio in attendance as papal legate. Luther came as near to the frontier as he could, and residing in the castle at Coburg watched the proceedings with sharp attention, now advising and now abusing the Protestant delegates at the diet.

The emperor, long absent from Germany and not realising that the Lutheran schism and the wider divergence of the Swiss Protestants was not to be healed by attempts at conciliation, sought in vain at the diet to win support for his policy: a united Church in a united nation. He saw Germany threatened by the Turks, with Sultan Solyman in possession of Hungary; by the French, with Swiss Zwinglians prepared for alliance with Francis for the overthrow of the Hapsburgs. Pope Clement still looking to France for security against the might of the emperor was not unreasonably suspected. (A year or two hence and the pope would give his niece, Catherine of Medici, in marriage to the Dauphin.)

Charles was conciliatory, bent on bringing Lutherans and other recalcitrant Protestants into line with the Catholics of the empire. His hopes were doomed to be frustrated from the first. It was the Feast of Corpus Christi when the diet opened and the customary procession — for Augsburg save for a minority of rich burgesses was a Catholic city — proved more splendid than ever. For two hours the emperor marched bareheaded behind the Sacred Host in the monstrance, through the streets of the city; but the Protestants deliberately kept away from the procession and from all Corpus Christi services. The emperor met this rebuff by the prohibition of sermons by Protestant divines while the diet was in session. But he persisted in conciliatory efforts, and Luther, nervous at the Zwinglian advance, favourable at that season to the principle of authority in general and to the imperial rule in particular — always provided the authority of the state, and ultimately of the emperor, would allow the Lutheran gospel to be freely preached and the Lutheran church to be protected in the possession of sequestrated Catholic property — expressed appreciation.

Melanchthon, too, the chief delegate from Wittenberg, has also left his witness of the character of the emperor at Augsburg and to the impression made by the emperor's conciliatory policy; a policy by no means to the liking of all his Catholic princes. "In this religious question," Melanchthon declared, "in which our adversaries with wonderful cunning strive to exasperate him [the emperor] against us, he has always heard us in a judicial spirit. His private life is a model of continence, temperance and moderation." This private life of the emperor, noted by Melanchthon, was something very unlike the private lives of princes and prince-bishops at Augsburg. Nor were Protestant princes more reputable in their private lives. Landgrave Philip of Hesse was the very last person whom friend or foe could call continent, temperate, or moderate.

The emperor in fact made a far more distinguished appearance than any of the delegates at Augsburg. Luther issuing manifestoes to his disciples from the safe retreat at Coburg is overshadowed. The emperor held the centre of the stage. Thwarted by the Catholics as he often was, continually flouted by the Protestants, Charles never lost his head. He retained his composure and stuck to the conciliatory attitude. It was by far the more prudent course in the face of hostile elements not to be pacified. But Charles was by nature a grave, cold man.

Melanchthon also was for moderation and conciliation — to be blamed by Luther for weakness and reproached by Zwinglians for betrayal of the evangelical cause. (Not that Zwinglians would have accepted any compromise proposed by the Hapsburg emperor. These Swiss Protestants were convinced that the empire must be overthrown in the interests of their religion; which they held to be the only true religion. The sultan and his Turkish army might be an instrument in God's hands for the destruction of the Catholic Church and the opening of a door for the entrance of the gospel of Zurich. The king of France, though a Catholic, might be equally a divine instrument for the overthrow of the empire; and as such was to be supported by all good Swiss Protestants.)

Melanchthon, the appointed representative of the new evangel, presented a confession of faith, an historic document that came to be known as the Augsburg Confession and to be preserved as a fundamental statement of Lutheran belief. To Luther has been attributed the original Latin version. Melanchthon was certainly the author of the German confession read at Augsburg. The twenty-eight articles of this confession are less a positive creed than an explanation of what was being taught in the territories of Lutheran princes. By skilfully omitting all denial of free will, of the pope's supremacy, of the character of the priesthood, of seven sacraments; by minimising in fact all the departures from accepted Catholic doctrine and practice, demonstrating plausibly that no essential matters of faith separated Lutherans from the visible church, Melanchthon endeavoured to come to terms with his Catholic opponents, to postpone the outbreak of civil war, and if possible to secure the support of Catholics against the dangerous propaganda of Zwinglians.

To safeguard his position Melanchthon laboured for peace. In pursuit of this pacific policy he deliberately curtailed the Lutheran theology and understated the extent of the schism. Luther following the discussions at Augsburg marvelled at the ingenious suppressions and yet while blaming the advocate, would not disavow him. But Zwingli would have none of this moderate half-and-half confession of faith; this tepid peace with the old religion that he was bent on destroying. And Philip of Hesse, rather than come to terms with the emperor, whose power he hated, left the diet when Melanchthon began negotiations for a common policy with the emperor's representatives.

Reconciliation and agreement were never really in sight. Keeping silence on doctrinal differences did not cause the differences to disappear. Luther had no intention of withdrawing from his position of hostility to Rome, and Melanchthon for all his horror of civil war, never contemplated return to the Catholic Faith; though many thought at the time such return was probable. What Melanchthon and Luther contended for then and later was the recognition of the new evangelical church as the true and genuine Catholic Church. Given that recognition with full and free opportunity to preach the new evangel, they professed willingness to live in peace with more backward Christians who still clung to "the old superstitions of popery." In fact Luther and Melanchthon were opportunists in their proposals for peace, now at one time expressing desire for mutual toleration, at another time declaring toleration of the "pope's religion" impossible. For Zwinglians — who came to be called Sacramentarians — Anabaptists and other Protestant sectaries, Luther would allow no room in the territories ruled by evangelical princes.

At Augsburg Melanchthon brought up once more with the Confession the old Hundred Grievances of the German Nation as a reminder that obedience to the papacy meant economic hurt.

Emperor Charles, himself no theologian, and never understanding the fundamental Lutheran dogma of justification by faith alone, called upon the Catholic doctors summoned to the diet to answer the Confession; this they did in a *Confutatio*.[2] (The emperor required the *Confutatio* to be revised before he would sanction its public reading. The controversial note was too sharp in the first edition. Charles, anxious to avoid provoking further dissention and to reunite, in the cause of the empire, the broken church, stuck to his conciliatory policy until it was plain there was no chance of the Lutherans yielding any real ground, or making any submission.)

The *Confutatio* having been read, the emperor declared that the Lutherans must now abandon their separation from the Catholic unity and return to their old obedience. Six months' grace was allowed. At the same time Charles, moved by the arguments of the Catholic princes, declared himself in favour of a general council. But a general council was the one thing Cardinal Campeggio, the papal legate at the diet, thought highly dangerous. Pope Clement was of the same opinion, holding that so far from mending matters a general council might well result in further separations. Besides, the political situation made it practically impossible for such a council to meet.

While it is no doubt true that a general council would not have brought Luther, Zwingli, or Philip of Hesse back to the Catholic Faith, it is clear that the immediate result of the Augsburg diet, with the refusal of the pope to give any hope for a general council that would amend the very grave scandals of the Church, enlarged the Protestant area throughout the empire.

---

[2] For a careful and detailed account of the Catholic and Lutheran doctrines enunciated at Augsburg see *The Reformation, the Mass, and the Priesthood,* by Dr. Ernest C. Messenger, London, 1936.

Melanchthon seriously alarmed at the rumours of imperial action to enforce against Luther the old decree of the Diet of Worms, and distressed at the possibility of open war, tried to effect some arrangement with Campeggio. The emperor on his part authorised seven Catholic theologians to negotiate with seven Lutherans for a basis of agreement. Both Melanchthon and the Catholic doctors made offers that could not have been fulfilled. The willingness declared by the former to submit to the jurisdiction of the Catholic episcopate and the promise by the latter of toleration to a married clergy and the chalice to the laity at Holy Communion, would inevitably have been repudiated. The negotiations came to nothing. All that Melanchthon could do was to publish an *Apologia* in reply to the *Confutatio*.

Four imperial cities — Strassburg, Constance, Lindau, and Meiningen — seized the occasion to issue a joint manifesto of their own, neither Catholic nor Lutheran, which they called the *Tetrapolitana;* in the main Zwinglian, for its authors were Bucer and Capito, the Strassburg divines. Two other cities, Nuremberg and Reutlingen, signed the Augsburg Confession and the number of Protestant signatories amongst the princes of the empire showed an increase.

Could the emperor have achieved any success had he attempted coercion against the Lutheran recalcitrants? His own natural caution must have answered in the negative. Who besides Duke George of Saxony and possibly Elector Joachin of Brandenburg cared enough for the Catholic cause to make war on its behalf? All that the emperor gained from the Diet of Augsburg was the promise of the majority that Ferdinand should be elected king of the Romans at a meeting of the diet at Cologne.

The six months' session at Augsburg closed with the reiteration of the edict of Worms, demand for acknowledgment of episcopal authority, orders for the restoration of ecclesiastical property by legal process. The *Reichskammergericht* was to function against all who had annexed church lands and appropriated church endowments for Lutheran ends. The emperor also promised to urge on the pope the necessity for a general council in order that the hundred grievances might be remedied.

The Protestant princes met at Schmalkald in the following year; examining their position they decided to resist by force of arms any imperial attack on the property they claimed as their own; to meet by violence any violent action to restore the old religion or displace the new. Philip of Hesse, ever ready to give battle to the emperor, joined the Protestant league of Schmalkalden, a league organised by lawyers and by John of Saxony and Duke Ernest of Braunschweig, that bound each member to make common cause with any member attacked on religious or indeed on any ground.

The Catholic princes had no such organisation as the Schmalkaldic league of the Protestants. They were not at all prepared to start a civil war to gratify an emperor of whose power they were for the most part jealous. Neither were they prepared to relax their sovereignty within their own dominions. The time would come, as it did in every other land where Protestant teaching penetrated, when the issue would be fought out in long and bloody wars; in Germany the time was not yet.

Luther, anticipating war, backed the military league of Schmalkald, publicly declaring that it was lawful to take up arms against the emperor. This was in contradiction to his former teaching on the subject and brought him into conflict both with disciples who could not agree to the change of view and with Catholic divines. In a little while Luther was so far from nonresistance to evil policy that he was prepared for all to be slain who threatened the evangel.

Charles, always alive to the peril of invasion by the Turks and to the hostile policy of France, aware, too, that the Schmalkalden league had no friendly intention toward Ferdinand, was compelled to make peace. The resolutions carried at Augsburg for the restoration by legal process of church property seized by the Lutherans were never enforced. The six months' grace allowed to the Lutherans expired without any threat of enforcing uniformity. Finally, at Nuremberg, in July, 1532, a definite peace treaty was signed. On the imperial side it was agreed that all suits before the *Reichskammergericht* for the restitution of church property should be annulled and that existing conditions of public worship should be respected. There should be no interference with the religious observances in Protestant territories until a general council was assembled. What the emperor gained in return was assurance of aid against the Turks, for Sultan Solyman was at the very gates of Vienna.

The peace of Nuremberg signed, Charles departed for Italy not to return to Germany till nine years had passed.

Luther agreed with the peace terms, supported resistance to the Turks and favoured for the time mutual toleration of Catholic and Protestant worship. Aleander, the papal legate at the diet, in his letters to Rome mentioned the peril to the empire from the Turkish advance and from French intrigues with German princes. Cardinal Garcia de Loaysa, the emperor's confessor, urged compliance with Lutheran demands for the sake of the defence of Hungary and Germany. Loaysa said frankly that religious uniformity must be sacrificed for the sake of political necessity.

Luther could afford to take a more confident view of the future of the evangel when the peace of Nuremberg was signed. The previous year had seen the death of his rival Zwingli, who fell in the battle of Kappel, fighting for Zurich in the war against the Catholic cantons of Switzerland. Another Protestant critic of Lutheranism, Oecolampadius, died a month later at Basle. Luther was satisfied that both these preachers of another gospel than that of Wittenberg were "damned," though with characteristic levity of mind he wrote subsequently to Bullinger, Zwingli's successor elected chief pastor at Zurich, as though he esteemed Zwingli and mourned his death.

Bullinger never had the influence of Zwingli in Germany though he corresponded freely with the Protestant reformers in England, and the Zurich doctrine and discipline consequently waned, yielding to Bucer's mistier creed of Strassburg or declining before the Lutheranism of territorial princes. Not till Calvin came to rule at Geneva would Luther again be opposed and his following disturbed by Protestantism bleaker and more logical than his own.

Calvin had but recently left the Catholic Church — in the year that Ignatius Loyola and his companions took their vows at Montmartre. At the same time the news came to Luther and to all Germany of an Anabaptist rising, a revolutionary movement that struck not only at the faith of Protestants but at the very existence of society ordered on Christian principles. Once more as in the Peasant War, Germany was shaken as by a volcanic eruption. Elements surged up from the underworld, in that year 1534, as hateful to Luther as to Catholic princes.

X

From Anabaptist Rising to Sanction of Bigamy: 1534–1539

THE DEMAND for a general council, heard so frequently in Germany in the years preceding the Diet of Nuremberg, was not stilled when the diet closed. Emperor Charles, never grasping the theological significance of the new evangel, still believed the differences between Catholics and Lutherans could be adjusted by discussion and the latter reconciled to the Church. Therefore Luther, not to be put down by excommunication nor silenced by imperial ban, maintaining an incorrigible obstinacy, with the disaffection of his equally incorrigible followers spreading gravely throughout the land, must be met and answered at a general council. Many of the Catholic princes agreed with the emperor.

Others cried out for a general council because they wanted the papacy reformed, the abuses, chiefly financial these, of the papal court corrected. Others, again, perhaps the majority, impatient that in Germany the moral discipline, notoriously lax and scandalous, of the higher clergy was not corrected, called for a general council for the sake of moral reform at home. It was useless, they argued, to take up arms for the Faith when Christian morality and common decency were violated by the chief shepherds of the Faith. The decay of morals in the empire that Luther witnessed was apparent to Catholic princes.

Confusion in religious belief assisted the decay when the people beheld the clergy, Catholic, Lutheran, and Swiss Zwinglian, in violent dispute. This, indeed, hastened in various territories the departure from the Christian standard. But the root of the disease, as more than one papal nuncio pointed out, could be traced to the shameless lives of German prelates. For their part the said prelates had neither liking for nor interest in the notion of a general council. Pope Clement on political grounds would not favour the idea. The Catholic princes, therefore, urged at Nuremberg a general council or national synod for Germany, to meet with or without the pope's approval. An impossible demand, recalling theories of conciliar authority that put the council above the pope.

Luther himself encouraged his disciples to support the cry for a general council because he looked for what he considered a reform of the doctrines of the Church. In his confidence that the papacy was doomed, that all Germany could be won to his evangel, Luther at times almost eagerly exclaimed that a general or at least a national council was needed. At other times his despondency and depressed mental condition expressed despair. He could hope for nothing from councils while the Catholic hierarchy resisted his gospel. And Albert, archbishop of Mainz, now cardinal, simply declined to be converted, preferring to continue in his easy morals, never allowing the Faith he professed to interfere with his private life, unwilling to hinder the Lutheran preaching and asking no more in return than that Catholics should be left undisturbed in their public worship. Humanist and lover of good literature (and lover of other things less good), the cardinal-archbishop, whose purchase of the archiepiscopal see had indirectly provoked

Luther's original Ninety-Five Theses, surveyed a troubled and distracted Germany with a cheerful indifference; undismayed by prevailing heresies and schisms, he could see no urgent need for a reforming council.

The general council for which earnest Catholics had for so many years pleaded was not to meet for another ten years. Schisms by that time were too deep and wide to be healed; heresies too strongly rooted to be got rid of. Schism and heresy were, by the time the council met, in fact already accepted by Protestants as part and parcel of the visible church of Christ. The subjective philosophy of Martin Luther, with its popular appeal to personal experience as the guide to truth, its constant harping on the theme that what we feel to be true is true — in contradistinction to the Catholic scholastic philosophy that man is given the power to believe and by the use of that power can lay hold of the Faith revealed by God, the Faith set out by divine inspiration in the creeds of the Catholic Church — had become a richly comforting way of life to all Protestants. It has endured, this subjectivism, the favourite philosophy of multitudes no longer calling themselves Protestant.

The arguments for and against the immediate calling of a general council — the arguments against being immeasurably the weaker — were forgotten when Philip, landgrave of Hesse, in the year 1534, made war on the absent emperor and brought back, unchallenged by diets of the empire, Duke Ulrich to Wurtemberg, whose dominion had been justly forfeited according to the decisions of imperial councils. Philip was backed by Francis, that most Christian King of France and Catholic ally of Pope Clement, in this attack on imperial authority, while Ferdinand, engaged in keeping off the Turk from the eastern frontiers of his kingdom, could only accept Philip's peace terms. These included the establishment of a Protestant faith in what had hitherto been a Catholic land. Protestantism for Wurtemberg, under Ulrich, meant the seizure of all church lands and the confiscation of all Catholic buildings and estates. Monasteries and convents were secularised and their members dispersed. Churches were no longer to be used for Catholic worship, while the clergy were to become ministers of the landgrave's religion. In this way Philip struck successfully at the emperor and at the Faith of the Hapsburgs.

Thus Luther's doctrine of private judgment was interpreted by the landgrave of Hesse.

It was interpreted in even more drastic fashion by the Anabaptists who in that same year rose in the lands of Westphalia and made themselves lords of the city of Munster. General councils and doctrinal differences of belief were by common consent of Catholic and Lutherans of minor importance in the presence of militant Anabaptists preaching revolution; men feverishly alert and possessed of unrestrained activity.

Feared and hated by all civil governments were the Anabaptists; feared and hated as enemies of God and man. However sincere the nonresistance of these sectaries who refused to bear arms; however irreproachable in conduct the personal character, suffusing as it often did both mildness and charity; however honest the intentions to the state, there was no denial that fundamentally the political and social creed of the Anabaptist was anarchism, incompatible with law and order administered in their respective dominions by princes and by oligarchies in free cities. Utterly at variance with all traditional opinions concerning relations of church and state was the communism of the Anabaptist.

Luther hated Anabaptists as fiercely as he hated Catholics. The downfall of the latter he took to be inevitable. The very existence of the former — intolerable. The Anabaptist challenged Luther's authority to determine what men should believe and derided his argument that by private judgment and study of the Bible all men would arrive at similar conclusions in faith and morals.

The vital and distinctive doctrine of the Anabaptist was obedience to the inner light; a doctrine that sprang from the persuasion that the individual Christian must be directly guided by the inner light alone; that God shed this inner light on all true believers. Inevitably this doctrine, extending the Lutheran private judgment to very far lengths, brought startling developments and unexpected diversities. With extreme individualism in religious belief went a lively communism in social and political ethics, a combination totally repugnant to princes whether Catholic, Lutheran, or Zwinglian. Not without reason. For strange and sinister elements were attracted to the Anabaptist community, as at an earlier date they had flocked to the peasants in revolt, and as they are invariably attracted to all revolutionary movements. Recognising that men and women, guided solely by the inner light, would hardly arrive at doctrinal unity, still less at uniformity, the Anabaptist communities were not impatient when the extravagant utterances of their adherents disturbed orthodox Protestants. To hear Luther denounced as but another pope, the creed and catechisms of Wittenberg repudiated by illiterate artisans — all this though very shocking to Lutheran Protestants struggling for mastery over Catholics — was well received in Anabaptist circles.

In truth Lutheranism had lost its freshness. Anabaptist agitation brought an emotional excitement that the Lutheran evangel could no longer provide. Again and again itinerant Anabaptist preachers found receptive audiences for their fervid promises of the speedy coming of Christ and the enthronement of His saints as lords of all the world. Hints of revolutionary action for the overthrow of rulers who would not accept the Anabaptist gospel were received no less favourably in many a north German town. In the south the annihilation of the peasant armies and the bitter reprisals that followed the peasant revolt had left dreams of social revolution and visions of social justice that now were no more than memories, memories of a dead and buried past. In the north, on the contrary, the experience of a revolutionary hope defeated and frustrated was unknown.

When revolution did come in the city of Munster men recoiled from the tyranny manifested, and shuddered at the destruction it wrought. In the manner of every social revolution, the perfectibility of man being assumed and the brotherhood of the human race the declared goal, the leaders of the revolutionary minority found it necessary to inaugurate the new order of society by the massacre of opponents — to kill, and kill, all hostile critics, until in due time the slayer became the slain. So it was in the walled city of Munster, a nominally Catholic city until the encroaching tide of Lutheranism capturing minds ill-prepared for resistance, spread diversity of opinion and civic disorder, to the undoing of the commonwealth.

Bernard Rottman, an ex-priest, was the orator of the oncoming Lutheranism. Knipperdollinck, by trade a draper, was the fanatical man of action. Both were to be absorbed into the ranks of revolutionary Anabaptists. Though Count von Taldeck, recently elected bishop of Munster, and not yet ordained priest, had no strong feelings against Lutheran beliefs and was always prepared to compromise, the portent of insurrectionary attack on property, ecclesiastical and civil alike, drove him to take up arms when the Anabaptists were in power in the city. But at the beginning of troubles the bishop agreed to an arrangement that gave the Lutherans, now a majority on the city council, a number of parish churches, while reserving the cathedral and other churches for Catholic worship. That was in 1532. The following year Rottman pronounced against infant baptism and declared the Anabaptists were right in insisting that baptism must in every case be administered to adults who had experienced conversion. The moderate Lutherans, constituting the wealthier body of Protestants in Munster, naturally became uneasy when Anabaptists from Holland, hearing of Rottman's word, began to arrive in the city. The emperor could prohibit Anabaptist and other Protestant sectaries from public preaching in his own dominions of the Netherlands, he could not suppress the secret propagation of strange beliefs. Munster, therefore, provided an outlet for disturbing activities that had been denied all open expression elsewhere. It also provided an opportunity for the dictatorships of two of the most amazing figures in the history of the reformation in Germany. Typical figures in the history of revolution they appear, these two: Jan Matthys, a baker of Haarlem, leader of the Anabaptists in Holland, and Jan Bockelson, journeyman tailor of Leyden. The latter, having wandered over Europe and lived in many cities in the course of his trade, was now a convert to Anabaptist communism, eager for the militant establishment of whatever Anabaptist communism might imply.

Lutherans and Catholics, still the considerable majority in the community, affected an alliance in the presence of these revolutionary elements in the city. Then, intimidated by the Anabaptist agitation, with its threats, promises, and contagious enthusiasm, they deemed it safer to offer terms to the sectarian forces. Mutual toleration was the form of agreement, with the result that Anabaptists, attracted by the preaching of social revolution, now flocked increasingly into the city from Holland and from many German towns in expectation of things happening. As in the first place the Catholics of Munster, by yielding churches to the more energetic Lutheran minority, hoped to preserve peace, and instead were merely reduced to a despised section of the community, so the combined Catholics and Lutherans now, by surrendering to the Anabaptist minority, contributed to their own undoing by this futile attempt to ward off the dreaded evil. To surrender ground at the demand of revolution is to invite extinction; to compromise with men resolved on absolute rule is to provoke self-destruction.

By February, 1534, the Anabaptists had a majority on the

city council and could do as they pleased. Matthys at once became dictator; Knipperdollinck, burgomaster and public executioner. The latter office no sinecure, for a reign of terror was promptly inaugurated to usher in the reign of saints. The immediate second coming of Christ justified, according to the doctrine of the Dutch Anabaptists, the death or expulsion from the city of all who resisted conversion. Numerous Catholics and Lutherans fled from a prospective general massacre. A crowd of men, women, and children — mere infants many of the latter — were driven out of the city to perish in the snow.

The siege of Munster began. Bishop von Waldeck — with some troops from Hesse — unable to dislodge the Anabaptists, was not prepared to abandon his temporal dominion. For nearly eighteen months the city held out while the unconsecrated bishop sought help from Catholic and Lutheran princes. But none of them were overanxious to do anything that might strengthen an independent neighbour. More anxious rather were these princes to avert the danger of the emperor, by coming in and subduing the rebels, adding the episcopal realm to his own vast territories.

Matthys was killed within a few months of his seizing power. His death was an illustration of the mad subjectivity of his mind. He felt himself subject to special revelations, the inner light was always driving him to do things as shocking as they were unreasonable. Under the influence of a wild and certainly depraved imagination the amount of destruction accomplished in Munster under the Matthys tyranny was appalling. A good deal of plunder went to the poor, but everywhere books, pictures, manuscripts, musical instruments, and church steeples were destroyed. (Church steeples were destroyed for the sake of military defence. Cannon could be mounted on the stumps of the towers.) Announcing that he had received a revelation to go out and overcome the enemy that besieged the city, Matthys rushed forth with a considerable force and was slain with all his company by the larger force of the besiegers.

Jan Bockelson — Jan of Leyden as we know him — immediately diverted attention from the dead leader to himself. A stronger character than Matthys, a far more efficient dictator, insane with the insanity of the complete egoist, grosser in the following of desire, undistracted by pity when the homicidal mood was upon him, Jan of Leyden ruled as tyrant of Munster for more than a year; holding the city against enemies without and making short work of opponents within. For he had opponents. The communism he decreed — and every decree was issued as a divine revelation, so that disobedience was a sin against God, therefore deserving death — gave him the administration of the wealth in the city. This involved no less than the surrender of every piece of personal property that had value, a confiscation naturally distasteful to persons theoretically sympathetic with communism. Still more, the decree of the dictator sanctioning and approving general polygamy was hated as a thing intolerable by Anabaptists in whom some roots of Christian tradition still survived. It produced a conspiracy against the dictator and the discovery of the plot was followed by the prompt slaughter of the discontented. "He does God service," cried Jan of Leyden when the conspirators were taken, "who fires the first shot."

The ability to defend the city from the besiegers was proved at the end of August, 1534, when an attempt to storm the gates and force an entry was repulsed with heavy losses.

By that time the dictator of Munster was plainly and dangerously mad, a megalomaniac whose instincts, savage and undisciplined, no one dared resist. A man named Dusentschur became his official prophet to declare the will of God. Then it was that Jan Bockelson, having announced that he was sent by God to set up the Fifth Monarchy of the Apocalypse and to become ruler of all the world, despatched messengers to neighbouring towns and cities requiring their inhabitants to come into the new kingdom. But these heralds, persuaded of their safety by the word of Dusentschur that no one durst touch them without fatal hurt, went in vain on this errand. In the city of Warendorf alone was any consideration given to the Munster proposals of alliance. Elsewhere the heralds were imprisoned and in most cases executed, so little heed was given to the words of the prophet Dusentschur.

This reign of terror in Munster, this Anabaptist dictatorship, endured till the midsummer of 1536. Even then the besieging army conquered only by the help of citizens who opened gates and brought ladders to the walls. The courage of the dictator failed at the sight of hostile troops within the city, yet a desperate fight was put up by his followers. Street after street was contested by the militant Anabaptists, but their defeat was inevitable. The professional soldiers outfought the townsmen and conquered. The dictator, Jan Bockelson, and his executioner Knipperdollinck, found in hiding, were tortured to death.

When it was over, this experiment at Munster in militant Anabaptist communism, not only princes and rulers in Germany but all governments in Europe were on guard against Anabaptist teaching. The quiet, respectable, average Lutheran felt the horror that law-abiding folk would feel when the full story of the reign of Jan of Leyden was unfolded. Catholics indifferent to creeds and sacraments saw in Anabaptist communism, a Protestant peril. In the crime and lunacy of Munster's Fifth Monarchy could be discerned what lurked in Luther's doctrine of private judgment; the seed of Anabaptist harvest at Munster was the Lutheran teaching that what a man must believe was revealed to him personally, that what he felt to be true was true. So Catholics argued.

Luther, of course, had from the first denounced the Anabaptists and disavowed all sympathy with their teaching. By this time, too, there were thousands of Protestants who accepted Lutheranism or Zwinglianism as an objective faith, holding it to be true not because they felt it to be true but because they were told it was true. Children and young persons in the Lutheran territories were impelled to adopt Lutheranism or Zwinglianism as their forefathers had accepted Catholicism, because it was the only religion they knew. Similarly in a few years Calvinism would become an official religion to be refused under pain of exile.

Militant Anabaptism, with its outcome of the reign of terror, called the rule of the saints, perished on that midsummer day when the streets of Munster were filled with the bodies of its exponents. Nor was any revival attempted. Henceforth the central doctrine of Anabaptists, that no infant, and none save the converted adult must be baptised, alone remained; to find continual response throughout the centuries to come and to flourish wherever Protestant Christianity flourished.

Munster itself, deprived of all rights under the empire, was made a Catholic city once more despite its lay bishop's tolerant views of Lutheranism. Protestant gains in other parts proved that the hurt done to Lutheranism by the bloody tyranny at Munster was not grave enough to upset the Schmalkaldic league. The league had its uses. Possession of church property alienated from its original purposes by the change of religion was guaranteed to Lutheran rulers by their membership in the Schmalkaldic league. But what of the city councils that had made themselves masters of Catholic houses of religion? of princes not yet positively committed to Protestantism who had forcibly possessed themselves of church lands? It was in these numerous cases that appeals to the supreme court, the *Reichskammergericht,* were lodged against the secularisation of ecclesiastical property. Hence theological divisions fell into the background, largely forgotten or obscured when the ownership of property was the burning question.

Alliances, truces, political action for economic ends, security through the balance of power — these are the phenomena of the ten years that followed the Munster terror. The issue in that conglomeration of principalities and free cities and Hapsburg dominions, called the Empire, and in the Hapsburg dominions of Austria that Ferdinand ruled, was power through ownership of landed property. Lutheranism, Zwinglianism, Catholicism, each is weighed, supported, or disowned by many a prince of the empire as it is judged to favour material gain and political security. Doctrines concerning justification by faith alone, the sacrifice of the Mass, the presence of Christ in the Eucharist, were of no particular interest to men engaged in eager pursuit of political power, or anxious to safeguard wealth gained in the conflict of creeds.

Politics, and this meant property — as it so commonly does— was the chief business of princes. Let clergy attend to religion, and order that religion as their princes decided.

Catholicism recovered no lost ground in these years of wide indifference to theological truth. The publication of Luther's complete German Bible encouraged disaffection from the old religion and from the papal obedience; since apart from its literary qualities — and these were rich and attractive — the translator's notes and glosses were strongly anti-papal and anti-Catholic. Writers on the Catholic side, Dr. Eck and Cochlaeus may be named, complained that publishers and booksellers would do nothing for them. In those years of confusion, years when populations suffered whatever change of faith their rulers decreed, the Catholic cause was, in Germany, everywhere depressed. Few looked to the pope for help, though Clement was dead and an old man, Paul III (Farnese), bent on Catholic reform, reigned in his stead. The politics of the papacy had been too definitely anti-German for princes and electors of the empire to turn hopefully to Rome.

But the new pope, cautious and watchful of the emperor, was in earnest for reform, and if he seemed to stick to the bad old ways of the renaissance papacy by making cardinals of two nephews, one aged fourteen and the other sixteen, he also gave proof of zealous intention by his choice of Contarini, Caraffa, Sadoleto, the Englishman Reginald Pole — four men known for their rare spirituality and all identified with Catholic reform — for the cardinalate. These four, with others, were appointed to act as a commission to report on the abuses of the papal court and suggest the needed reforms. The result of their deliberations was the famous *Consilium delectorum cardinalium et aliorum praelatorum de emendanda ecclesia.*[1]

Paul III, believing that Lutherans and Zwinglians might be brought back into the Catholic unity by means of a general council, sent a nuncio, Vergerio, into Germany to urge persuasion on the Protestant leaders in favour of such a council. Vergerio was most conciliatory, inviting Luther and Bugenhagen to breakfast and ignoring Luther's outbreaks against the papacy, while making much of Luther's willingness to attend a general council. Luther, at this interview with the nuncio, was full of the success of his teaching and the mood of boastfulness grated on his host. But the eyes of Luther fascinated him and he wrote of these "uncanny eyes." (The subsequent career of Vergerio suggests that the nuncio of Paul III was a queer character. For after achieving a bishopric in Italy he lapsed into Lutheranism himself and died a Protestant at Tubingen thirty years later.)

The mission of Vergerio was a failure. No general council could be assembled, though the pope wanted it to be held

[1] This document, of high value in the history of the sixteenth-century papacy, must be discussed in the chapters on the Counter-Reformation.

at Mantua. Internal conditions remained unaffected in Germany, where with the general decay of authority in religion personal morals still further decayed. Since power through property was the main thing, the thing that mattered to men in high estate, the securing or retention of it was far more exciting than a theology that had no bearing on disputed points of ownership. Hence morality inevitably suffered.

The German Reformation is seen to have passed from its first phase. Visible to all was the preoccupation with rights of ownership, with schemes and party strife for possession of property. Faith, it might well be judged, was moribund, Christianity, Catholic or Protestant, of diminishing account. Yet in that same year, when Anabaptist madness raged in Munster and Philip of Hesse severed Wurtemberg from Ferdinand's territories and brought back Duke Ulrich, history notes how at Montmartre, outside Paris, a Spaniard of high family, by name Ignatius Loyola, with certain companions took vows that were to renew Catholicism throughout the world. In that same year, too, a certain French lawyer named Jean Calvin, impressed by Lutheranism, decided that he must leave the Catholic Church which had educated him; and his going out is the prelude to a new version of the Lutheran belief, a bleaker, stricter, more logical version that also would make its influence felt throughout the world; at least throughout the Protestant world.

Christianity was by no means moribund for all its bedraggled plumage. The end was not yet.

Yet the dawn of better times was not perceptible. Fear, root of persistent evil among mankind, and hate, its frequent offspring, are the dominating motives of the ten years in Germany that preceded the Council of Trent. Fear and hate concerning earthly possessions. Treaties were made and broken, principles laid aside at the call of politics, former theological enmities forgotten. The commercial cities preferred Lutheranism and the war of Lubeck against Denmark, as well as the trade policy of the once famous Hanseatic League, belong to general European history.

Lutherans and Zwinglians made peace in 1536, agreeing to a formula, the concord of Wittenberg, which left their differences unreconciled. They were to be discussed in local congregations, without disturbance of the common agreement that made Lutheranism the nominal religion of princes and other territorial rulers who had repudiated all obedience to the pope, and who had renounced all belief in the sacrifice of the Mass and the doctrine of the priesthood. Henry VIII sent representatives from England to the Wittenberg conference, being at that time inclined to join the Schmalkaldic league for his own ends.

Catholicism seemed a lost cause in the empire, its vitality ebbing away in Ferdinand's own Austria. In the diocese of Laibach no more than seventeen priests were ordained in eight years, while at Passau, the Bavarian diocese on the Austrian border, there were but five priests ordained in four years. In these circumstances Charles and Ferdinand saw that some working arrangement must be made with the Lutherans. Self-defence and the preservation of their respective dominions from external foes compelled alliance, or at least a truce or armistice, with these petty rulers who were always ready to join any movement hostile to the imperial power; who in fact were as fearful of curtailment of their rights or loss of territory as was the emperor himself of curtailment of imperial rights and loss of Hapsburg territory.

Mutual toleration of public religious worship was the basis of agreement that Charles and Ferdinand proposed to the Protestant princes, and this was the condition of the truce of Frankfort, which made of no account the Catholic league of Nuremberg. Toleration of Lutheran worship throughout all Hapsburg dominions and Catholic principalities was guaranteed by this truce of Frankfort, but its counterpart, the toleration of Catholic worship in Protestant parts of the empire, was never fulfilled.

The death of George, Duke of Saxony, removed the one man conspicuously loyal to his Catholic convictions in a time when the policy of his contemporaries was deflected by fear; when principles, religious and political, were changed as occasion demanded and as the more profitable course dictated.

Among the ruins of a broken Christian unity, in an empire threatened by civil war, in an age when the corruption of public and private morals startled Luther himself, Duke George was consistently faithful to the Catholic religion, without making any concealment that reform was needed in Rome and elsewhere. Neither did he conceal his resolute conviction that the Lutheran dissent from the Church was ruinous to the country. Blameless in private life, personally devout, prudent in his rule, yet not without courage when danger pressed, Duke George sought for unity as the one thing needful in Church and state. Unity of the empire, unity of the German nation, unity of the Church; otherwise came disaster, with the downfall of all that a Christian man counts good. In this belief George, duke of Saxony, lived and in this belief he died. Not a great leader, no brilliant military commander, but a plain and conscientious man, aware of his responsibilities, who sought to fulfill them as best he could.

To keep Catholic his ducal Saxony, George had bequeathed his territories to the Hapsburgs in case his successor, his brother Henry, should turn Lutheran. It was vainly done, for Henry was already Protestant and no legal authority could disinherit him. His subjects accepted without any display of regret the change of religion decreed by their lord, the Catholic nobles of ducal Saxony acquiesced, and the bishop of Meissen alone objected. On Henry's death his son Maurice who, to Henry's annoyance, had married a daughter of Philip of Hesse, reigned. Saxony was lost to Catholicism.

At the same time Joachim II, Hohenzollern, elector of Brandenburg, decided that he would rule the church in his territory as Henry VIII was doing in England; to that end, with Agricola for his court chaplain, he established a Lutheranism that combined much of the old Catholic ritual with the doctrines of Wittenberg. Luther flung contempt on his former disciple, John Agricola, for compromising the evangel, and separation followed.

Duke William of Cleves also fancied a similar policy for his dominions and joined the Schmalkaldic league. Negotiations proceeded for an alliance with the king of England; to provide a common front against the emperor. But the negotiations came to nothing, for Henry VIII, irritated by the bride sent to him from Cleves, Anne, William's sister; never at heart friendly to Lutheranism; and seeing no gain in the project, dissolved the schemes for bringing England into a Protestant alliance.

On all sides disintegration is observed in the Empire, as secular princes and prince-bishops, with opulent city councils, openly changed their faith, declaring for Lutheran Protestantism. Without such change, how were the church lands, and especially the rich properties of the monasteries, untenanted for the most part save for a handful of elderly and pacifically minded men, to be secularised? Vocations to the religious orders had for years dwindled so that it was said there were more monasteries than monks in Germany.

A check to the triumphant Protestant advance came when Philip of Hesse, champion of the Protestant cause, indulged in bigamy. The ways of Duke George of Saxony, contrasted with the manners and morals of Philip, left the latter at a disadvantage. It was the year of Duke George's death when the landgrave, never a continent man, felt constrained to commit bigamy and required Luther and Melanchthon to bless the performance. Which they did; yet reluctantly and not without distress at more than scruples violated. Philip, whose matrimonial infidelities no Lutheran or Zwinglian gospel could check, insisted upon a bigamous marriage with a young lady residing at his court, Margaret von der Sale. The pious reason given was that not otherwise, living in adultery as he was, could he with quiet conscience receive the sacrament at the Lord's Table. Bucer — no man readier to act as intermediary — was employed to arrange at Wittenberg the approval of Luther and Melanchthon. This he did successfully, returning with testimony signed that Philip might proceed as a "necessity of conscience" to this bigamous marriage. The document also contained advice to keep the marriage and "testimony" secret, lest it should be taken as a general encouragement to polygamy. Melanchthon himself was present at the marriage ceremony, with Bucer and other ex-Catholic clergy, in March, 1540.

Luther saw the danger of making public this bigamy, saw that scandal would be given, and it seems really believed the landgrave would keep it secret. Obsessed by the Old Testament stories of the patriarchs and their numerous wives, Luther could find no natural objection to polygamy, no direct prohibition in the Gospel. He had advised Henry VIII to make Anne Boleyn his second wife and could hardly do less for Philip of Hesse than give similar approval. Besides, the vital thing was to keep Philip loyal to the Protestant cause. To thwart him was to run the risk of sending him over to the side of the emperor; a disaster that would be fatal to the Schmalkaldic league and the fortunes of Lutheranism. At the same time secrecy must be observed. Bigamy might be permitted as a "necessity of conscience," it should not be told to the world that Luther and Melanchthon had given their consent, in writing, to such a step.

Of course the affair was not to be kept secret. It is doubtful whether Philip supposed that it could. Luther braved the scandal and brazened out his part in it when the news was openly told. Melanchthon was miserable in shame.

Bigamy sanctioned by Luther and Melanchthon was still bigamy. The moral influence of Luther was diminished by the sanction given, the legal consequences of Philip's act were unaffected. To the embarrassment of all parties concerned the landgrave's bigamy became a matter of high politics in Germany. By the law of the empire the penalty for this offence had but recently been made capital and the Elector John Frederick of Saxony (himself charged with grave and scandalous crimes against purity), with Duke Ulrich of Wurtemberg (whom all contemporaries judged disreputable), were both furious with the landgrave at the violation of the law when publicity came.

In the end Philip was driven to make his peace with the emperor, agreeing that the lady should not be regarded as his wife, promising soldiers for the imperial army, and withdrawing his support from the Schmalkaldic league. Politically the result was a mortal wound to the league. Morally the result was deplorable. Bucer was probably right when in a letter to the landgrave he declared that, with everybody discussing the conduct of their rulers, "the people are lapsing into barbarism and the lascivious state of affairs goes on increasing."

Philip, no more a theologian than was Charles, was not prepared for the sake of a scruple to forfeit territory. Nor was he inclined to run the risk of defeat. The Protestant side, for all the breakup of Catholic unity, was not obviously the winning side in a war with the emperor. Personal animosity against Charles did not justify war. Peace was the better policy. Philip remained a Protestant, but in self-defence became a supporter of the emperor; the emperor for so long hated as an enemy.

The conference and diet at Ratisbon, in 1541, put Philip right, legally, in the eyes of the world.

XI

From Diet of Ratisbon to Death of Luther: 1541-1546

LUTHER DIED in 1546 and for the last five years of his life the course of the Protestant reformation in Germany was so dominated by political issues that the religious question is only discerned in the background. Charles, persistently seeking to preserve the semblance of unity in the empire, made overtures to the Lutherans for peace. Without budging from the Catholicism, that was for him personally the only possible faith, he promised concessions, as unacceptable at Wittenberg as at Rome. Lay princes and prince-bishops of the empire found in imperial interests and the interests of the Hapsburg family, distinction without difference. Whether professing the Lutheran creed or the Catholic Faith of old Germany, these territorial rulers were for ever intriguing for increase of power or defence of vested rights; willing enough at times to engage in war provided the expense fell on others, equally willing to change from Protestantism to Catholicism, from Catholicism to Protestantism, did circumstances appear to make the change profitable.

Pope Paul III, watching events in Germany and never

completely trusting Charles, determined to effect reforms in the Church, in especial reforms in the papal court, without a general council. If it were possible.

But Charles had promised a general council to his Hapsburg subjects and to all the Catholics and Protestants of the empire; had further promised that it should meet in Germany. While composed of Catholic representatives, according to the tradition of general councils in the past, an opportunity would be given for the free expression of Protestant grievances. Charles wanted a settlement of theological disputes, in which he was not interested. Believing that the doctrine of justification by faith could be defined in a manner that would satisfy all but the most bigoted sectaries, he hoped that some compromise might be arranged that would allow the clergy to have wives rather than concubines, allow also public worship in the vernacular rather than in Latin, since it was in the vernacular in the Slavonic countries and in Eastern churches; and that by mutual concessions, the dispute about giving the chalice to lay communicants at Holy Communion might be ended. That the Mass should be abolished or the pope's headship of the Church denied was never in the emperor's mind. The pope's authority might be strictly limited in Hapsburg lands — it was as a matter of fact very strictly limited in Spain and by the royal power in France — the notion of imitating the example of King Henry VIII of England did not appeal to Charles. Lutheran princes and Scandinavian kings constituted themselves supreme in church as in state after the fashion of the Tudor monarchy in England; not so the Hapsburg emperors in this matter, or in that other matter of dissolving religious orders.

The royal supremacy over the church in Protestant lands brought invariably the suppression of the religious orders and the seizures of abbeys, priories, convents, and all the treasure accumulated in the past centuries within these religious houses, as prerequisites of the crown. It was not only covetousness, that induced this annexation of monastic property; neither was it due to the preaching of Protestant clergy against chastity, though undoubtedly this encouraged and sanctioned the abolition of religious vows. The essential ground for suppression was the absolutism of the state. In the absolute or, as it is called to-day, the totalitarian, state the presence of religious orders is a witness to internationalism, since monks and nuns, friars and all regular clergy belong to societies that admit no national frontiers, and have their headquarters in Rome. This is resented by dictatorships. A secular clergy can become as ardently nationalist, as fiercely patriotic as the laity. The religious orders, whether contemplative or active, are by their very existence, by their customs and traditions international; knowing no abiding city, relying indeed on the state for protection in temporal matters, but indifferent to the form of government.

Charles, not proposing to make himself head of the Church, was no confiscator of monastic wealth. On the contrary, he endowed monks and nuns with property. But his political interests are the measure of his activities in European history, the record of the years in Germany that preceded Luther's death is a record of imperial policy directed to imperial ends.

The emperor — all his efforts at enforcement of the original ban placed on Luther at the Diet of Worms rendered futile — could not save the empire for the Catholic Faith. That was impossible when princes nominally Catholic were ready at any moment to join his enemies, and bishops, also nominally Catholic, evaded obedience to the Christian moral law. Diets and conferences were convened by the emperor, searching for a guarantee of internal peace, while the Turks threatened both the Mediterranean Sea and the Austrian dominion, while Francis prepared for his last war against the Hapsburgs.

Therefore to Ratisbon, in 1541, came Melanchthon and Bucer — the latter an accomplished delegate at conferences

— representing the Protestant interest, and Dr. John Eck — from the first, Luther's stoutest opponent — with John Gropper of Cologne on behalf of the Catholics. Both sides brought supporters. The diet was in session and the emperor had adjourned this theological conference from Worms. Cardinal Contarini, ardent in the Catholic group for reform within the Church, was also present as papal legate. No agreement was possible because, as Eck was aware, the real issue was the authority of the pope and the general council over the Church. Then, too, on the doctrine of the Mass, on the true teaching of the Church concerning sacramental confession and absolution, and on the practice of invoking the saints no common formula was possible between Catholic and Protestant. Conciliation was the note of the conference, that indefatigable controversialist Dr. John Eck alone declining to cry peace when it was all too obvious there was no peace. Bucer and Melanchthon were ready for any accommodation that left them undisturbed in their Protestantism. Both men sincerely desired reunion; only their idea of reunion was that Protestants should retain their Protestant beliefs and Catholics give up all that Protestants disliked. (Talk in Anglican circles of reunion in this twentieth century similarly assumes that Catholics will some day abandon the pope's supremacy, and with it any doctrine unacceptable to "separated brethren.") Luther never deceived himself by supposing reunion with the anti-Christ of Rome possible nor did he deem it desirable.

At Worms no one could have been more conciliatory than Martin Bucer, except perhaps John Gropper, when it came to a formula on justification by faith. Too conciliatory appeared the latter to theologians in Rome when the article was subsequently submitted to them. No less objectionable to Luther, deaf to all pleading for compromise, was Bucer's contribution. Cardinal Contarini, as anxious as the emperor to accommodate the Lutherans, put in a "Letter on Justification," which brought down upon the writer a storm of disapproval from the theologians who disapproved of Gropper, but left his relations with Pope Paul III undisturbed.

At the Diet of Ratisbon Contarini came to understand that no agreed formula on justification by faith would heal the divisions of the empire. Ignorance and neglect of Christian principles were the roots of the disease that had split the Church in Germany. In his letters to Rome the Venetian cardinal stressed the need for reform in the German episcopate, the need for trained preachers, above all the need for education. As for the Catholic princes of the empire "there is scarcely a man, or at the best very few (among them) who serve God with honest heart," wrote Contarini. "These dukes, Catholic and Bavarian, have observed that Philip of Hesse and the elector of Saxony have become great persons by leading the Lutherans and so they want to become great Catholic leaders, and are ready for war. Only as they have no money they want to wage war at the expense of the pope and the prince-bishops of the empire."

Religious disunion was mixed inextricably with political aims. John Frederick, the last Ernestine elector of Saxony, did all he could to get the Catholic princes to act with him against Charles in order to help the duke of Cleves to hold Guelders. Luther, for a while past favourable to the emperor and ready to allow reverence to imperial authority as a safeguard against Anabaptist rebellion and the possible invasion of Germany by the Turks, now broke out in a characteristic denunciation. The emperor was "a false, lying man; a man who had forgotten his good German morality and held the papistical, cardinalistic, Italian and saracenic creed." (No good German was Charles V, the emperor, according to Luther. But Charles never had been German. His offence in Luther's eyes was in sticking to the Faith of Rome instead of embracing the gospel of Wittenberg.) Luther uttered an equally emphatic condemnation on the character of Albert, archbishop of Mainz, that scholarly and worldly minded prelate, for resisting the new evangel. The archbishop was now, Luther decided "the devil himself and the real emperor; the pestilence of all Germany."

Charles strove at Ratisbon as on other occasions for religious union because of impending foreign wars. The princes as on other occasions favoured disunion and a wider breach between Catholics and Protestants out of fear of all Germany rallying to the emperor and thereby greatly increasing the imperial power. If religious agreement could not be effected, then, Charles suggested, let there be mutual tolerance until a final settlement of theological differences was made at a general council of the Church. But to this Contarini was opposed, declaring the imperial recognition of what was after all heresy, to be a sign of weakness. Better to admit frankly that Catholics and Protestants were doctrinally separated, the cardinal argued.

Confusion of politics and religion at Ratisbon is perhaps displayed nowhere more obviously than in the intrigues of the Catholic chancellor of the Catholic duke of Bavaria, who urged Charles to suppress heresy by force throughout the empire and at the same time busied himself in trying to get the Lutheran princes to form a league under the protection of Francis, against the emperor. Inevitable and imminent with such a league in existence was a fresh war.

In the interests of peace the diet, with the approval of Charles, conceded to Protestants the right to sit in the imperial chamber. Charles liked heresy no more than Contarini did, but was bound to keep the peace with the Protestants of the empire. For Solyman and his Turks had taken Buda-pesth, overrun all Hungary, and incorporated its rich lands within the sultan's dominion; Francis was in alliance with the Turks, and the pope more favourable to France than to an emperor who demanded a general council and threatened to call one himself if the pope delayed much longer.

Charles in self-defence made his private treaty with Philip of Hesse; a treaty that promised political security to emperor and landgrave and washed out the latter's bigamy. Exclusion of France, England, and the duke of Cleves from the Schmalkaldic league by Philip's influence averted danger from that quarter, and made the league comparatively innocuous; while Joachin of Brandenburg promised on his part not to join the league if the emperor would sanction the particular form of Lutheranism established in the Hohenzollern territories. Under these conditions Charles could once more face his old enemy Francis without misgivings. War with France came in 1542 but it lasted only two years and at the end the advantage was with Charles, who compelled the duke of Cleves to surrender Gueldersland and thus increase the Hapsburg patrimony. The Franco-Turkish alliance, with the advance of Solyman to the very walls of Vienna, compelled German princes, Protestant no less than Catholic, to support the emperor, to regard the war as an imperial war, in which the whole empire was involved. It brought no favourable change of attitude on the part of German Protestants to the papacy. For the pope was known to be pro-French and therefore held to be pro-Turkish. Besides it was openly reported that the Turkish fleet was allowed to purchase supplies at ports in the papal states.

But the pope was neither pro-French nor pro-German. In earnest for reform of papal abuses, for the return of Protestants to the Catholic unity, for the renovation of the spiritual life and the better education of the clergy, Paul III never forgot the interests of sons born to him when he was a young man, of his nephews, and the safeguarding of the papal states. When Barbarossa and his pirates from north Africa ravaged the coasts of Naples and Tuscany, co-operating with Francis against the Hapsburg emperor, the pope did the best he could for his own subjects. It was not to help the Turkish pirates but to protect his people that supplies were sold to the fleet that threatened all Christian nations sailing the Mediterranean Sea.

For political ends the Protestant princes might for a time support the emperor against France and the Turk, such support did not hinder the Lutheran advance. The bishoprics of electoral and ducal Saxony were all in Lutheran hands in the year after Ratisbon, and Luther in that same year committed what he called a "daring act" in consecrating a Protestant bishop, Nicholas von Amsdorf, an ex-Catholic priest to the vacant see of Naumberg, hitherto directly under the emperor. The chapter had elected their devout and learned provost von Pflug, but when John Frederick the elector swooped down upon the city and required it to turn Protestant, the scruples of those who had sworn to preserve the rights of the chapter were swiftly brushed aside by Luther's dictum that such oaths were nothing but oaths taken by sheep in the presence of wolves, and that "no duty was binding which conflicted with the commandments of God to banish all idolatrous doctrine."

This "daring act" was entirely in accordance with the theory of holy orders set out by Luther years before; a theory which in various formulas was accepted by all Protestant churches and, still acted upon, marks the distinction between the Catholic priest and the accredited minister of Anglican, Lutheran, Presbyterian, Methodist, and other Christian bodies. The priesthood of the laity was so regarded by Luther that it denied the sacrament of orders but required that the minister of the gospel must be duly called and, set apart to preach, and administer the sacraments; called by the congregation or by the prince as the case might be, and set apart desirably (necessarily some Protestants held) by the laying on of hands in the presence of the whole community. As for bishops, they were no more than superintendents of the churches of true believers; convenient but not essential to the government of the church, to be retained or discarded as circumstances dictated. The doctrine of apostolic succession Luther dismissed as false. Bishops, if desired, were as validly set apart by ordination at the hands of ministers or laymen as by fellow members of the episcopate. Hence the communion of episcopal Lutheran churches, of Sweden, for example, with the non-episcopal Lutheran churches of Germany, was never disturbed.

Luther himself only "consecrated" one other bishop, Prince George of Anhalt to the see of Merseberg in the territory of the elector of Saxony. To prove, however, that he was qualified to perform all offices hitherto reserved for the hierarchy Luther accepted the invitation of the Elector John Frederick to dedicate the first Protestant church at Torgau on the Elbe. All the ancient rites of consecration were on that day dropped and Luther's sermon, in which he identified the assembled congregation with the preacher, was sufficient for the hallowing of the elector's new church.

Lutheranism had conquered all Saxony, it now made an unexpected appearance in the west in Cologne, the city of Archbishop Hermann von Wied. A Catholic city it was where a provincial council, summoned by the archbishop, answered the Protestant teaching of Augsburg by plainly declaring the doctrine of the sacrifice of the Mass and followed up this statement by a fuller piece of writing, the *Encheiridion,* which dealt with transubstantiation, the Mass, and the Catholic doctrine of the seven sacraments and holy orders.

But the archbishop wavered as he read the works of Melanchthon and Bucer and gradually passed over to the Protestant side. Three years after the provincial council had met, the archbishop published a Lutheran service book called the *Simplex et Pia Consultatio,* depreciating the sacraments and abridging the Mass by an arrangement that left out the Canon.[1]

Here the Protestant encroachment was repulsed. For the

[1] For the importance of this service book of Hermann von Wied because of its influence on the compilers of the Church of England Book of Common Prayer see *The Reformation, the Mass, and the Priesthood,* by Dr. Ernest C. Messenger, London, 1936.

cathedral chapter of Cologne, helped by the learned John Gropper, replied to the archbishop's arguments and would not yield. The archbishop, subsequently excommunicated by the pope, put to the ban of the empire, refused to depart from his Lutheranism. As long as the Schmalkaldic league protected him he was safe, but the victory of the emperor over the league in 1547 ended his rule. Cologne had shown no inclination to the Protestant cause and on the deposition of the archbishop a Catholic successor was enthroned. Hermann von Wied, for more than thirty years archbishop of Cologne, when excommunication fell upon him went into retirement and died five years later. In his own way he had assisted the breakup of Christendom, although unsuccessfully in his own dominions.

The overthrow of Henry, Catholic duke of Brunswick, an eccentric, violent, and tyrannical man upon whom Luther was never tired of heaping abuse, brought about by Philip of Hesse and John Frederick of Saxony, the division of his territory and the installation of the indefatigable Bugenhagen as Lutheran superintendent, increased numerically the Protestants of Germany and enlarged the confusion. A few years later Henry turned the tables on his enemies and recovered his duchy. But the Protestant teaching had by that time taken root.

In these years of strife, of alliance, and agreement made and broken, the progress of the Reformation is seen through fog; the picture continually blurred. Persons and events emerge. It is the muddle of war. The tangled skein of politics and religion cannot be straightened. Well might Cardinal Morone, the papal nuncio at the Diet of Spires (1544), write to the pope of the indifference of the German prince-bishops to all save their worldly advantage, and their readiness to compromise with Protestant demands for the sake of present ease and carnal enjoyments. "The bishops rush full tilt towards comprehension in the hope of peace for themselves," wrote Morone. "They care only for drink and for concubines; they have no interest in theology, no respect for the holy see; they even wish to free themselves from the authority of the pope." With such men for bishops it was not to be expected that the lay princes would display nobility of character or high principle. Nor is it matter of wonderment that so many bishops turned Protestant and thereby kept their landed estates, their palaces, their mistresses, and petty sovereignty.

Charles was driven at that Diet of Spires to offer terms of peace to his Protestant princes, for Philip of Hesse and John Frederick of Saxony were present and there was much anxious diplomacy concerning matrimonial alliances and combinations for mutual aid. The emperor promised a free and general council on religion to be held in Germany and undertook that a preliminary diet should be held to make arrangements for settlement of the religious question; if such settlement were by any means possible. This undertaking brought down the wrath of Pope Paul III on the emperor and roused Luther to write in his defence. A further promise that all proceedings against Lutherans taken under the edict of Augsburg were to be suspended for the time, foreshadowed the coming peace of Augsburg ten years hence.

It was in February when the diet met and the decision taken that the campaign against France must be recognised as a war of the empire, to be waged by the whole empire, and not by the Hapsburgs alone. By September Charles had ended the war with the treaty of Crepy, and its secret clause that bound Francis to help the emperor in joint action against Protestants, should the latter resort to arms.

And now at last the long deferred and greatly needed ecumenical council was summoned to assemble by Pope Paul III, on German soil, at Trent, as near to Rome as any German city that could be named. It did assemble at the end of 1544 and after a brief interval resumed its work the following March, with thirty-four bishops from Italy and

Spain in addition to various theologians. A diet summoned by Charles for the need of assistance against the Turks also assembled at Worms in that same year.

It was little help the emperor got at this diet. The elector of Saxony refused to attend unless a free Christian council was summoned in place of the council at Trent. Recriminations were plentiful. The Council of Trent instead of starting on a reform of the abuses at the papal court had taken the doctrinal question for its first item and was not by any means the assembly of free Christians the Protestants had set their hearts upon. The general council that Luther, Bucer, and their disciples had in mind was a gathering in Germany where all good Protestants could be represented on equal terms with their papal adversaries; where the doctrine of justification by faith alone could be argued triumphantly; and the old Catholic doctrines of the sacrifice of the Mass, of the priesthood, of the papal supremacy refuted, with their defenders ignominiously discomfited.

The council in session at Trent was not in the Protestant view a national German council, still less a general council of the whole church. It had no authority at all for Protestants, and the Lutherans declared that the emperor had played them false. The "Wittenberg Reformation," a document drawn up by Melanchthon in conjunction with other Lutheran divines and published as a counterblast to the proceedings at Trent, at the request of the elector, restated in moderate language and in mild terms (even the papacy is called nothing worse than "idolatry") the minimum of the Protestant program of reform. No objection was made to episcopacy in this manifesto, provided the bishops accepted the new evangel.

In the mood of this "Wittenberg Reformation" the Lutherans at the diet declined to give any help to the emperor against the Turk without a guarantee of permanent peace throughout the empire; a guarantee irrespective of any decisions made at Trent. That it was a "small matter whether their children were taken captive by Turk or Catholic," was presented as the ground for refusing a subsidy for the Turkish war.

The Catholics pointed out in reply to this demand for peace that Lutherans, where they had power, had everywhere plundered and persecuted their Catholic subjects and neighbours; that all the troubles in the empire were due to the contempt for authority inculcated by Protestant preachers, to the decay of schools and charities through the same preachers who indulged in raving abuse rather than the delivery of homilies, and to the pamphlets against Jews and usurers that were nothing but incitements to plunder and bloodshed.

Charles was utterly powerless at the diet, but he planned to subdue by arms this Lutheran rebellion that would not acknowledge either pope or emperor and was steadily penetrating every part of the empire, bringing dissension and heresy within the very Hapsburg dominions, and like an all-devouring fire or oncoming tide was consuming and destroying the goods of faithful Catholics. If the Schmalkaldic league was not put down — and this league was the efficient bond and source of strength in the regions of militant Protestantism — the empire would crumble. A house divided against itself could not stand.

Luther preached war against the pope while Charles thought of war against the Schmalkaldic league to save the empire from dissolution. Luther abated none of his hatred of the papacy. He put no restraint on the violence of his words, written or spoken in the pulpit, in that last year of his life. A twenty years' hostility to the Jews, rooted in disappointment because the Jews had not embraced the evangel of Wittenberg as Luther had confidently expected, broke out in one of his very last sermons. Jews should not be tolerated but should be expelled, Luther cried, and acting on this the Elector John Frederick had expelled them from

Saxony, driving them across the borders into King Ferdinand's dominions where they were allowed to remain.

With denunciation of the Jews came denunciation of usury. On this latter point Luther would hear nothing in favour of taking interest on loans.

All money lending that involved payment of interest he found utterly reprehensible. In an age when commerce and finance were developing, what we call capitalism and money loans were finding a brisk demand, Luther to the last preached against the whole business with the ferocity that characterised his lifelong utterance when hostility was aroused. Only on one condition might interest be taken. Old persons, widows, and orphans, if they were in need, might take interest on loans. Otherwise the practice was to be condemned. This Luther maintained in one of the sermons preached at Eisleben a few days before his death.

Eisleben was his birthplace and there Martin Luther died in the sixty-third year of his age. He had been troubled with heart disease and the journey in mid-winter to help adjust the legal disputes of the Protestant counts of Mansfeld was not at all to his liking. Death came suddenly. Luther, with his fits of profound melancholy, talked frequently of death but there was no expectation of its immediate coming. Jonas of Wittenberg and another friend, Coelius, the court preacher to the count of Mansfeld, were with him when the stroke came, and pressing the dying man for an answer to their question whether he died faithful to the doctrine of Christ which he preached, received a whispered "Yes" for the reply they sought.

So died Martin Luther, and many fantastic legends sprang up concerning his death as friend or foe sought to glorify or defame this extraordinary man. Not so died the movement which he, and he alone, had created. Directed by other minds the movement swept onwards, abridging or expanding the Lutheran doctrine, annulling all anti-usury notions. Under Calvin and Bucer Protestantism fastened on Great

Britain — its influence to remain. The followers of Zwingli inveighed against by Luther as "Sacramentarians" persisted.

For the next ten years in Germany the struggle between Protestant and Catholic was to continue, but with Luther's death and the death of Francis, king of France, the Emperor Charles had two enemies the less in the world. Protestant advance he could not subdue. Political intrigue, the rise and fall of princes, bewilderment concerning the aims of the petty sovereigns of the empire, confusion that broods over the history of Germany in Luther's last years, none of these things, not even the bigamy of Philip, landgrave of Hesse, stayed the activities of Lutheran preachers. For these preachers, for the most part brought up in the Catholic Faith and ordained as Catholic priests, must needs justify their change of religion, while the genius of John Bugenhagen for organisation had immense outlet.

Then, too, the Protestant universities, Wittenberg, and Marburg, founded by Philip of Hesse, and the commercial cities of the Hansa in the north, were vital centres of evangelistic teaching, strongholds of the anti-Catholic recruiting agents, places where it was constantly maintained that the pope was anti-Christ, the papacy a diabolical invention.

True the Protestant advance was not allowed undisputed progress. At Cologne it was definitely repulsed. Dominicans and Franciscan clergy in many places did what they could to preserve the Catholic unity. Numbers whose names are no longer recalled continued to walk humbly before God in the old paths of Catholic Christendom. Unknown to the historian are the many who daily persist in their callings, despite all strife of princes, saving the world by their patient labour and their charity to God and man.

But with Protestant princes — the pettiest of them ruling in sovereign state — refusing to allow any form of Catholic worship or the ministry of Catholic priests within their dominions, with Catholic princes more or less indifferent as to what their subjects believed or where and how they prayed, with the Catholic episcopate so often attentive to carnal appetites to the neglect of spiritual things, the position in Germany could hardly be otherwise than favourable to Protestantism. The wide and much-noted decay of morals deplored by Luther was no particular hindrance to the establishment of the "evangelical" church.

The Council of Trent had begun its historic sessions, but the counter-reformation had not reached Germany; neither was it at all apparent that the era of Catholic reform was at hand. Yet there were signs of awakenment even among the worldlings of the German hierarchy. That scholarly prince-bishop of renaissance tastes, once the friend of Erasmus and correspondent of Pope Leo X, Albrecht, cardinal of Mainz, whose easy-going sensual life provoked and irritated Luther to write the coarsest indictments, which grew stronger and more violent in language as the hope of converting the archbishop to the Wittenberg evangel receded, started to amend his ways before death took him in 1545. The papal legate, Cardinal Morone, and Peter Faber, one of the early companions of Ignatius Loyola, were chiefly responsible for this change which affected not only the archbishop himself but the princely archiepiscopal court and the city.

The power of law and the strength of armies might enable the emperor to overthrow militant Protestantism in many parts of the empire. The spiritual strength of the new religion could only be met by the spiritual forces of Catholic reform, and the surest, bravest, and best equipped of these forces was the recently instituted Society of Jesus.

XII

From Death of Luther to Peace of Augsburg: 1546-1555

LUTHER DIED in February. The emperor supported by the pope and in secret agreement with Maurice of Saxony was at war with the Schmalkaldic league in July. John Frederick, the elector, and Philip of Hesse, the latter once more a recognised leader of Protestant movements, his bigamy not to be remembered against him, his submission to the emperor an affair of the past, were declared outlaws, the ban of the empire placed upon them. For Charles insisted that political necessity and not differences of religion occasioned the hostilities; though he was fully aware that politics and religion were still inextricably mixed and personal ambition as powerful a motive as ever with men like his present allies Maurice of Saxony, landgrave Philip's son-in-law, and Joachin, the semi-Lutheran elector of Brandenburg. The pope sent troops and money to the emperor because at the outset he saw the war as a crusade against heresy. He changed his mind the next year, even before the Protestants had been routed at Muhlberg on the river Elbe in Saxony, on April 24, and John Frederick taken prisoner. For this victory, followed by the surrender of

Philip to Maurice and Joachin, left Charles all powerful as it seemed in Germany; far too powerful in the eyes of Paul III, far too ready to intrude the imperial will in the councils of the Church, where no layman's voice was wanted. For the sake of peace within the empire Charles was prepared to meddle with theology, to arbitrate on questions of Church discipline — so Paul III judged. With plague rife in the neighbourhood of Trent, the pope transferred the council to Italy, to the city of Bologna.

This move the emperor countered by positively forbidding all German bishops to attend, and, as it turned out, nothing was done at Bologna. Relations between pope and emperor were further strained by the diet which Charles opened at Augsburg in September and by the murder of Pierluigi Farnese, duke of Placentia, the son of Paul III to whom the aged pontiff was greatly attached. The murder was done by imperialists, out of political hatred, but it was said at Rome that the emperor's governor of Milan and the emperor himself were accomplices.

Victorious over the recalcitrant John Frederick, the landgrave Philip a prisoner, the duke of Brunswick restored, and Duke Ulrich of Wurtemberg once more put down and removed, to the unqualified relief of his subjects, the emperor now turned to settle the affairs of the empire on a peaceful basis at Augsburg, prepared to meet his Protestant princes with conciliation and effect political unity as best he could. The *Interim* was the outcome of this diet, the inevitable compromise drawn up by a small consultative commission appointed by the emperor, which included von Pflug, now bishop of Naumberg, and John Agricola, Joachin's special chaplain. Under the *Interim* the Catholic Faith remained the faith of Germany, but the clergy were allowed to marry, the laity were to receive the chalice at holy communion and the doctrine of justification by faith was defined in words that it was thought by Charles no reasonable Catholic or Protestant need object to. Certain reasonable Catholics, including Pope Paul III, thought otherwise. Certain reasonable Lutherans, and these ministers of religion and preachers to whom the Mass and the whole Catholic system of worship were abhorrent, departed from Germany rather than submit.

The college of electors approved the *Interim,* the college of princes, the majority Catholic, gave a qualified assent. Charles still not realising that the cleavage between Catholic and Protestant was too wide to be bridged by the concessions of the *Interim*, believing also that his Lutheran subjects would now be ready to stand by him against the pope should the latter make trouble, and relying on his efficient Spanish infantry, determined that the *Interim,* a decree of the imperial diet, should be enforced throughout the empire. Very considerably he succeeded; compelling a nominal obedience over the greater part of Germany, for the Protestants, without leaders, were divided. Melanchthon at Wittenberg advised submission, but characteristically in lukewarm fashion; publicly conforming to restored Catholic rites while privately expressing doubts whether resistance was not the better way. In every Lutheran city, in every Lutheran dominion some were for carrying out the *Interim* others for ignoring it. None were for more than yielding passive obedience, giving way to the imperial will in external observance. No return to the Catholic unity was seriously discussed. The compromise was not popular; nor was it hailed as a contract that promised lasting peace. The *Interim* was at the best a truce — to be very soon broken.

Maurice of Saxony, created an elector of the empire by Charles in place of John Frederick, and receiving much of the territory of the latter (in whom died the Ernestine line of the Wettin family), after abandoning the Lutheranism of his early youth and at the exactly opportune moment going over to the emperor, now thought the time had come to change sides again and revert to Lutheranism. That a Catholic elector could be acceptable to Protestant Saxony after twenty years of Lutheran ascendancy, it seemed was impossible. Therefore Maurice quietly and steadily intrigued with princes of Lutheran persuasion and raised troops; at the same time coming to an agreement with the new king of France, Henry II, son of Francis. For Henry who would have no heresy tolerated within his own kingdom was ready to ally with heretics for the ruin of the empire. (Thereby anticipating the policy of Richelieu — security of France through alliance with the Protestants of Germany.)

Neither religious apostacy nor grave change of religious belief need be inferred from the conduct of Maurice. There is no evidence that he adopted Catholicism through any conviction that the Faith of the Holy Roman Church was the faith of divine revelation, that the Catholic Church was the body of Christ, one and indivisible. There is indeed no evidence that this young ambitious prince cared anything at all for religion or expressed the slightest interest in theology. Lutheranism may have been preferred because it made less demands on its adherents than did the religion of the emperor; for one thing it had no pope to interfere with and obstruct the policy of temporal rulers. Maurice turned back to the Lutheranism of his youth, so far as it can be judged, because the political situation demanded such reversal of creed. Conscience did not dictate the change, it acquiesced. It was obvious to Maurice that, *Interim* or no *Interim,* the imperial will could not bring back the empire to the old religion however strenuously the emperor exerted it. Besides as real and effective ruler of all Germany Charles threatened the sovereignty of princes; threatened particularly to check the forward career of Maurice.

The success achieved in forcing the *Interim* on all Germany was more apparent to the emperor than to his Lutheran princes. It brought no popularity. It produced misgivings. There were many reasons why Maurice should lead his fellow Lutherans, in conjunction with the forces of Henry II of France, to pull down the emperor from his high estate. Maurice, at thirty, conscious of military abilities, aware of talents that surpassed the modest intellectual attainments of his princely contemporaries, prepared for war; war that would curtail the imperial rights in Germany, reduce the overweening sovereignty of the Hapsburgs, and enlarge the powers of Maurice of Saxony at the emperor's expense.

The expectation of a victorious plan of campaign was very nearly fulfilled. For Maurice and his troops were ready for action when the French armies crossed the frontier of Lorraine, while the emperor, distrusting Maurice, was unprepared. Augsburg was taken and Maurice pressed the pursuit of the emperor. Only by hasty crossing of the Brenner Pass into Austria and finding safety at Villach in Carinthia did Charles escape and leave Maurice frustrated, to recognise that with Ferdinand insisting on peace further civil war might bring ruin.

The peace of Passau followed and the terms drawn up by the assembled princes, Catholic and Protestant, included the liberation of John Frederick and Philip of Hesse, admission of Lutherans to the imperial council chamber, and the promise of yet another diet for the permament settlement of religion. The deposed elector John Frederick, an entirely sincere Lutheran, though contemporaries found his personal morals unstable, with a resolution to stand by his faith that matched the emperor's adherence to Catholicism, expressed the utmost disgust at receiving freedom at the hands of Maurice—Maurice of the Albertine line—who as the reward for changing his religion had obtained the electorate of Saxony and much landed property.

The electorate never returned to the Ernestine Wettins, but the supplanter of John Frederick had but short enjoyment of it. For Maurice was killed in battle at Sievershausen, in July, 1553, waging war against the utterly lawless Albrecht Alcibiades, margrave of Brandenburg-Culmbach, whose robber bands pillaged and murdered throughout Franconia, sparing none and harrying in especial the lands of bishops. So at thirty-two died Maurice of Saxony, at the very outset of a high career. Political opportunism and military capacity were joined together and dominated by ambition in Maurice; hence neither friend nor foe could be sure of him. The electorate passed to his brother Augustus, an inoffensive man.

Eight months later and John Frederick was dead. Emperor Charles, with four years yet to live, had already decided on abdication, leaving his brother Ferdinand to succeed to the imperial crown. Despairing of the unity of Germany, the emperor departed—never to return. Proceeding first to Brussels before his final resignation, he then retired to the monastery of St. Juste near Valadolid in Spain. His son Philip II inherited the Hapsburg rule over Spain, Naples, and the Netherlands.

Luther, Erasmus, Henry VIII, Francis I, Zwingli, Archbishop Albert of Mainz, Popes Leo, Clement, Adrian and Paul III, all were dead. The principal actors in the tragedy of the Reformation had departed from the stage. Charles would leave the world; lay down the burden of authority; escape from the troubles of heresy and schism within the empire he had been chosen to rule, before death also came for him. Ferdinand, king of the Romans, emperor-elect, sovereign of Austria, would preside at the diet summoned to meet at Augsburg in February, 1555, and in the emperor's stead settle finally an accommodation with the Protestants of Germany. Yet Charles firmly insisted that no responsibility was his for the decisions to be arrived at. To the last he could not bring himself to sanction a divided Church, to grant a permit to heresy.

Since we must limit every period of history and mark the boundaries by positive events, this Diet of Augsburg is widely and very properly taken, so far as Germany is concerned, as the end of the revolution we call the Protestant reformation. Nearly forty years had passed since Martin Luther's first challenge, all unwittingly as far as the challenger was concerned, began the movement from obedience to Rome, the movement that brought disruption to so vast a portion of Christendom. Nearly thirty years back a diet of the empire at Spires had concluded, as the present diet would conclude, that no compulsion could restore the old religion in the territories of Lutheran princes.

At Augsburg, in 1530, had been drawn up the classic confessions of the new evangelical Protestant church of Germany. At Augsburg, in 1555, came the declaration of the imperial diet that the Lutheran confession of faith must be accepted wherever the state so ordered it.

The diet of 1555 was not fully attended. It was said that there were more princes of the empire at the Lutheran convention then assembled at Naumberg. Numerically the majority was Catholic at Augsburg, but Catholic and Protestant alike wanted peace; peace at any price compatible with security. The discussions and arguments lasted for months, and not till the end of the summer, and then chiefly through the efforts of Ferdinand and Augustus, Lutheran elector of Saxony, was a compromise arranged and a settlement embodied in the *Recess* published in September. Seeds of future strife, of the Thirty Years' War certainly, were embedded in the settlement of Augsburg, but for a season peace was ensured and the Protestant reformation recognised, within prescribed areas, as an accomplished fact. Differences of religion were not to be made the occasion of war within the empire; that was the first and most urgent point agreed upon at the diet.

Questions of ownership of church property provoked long and bitter discussion before the contending sides finally decreed that:

1. Present owners, whether Lutheran or Catholic, were to remain in possession of the ecclesiastical property they held. Secularisation of church property accomplished by 1552 not to be upset.

2. Prince-bishops or other clerical rulers must in future,

on giving up Catholicism, surrender all the property that belonged to their office; that is all the endowments given by Catholics for Catholic worship.

This second article in the peace treaty, the forfeiture of estates required of Catholic bishops on becoming Protestant, was never agreeable to the Lutherans. It remained a rock of offence; for in their hearts the Lutherans held that church dignitaries on abandoning Catholicism for the new evangel should not be penalised but rather rewarded. For a time, and only for a time, this "ecclesiastical reservation," as it was called, might be allowed to stand; Protestant resistance to its enforcement would one day ultimately put an end to so stout an obstruction to Lutheran progress. Deprivation of property was neither more nor less than persecution from the Lutheran point of view. It was without doubt an obstacle to the free play of the acquisitive spirit.

The third and most memorable decision at Augsburg laid it down that the religion of the ruler must be the religion of his subjects. *Cujus regio ejus religio.* The ruler whether prince of the empire, petty sovereign, or the governing body of a free city, having made choice between Lutheranism and Catholicism, the people inhabiting the territories of these rulers or dwelling within the city must abide by the result. There could be no two religions practised within one state. As the government worshipped so must the governed. The creed of the sovereign must be the creed of the subject; and this in every territorial dominion, great or small. Those who would not conform were free throughout the empire to migrate elsewhere.

"No estate shall try to persuade the subjects of other estates to abandon their religion, nor protect them against their own magistrates. Such as had from olden time the rights of patronage are not included in the present article.

"In case our subjects, whether belonging to the old religion or to the Augsburg Confession, should intend leaving their homes with their wives and children in order to settle in another place they shall neither be hindered in the sale of their estates, after due payment of the local taxes, nor injured in their honour."

So ran the terms of the Peace of Augsburg.

The triumph and emergence of the Protestant princes as absolute rulers in Church and state within their own dominions, was fatal to the imperial monarchy, fatal no less to German unity. "Henceforward Germany was not a kingdom but a collection of petty states whose rulers were dominated by mutual jealousies."[1] Charles V had foreseen as inevitable and as disastrous the peace of Augsburg. He, almost alone, had the foresight that recognised the doom of imperial Germany.

Yet in that year 1555 the principle *cujus regio ejus religio* neither startled people as a novelty nor invited resentment as tyranny. Absolutism had come in with the renaissance; the middle ages with their constitutional checks and political philosophy were over. By Catholic and Protestant alike the supremacy of the state seemed in the natural order. Catholics generally supported an absolute supremacy of the state in temporal affairs because they put their trust in princes for the protection of their Faith. A Catholic sovereign was a sure stronghold against disruptive forces. With Lutherans sternly excluded, the peace of the Church was assured. Anabaptists and other revolutionaries were no longer a hidden peril when their very presence was forbidden.

Charles, knowing that a house divided against itself cannot stand, sought by every means in his power to save Germany from the impending dissolution. He failed. The area was too vast to be controlled, the conflicting interests too diverse to be reconciled. His own attention was too often distracted from Germany, years of absence are recorded, the Hapsburg dominions demanded care and safe guardianship

---

[1] A. F. Pollard, *Cambridge Modern History,* Chapter VIII.

and had the prior claim; a claim exercised it must needs be at the expense of imperial welfare.

He had done what he could, Charles V, for the unity of Germany; it was not sufficient. Lutheranism proved too powerful a solvent of traditional beliefs; it established a mastery over the minds and feelings of men that local authority might coerce and perhaps expel. But no vague shadow of an absent emperor could subdue the preachers of the new evangel of Wittenberg; no reverence for the conglomeration of states called the Holy Roman Empire destroy the conviction that Luther was inspired by God to reform the Church of Christ.

Because the unity of Germany had perished there was more urgent reason for preserving unity in each petty state, in each self-governing municipality. The liberalism that sees in religious freedom a positive good and in religious toleration the very beginning of a neighbourly life, was a doctrine not acceptable to Protestant or Catholic in the sixteenth century. On the contrary the idea was positively repugnant, since everywhere in Germany religious toleration meant religious strife; a strife of tongues that sooner or later brought strife of arms and war. The time had passed for the settlement of religious differences by debate. Private judgment put an end to peaceful and reasonable settlements. For private judgment repudiated decisions of general councils; denied that God guided the Christian Church when such general councils were assembled. Private judgment concluded that what each man felt within himself to be true, that for him was true if he could show grounds for belief in the Holy Scriptures.

Private judgment, therefore, it was evident to sixteenth-century rulers, had become a danger to the state, since it implied the divine right of subjects to refuse obedience to the law on conscientious grounds, gave free play to scruples that would undermine all civil authority, and made passive resistance to government, a sublime and godly work. Nor did commendation halt at *passive* resistance. Active resistance, that included civil war and the assassination of tyrants, was assumed to be fulfillment of the will of God, when private judgment was convinced of the propriety of violent measures.

Private judgment, according to the mind of the rulers, must be restricted in its operations, limited to its lawful functions. The one and obvious business they would allow to private judgment was to bring a man to the faith of the Catholic Church, where the government was Catholic; to the faith of the Augsburg confession, where the government was Lutheran. (At Geneva, to the dogma and discipline of the church instituted by John Calvin.) When private judgment failed to lead men to conformity, private judgment must be discarded, shunned as a device of the devil for the ruin of mankind. The church established was the true church, the religion of the sovereign the true religion for true subjects. All else was treason to the state. Civil authority was the safeguard of orthodoxy. Let those who could not worship with their rulers, their divinely appointed rulers, depart and dwell in another land.

The sovereignty conceded to the emperor in earlier ages was now vested in the head of each small German state. Where the head was Catholic all the old forms and rites of the Catholic religion were maintained, the Mass celebrated, the feasts and fasts observed.

Lutherans were as content as Catholics with the peace of Augsburg — for the time. Although Luther at the outset of his campaign for the changes that meant for him reform in the Church never suggested that disciples of his evangel should take their credo from their sovereign, he arrived at the conclusion *cujus regio ejus religio*. His innate conservatism — that same conservatism that made him distrust all novelties in faith and worship not originating in himself — made him prejudiced in favour of a state church. The ancient discipline of the Catholic Church had gone; its episcopal rulers deposed, rubrics and ordinances dismissed as being without authority, the body of canon law burnt with papal bull in contempt as a thing of no account, the pope himself contemned as anti-Christ — what then remained to compel obedience to the moral law, to enforce respect for the ministers of religion, to see that to Caesar should be rendered the things of Caesar, to God the things of God?

Caesar and Caesar alone remained.

Not Charles, imperial Caesar; a man hostile to the gospel of Wittenberg, a servant for the most part of the anti-Christ at Rome, but the ruler of the territory where Luther lived was Caesar. And every ruler who embraced the Lutheran gospel was Caesar. The elector of Saxony, Philip, the bigamist landgrave of Hesse; Albert of Brandenburg, last grand-master of the Teutonic knights; various prince-bishops — in such rulers Luther trusted. To such he was willing to give the overlordship of the new evangelical church. These princes, not being averse from the exercise of power, accepted the overlordship; with the result that Lutheranism was nourished in bondage to the state, never in Germany to be released.

"The abhorrence of Luther for the visible organization of the Church inclined him from the beginning to respect the temporal power, but it was from the experience of his later life that he derived the sacred character of the civil authority. If secular thinkers regarded the state as the most beautiful and most complete human institution, it remained for Lutheran divines to find it god-like. The abolition of the universal Church was compensated by the deification of the only remaining power, the regional state. The territorial unit was conceived as the only external institution consecrated by God, outside of which human and divine aspirations could not decently be fulfilled."[2]

Compensations for this state supremacy were evident to

---

[2] John Armstrong, M.A., in "Church and State," Cambridge Summer School Lectures, 1935. London, 1936.

all active Lutherans at the time of the peace of Augsburg. For one thing the confessions and catechisms of the evangelical church would not be disturbed by criticisms of Swiss sectaries, adherents of Bullinger at Zurich, or of Calvin at Geneva. Provided that no attempt was made to set up rival Protestant churches Protestantism in Germany was Lutheran, but an inclusive Lutheranism and nothing else. Calvinism found congenial soil in the Netherlands territory of Spanish Hapsburgs. It was never suffered to take root in Germany. Verbal departures from the Wittenberg formula of sacramental belief, departures authorised by Zwingli and Bucer, once so acrimoniously opposed by Dr. Martin Luther, no longer burning questions among Protestants, shrank into insignificant discrepancies, into the merely trivial. Within the loose organisation of the evangelical church of Lutheran Germany there was room for every kind of sacramental belief (and disbelief) except transubstantiation and the sacrifice of the Mass. Luther's personal formula of consubstantiation was to be respected; it must not become a burden imposed on earnest Protestants as a text of orthodoxy. As in the Church of England and throughout the Anglican communion no inquisition was made as to what men did or did not believe concerning the presence of Christ in the eucharist. Protestant governments in Germany outside the Austrian and Hapsburg Holy Roman empire of Ferdinand were officially Lutheran. The established church of each of these Protestant governments was evangelical and Lutheran; not modelled on Swiss or Bucerian lines.

Protected by the state the Lutheran evangelical church survived as a distinct organisation of the Protestant world. Not so did the congregations of Bullinger and Bucer survive. Swiss Protestantism in various cantons claims Zurich for its birthplace — that is all that can be said.

But the Lutheran survival in Germany has been accompanied by the steady elimination of all that was vital in Luther's revolt. Augsburg confessions and catechisms, the whole body of sixteenth-century Lutheran theology, came to be studied by German Protestant divines as documents of no more than historic interest, to be freshly interpreted in each age by the modern spirit of that age; or cast aside — salt that has lost its savour.

For the decay of dogmatic belief and undermining of traditional Christian doctrine in the evangelical Lutheran church of Germany Luther himself is, of course, primarily responsible. His fluid vision, his flexible intelligence were ill-adapted for the propounding of articles of dogmatc faith. Luther's one article was "Justification by Faith Alone"; the Christian is saved from eternal damnation by believing that he is saved through the death of Christ. This assurance of personal salvation was the abiding strength in Luther's troubled life. It remained the abiding strength of evangelical Protestantism in the centuries to come. But Luther had not the constructive mind that could devise a new and positive form of Christian doctrine and bind multitudes to its acceptance. The evangelical church inherited the mutable qualities of its founder: comprehension of variety of belief — for justification by faith alone was fundamental but not exhaustive — distrust of the processes of thought, sentiment predominant over objective faith, feeling over the will. Even the rationalism of nineteenth-century German Biblical criticism, repugnant as much of it would have been to Luther, has the characteristics of the Wittenberg method; an arbitrary assumption that an hypothesis is necessarily to be acknowledged as a fact; a persuasion that what may be true, must be true; bias against existing and traditional interpretations of documents.

With the peace of Augsburg Lutheranism is seen established as the official religion of the larger part of Germany, with Catholicism retained in Austria and Bavaria. The political boundaries, frequently moved since that temporary settlement and liable to further change, still roughly indicate the prevalent religion of the majority. The inhabitants of Prussia, Saxony, Wurtemberg — Protestant; Austria, Bavaria, the Rhine lands of Westphalia — Catholic. Substantial minorities exist in every part, not to be left out of account.

Lutheranism in Germany gained on the terms of Augsburg where Protestant rulers extended their territories, profiting by the absolutism of the state.

Catholic reform, the counter-reformation, already at the time of Augsburg a living principle within the Catholic Church, recovered by spiritual means much of the ground lost to the Lutheran evangel; it could not restore the crumbled and shattered unity of the Kingdom of Christ, nor undo the work started by the Augustinian monk of Wittenberg.

XIII

Developments and Extensions of Protestantism in Europe

LUTHERANISM, embodied in the new evangelical church, satisfied the German people in those lands where the state imposed it. The appeal to religious experience, that essential item in the Lutheran gospel, won response as it always does when the heart is touched and the feelings moved. From the very beginning of Luther's public work there is evidence how many were suited by his exposition of Christianity. In his own lifetime Luther could see the gospel first preached at Wittenberg carried to wide areas of Germany and to Scandinavian countries, and note its acceptance by clergy and civil rulers. He could further note, but with less comfort, deviations from Lutheranism cropping up in Switzerland. After his death developments in Protestantism sundered the church of Luther from the church of the Swiss reform, sharply dividing German Lutherans from the Calvinists of Geneva.

For Lutheranism, while it gratified many German minds and the minds of many in Denmark, Sweden, and Norway, exercising also an influence on the leaders of the Protestant reformation in England — notably Cranmer and the Elizabethan bishops — took no root elsewhere.[1] Lutheranism flourished in the lands where it was established, and those lands were exclusively German and Scandinavian. It exists to-day as the faith of German people in far-off lands, much as Anglicanism expressed in the Book of Common Prayer exists for English people living remote from England.

John Calvin brought to German Protestantism an intensity of intellectual conviction, a logic, and a political ethic that were outside the Lutheran conception of evangelical religion, and unpalatable to Lutheran minds of the middle class. A Frenchman and a layman, trained in Catholic schools, enamoured of learning as a young man, diverted from holy orders to the study of law, Calvin at twenty-four passed from the influence of Erasmus to ponder and accept the doctrine of justification by faith alone which he read in the sermons of Martin Luther. France being at that time no safe place for Protestants, Calvin went to Switzerland and at Basle wrote and published the first edition of his famous version of the Christian religion, *Christianae Religionis Institutio,* often but erroneously described as the "Institution of a Christian Man," addressing it to Francis I. Calvin was twenty-six when he thus laid down to the king of France the duty of a sovereign to his subjects, emphasising the duty of toleration to separatists from the Catholic Church. The *Institutio* was many times revised and with every fresh revision came considerable additions but no change in doctrine. The last edition, published in 1559, stretched from the modest six chapters of 1536 to no less than four books and eighty chapters. Far more words but the same doctrine.

In the city of Geneva Calvin was given opportunity for the full practice of his reformed Christianity. Not at first. For two years (1536–1538) this young French layman tried in vain with the more elderly Farel, also an exile from

[1] For the success of Lutheranism in England see the author's *Protestant Reformation in Great Britain,* U. S. A., 1934.

France, to reform the unwilling people of Geneva, Protestant, but disliking the strict sobriety of this new French religion. Failing in this enterprise, the city council advised Calvin's retirement. Three years at Strassburg followed, years of preaching and a professorship of theology in that Protestant city. Then came recall to Geneva, a self-governing community which had cast off all allegiance to the bishop and to the ducal house of Savoy, ranging itself with the reformed Bernese. There, until his death in 1564, Calvin legislated and ruled; to divert, by power of pen and forcefulness of character, the course of Protestantism, to produce that immensely impressive thing called Calvinism, the religion of the reform.

At the age of twenty-six John Calvin fixed once and for all the doctrine that went out from Geneva. It was a development of Lutheranism and it remained unchanged. He could do no more than enlarge the argument, as he did with the increasing volumes of the *Institutio,* and expound at greater length the ecclesiastical ordinances of the church of the reform. At twenty-six Calvin was sure that he had from God, through a study of the Sacred Scriptures, the truth, the whole truth, and nothing but the truth. Doubts and scruples, anxieties and depressions might torture Luther; they were allowed no entrance into Calvin's mind once his creed was settled. Given the opportunity that the city council of Geneva provided, Calvin had the rare satisfaction of compelling his neighbours by force of law—himself the lawgiver—to submit to a code of morals drawn up once and for all; a code weighted with the author's assurance that the work was of divine sanction. To the natural confidence of youth was added, in Calvin's case, as in Luther's, an irrepressible conviction that he was called by God to renew Christianity by reforming the Christian Church.

Calvin's personal interpretation of the will and purposes of God became the legal and theological system of Geneva, and the city council aware of an immediate need of unity welcomed a dictatorship that would weld the people into a disciplined community. Absolute obedience was required of all citizens. Otherwise, divided by faction, rent by opposing opinions, Geneva might too easily fall a prey to the house of Savoy.

Morals and faith alike were decreed by Calvin to the citizens of Geneva; for this young French lawyer, a classical scholar educated in Catholic studies, had no illusions that conduct could be divorced from belief. Not for a minute would he consent to the notion that man, adolescent or adult, may be left to believe what he likes as long as he behaves himself with decency. No more would Calvin tolerate the alternative that orthodox belief excuses lapses in morals. Every man, woman, and child in Geneva had to conform to the Calvinistic worship — which mostly consisted in attendance at immensely long sermons — and obey without questioning the commands of the magistrate. Calvin's political ideal was theocratic. A return to the early Hebraism of the Old Testament would bring in the model state. As Calvin saw it, God ruled His people directly through the authority of the state; to the magistrates of the state was committed a sacred charge, the law of God, with grave responsibility for the punishment of all who violated, infringed, neglected, or cast ridicule on that law. The New Testament might be read, in especial certain epistles of St. Paul, by true Christians of the reformed church, but the Old Testament must be read and pondered; for the Old Testament contained the Ten Commandments given to Moses from Mount Sinai and the Ten Commandments explained by John Calvin covered every detail of human conduct.

All this was something very different from Lutheranism and in startling contrast to the Catholic Faith of Christendom. For Luther never could draw up a hard-and-fast theology; nor could he take a strong line on morals, filled as he was with the conviction that however deeply a man sinned, God would pardon him if he believed that he was saved by the justifying death of Christ.

Even more marked than the departure from Lutheranism was the revolutionary change from Catholicism expressed in the Geneva system of faith and morals. The Old Testament, apart from the psalms, was then as now, but little read by the Catholic laity. While every Sunday at Mass throughout the world, in these times, Catholics will generally hear some portion of the New Testament read aloud, in the sixteenth century ignorance of the New Testament was considerable. A host of ill-instructed Catholics existed in every land of Europe. But the faith of the millions, of the simple, the humble of heart who, following their callings, make no figure in history, was Faith in Christ, the Christ of the New Testament, and in His Mother. Nowhere but in the New Testament was the story of Christ's Incarnation, Passion, Crucifixion, Resurrection, and Ascension to be found. To put all this gospel of the New Testament into a second place and give the Hebraism of the Old Testament a priority of importance was an astounding deflection of Protestantism from the Wittenberg evangel, a devastation, in some lands a total submergement, of Catholic Christianity.

And Calvinism was precisely this, neither more nor less: An exaltation of the Old Testament at the expense of the New.[2] The Christian and Catholic Sunday became the Hebrew Sabbath, with dire penalties inflicted entirely in the rabbinical spirit on all who transgressed, however minutely, the letter of the law. Calvin's theology has been left to perish for want of readers, though still surviving in obscure churches and preached in out-of-the-way places; the

---

[2] It must not be inferred that Calvin and his disciples admitted this exaltation. There is no evidence that Calvin supposed he was conscious of doing anything of the kind. He believed he was "reforming" the church according to the doctrine of St. Paul and, in a lesser degree, of St. Augustine.

Sabbath observance, however, enjoined at Geneva and strictly carried out by civic authority, remains in Protestant countries the strongest memorial of the Old Testament dispensation. Inquisition into private morals, the making of laws for the regulation of personal conduct, the prohibition by the state on ethical grounds of habits and customs common to mankind but judged contrary to national welfare — these things, too, are memorials of Calvin's rule at Geneva.

Politically Calvinism was at variance with Lutheranism. Both systems were agreed on the principle *cujus regio ejus religio*. One form of worship and one only could be tolerated by the state. Neither from Calvin nor Luther is the beginning of religious toleration derived, though Protestantism with its varieties of belief ultimately forced toleration. Lutheranism made the state protector and governor of the church; hence in Germany and in England the state is still the supreme ecclesiastical governor; of the evangelical church of the former, and the established Church of England of the latter. Whereas in Scotland the established church, Presbyterian and of Calvinist extraction, remains self-governing; subject to no state overlordship in the appointment of its clergy, in the revising of its formularies.

To Calvin, with his ideal of the theocratic state, religion was no substitute for an efficient police, no handmaid or magistrates to be employed in the interests of law and order. The reformed religion was absolute and infallible, directly revealed by God to His chosen servants in these latter days, as positively as it had once been revealed to Moses and the prophets. Calvin might declare his own unworthiness, he never disguised from himself or from others that he was by no means the least of God's chosen servants; holding himself indeed a prophet of God whose words were not to be ignored save at grave peril.

The state therefore — and Calvin was not greatly exercised as to its form; in republic or kingdom alike, the state could protect the reformed religion and allow it to flourish

— must keep strictly to its own province the execution of the law given to its keeping by the Church. Magistrates were ministers of God no less than the official preachers. The latter expounded the law, the former were required to see it obeyed. Religion under these conditions, with the state really subordinate to the church, was a far more serious matter than it was in Lutheran lands. Calvinism shaped and gave hard distinction to the Scottish character, as Anglicanism never did to the English people, or Lutheranism to the German nation.

Calvin's terrible, to millions terrifying, doctrine of predestination made levity impossible to those afflicted by it. Luther denied that man had free will, maintaining that the will of God did everything; but he refrained from working out, as Calvin did, a close and reasoned argument of man's foredoom. Good works according to both Calvin and Luther could never affect the salvation of any man. Personal righteousness according to the former was no proof of predestination to heaven, of no avail according to the latter without justifying faith. But both were agreed that good works were a sign of right belief.

Luther held the pope to be anti-Christ and quite cheerfully, often boisterously, consigned his enemies to hell for opposing the evangel of Wittenberg. Calvin laid it down as part of God's plan that from all time the vast majority of human beings were consigned to an eternal punishment in hell. That nothing a man did could avert that punishment. Nor if he was of the few elected by God to salvation could his misdeed bring any forfeiture of heaven. It was obvious, Calvin pointed out, that the elect would be members of the reformed church; and obviously impossible that any "papist" could be saved.

This strange view of Christianity — a very travesty it seems to educated twentieth-century Presbyterians who derive from Geneva through the ministry of John Knox — was Calvin's development of the Lutheran theology; created by dwelling on certain texts in the Bible to the exclusion of other passages complementary, and by similar process extracted from the works of St. Augustine. It was, on the face of it, a dogma that once firmly held might be tremendously forceful. Forceful it was. Calvinists, self-persuaded that they were the elect, filled with Old Testament stories of Jewish warfare, identifying themselves with the children of Israel chosen by Almighty God to destroy the idolaters, proved great fighters. Calvin himself might uphold nonresistance to "idolatrous" rulers in Holland and in France, Dutch Calvinists and French Huguenots waged long and destructive wars against Catholic sovereigns; the former finally achieving political independence of Spain, the latter subsiding into a peaceful, respected, and not unlearned minority.

Wherever the Dutch or the Scots have settled, there the dogma of predestination has fastened on the land; and with the dogma went the assumption that the Calvinists and the descendants of Calvinists are of the elect, appointed as the Jews were of old to come in and possess the land.

The greatest exponent of the doctrine of predestination, the most powerful of its advocates, an American, Jonathan Edwardes, perhaps surpassed his master Calvin in sheer dialectic. In New England as sharply as in Scotland or in Geneva itself, the reformed church, through the magistrates, compelled the strict letter of the law to be observed. In South Africa the Dutch Boer farmers held to a strict Calvinism that brooked no mitigation. (But of course all this strict observance of laws and promulgation of habits that Catholic Christianity for more than fifteen hundred years had known nothing of, inevitably brought hypocrisy in its train. It could hardly be otherwise.)

Politically, then, Calvinism is a development of Lutheranism by its exalting the church above the state. Doctrinally it placed on Protestantism the burden of predestination with its utter doom of all mankind from the beginning of the world to an eternal hell, a tiny remnant of the reformed church alone, to be saved. The actual controversy between Calvinists and other Protestants turned mainly on the attitude to the authority of the Bible. A never-ending controversy, provoking, as it was bound to do, strife and sharpest antagonism between rival churches of Protestantism.

Lutheran and Anglican were content that articles of faith and church rites and ecclesiastical ceremonies should not be expressly forbidden in the Sacred Scriptures. The Calvinist required a plain and unequivocal authority from the Bible for his doctrine and discipline and for every church ordinance. What the Bible does not forbid we are free to practise, said Anglican and Lutheran. Unless the Bible tells us to do this we are not free and it is not lawful for Christian men, the Calvinist rejoined. In Great Britain the issue was fought out, in the civil war of the seventeenth century and for a while under Cromwell and his soldiers, Calvinism triumphed; tumbling down an established Anglican church at the time avowedly Protestant,[3] and sending Anglican king and Anglican archbishop to the scaffold. But the Protestantism of the English people was far too varied and flexible for Calvinist absorption. It could neither assimilate the logic of Geneva nor be assimilated into the theological system preached by Puritan and Presbyterian under the commonwealth.

England returned to a monarchy and an established Anglican church subordinate to the state; with a Protestantism of wide and loose theological interpretation, of undirective ethic in private life. Calvinism had its place in the Church of England but it never got the upper hand. In the main it was cherished by nonconformists and dissenters, excluded from all public office as rigorously as Catholics were, and denied, as Catholics were denied, all share in political citizenship. Yet depression of Calvinistic Protestantism could not extract the anti-papal prejudice introduced into Great

[3] Archbishop Laud, an earnest Anglo-Catholic insisted that he was Protestant.

Britain and into America by Puritans schooled in the doctrine and ethics of Geneva. The modern Lutheran will hardly endorse the Wittenberg dogma that the pope is anti-Christ. The Puritan of Calvinist antecedents is still in many places consumed with a mortal hatred, not alway articulated, of Rome, and is conscious of repugnance, often inexplicable repugnance, to the Faith of the Holy Roman Church.

Enthusiasm for the positive doctrine of Geneva is no longer found among Protestants of education and intelligence. The bitter hate of Catholics engendered by that doctrine survives chiefly in Protestant lands in the distrust of Catholics; distrust openly expressed, or silently, often subconsciously retained. As for the exuberant exclamation of John Knox, that Geneva under Calvin's rule was "the most perfect school of Christ that ever was on earth since the days of the Apostles," it may not be dismissed as the wild and incredible fancy of a Scot; for it does represent the attitude of Calvin's fervent disciples in the sixteenth century and for a hundred years or more to come.

Not at the time did Calvin's Geneva appear to Lutherans and moderate Anglicans of the Elizabethan Church of England as "the most perfect school of Christ." Still less did it so appear to the wandering heretical scholar from Spain whom we call Servetus.

A cleric of theological opinions that, clashing violently with the Calvinistic formularies, were not to be comprehended in any existing Protestant church, and would to-day be denominated Unitarian, Servetus, after controversy with Calvin, was denounced by the latter to the Inquisition in France. Servetus escaped only to halt in Geneva on his way to Italy, and thus fell into the hands of his enemy by whom he was burnt as a heretic. For wherever Calvinism was the established religion it was sternly repressive of nonconformity, holding heresy to be treason to the state. And it is due to Calvin to remember that the mild-tempered Melanchthon,

Peter Martyr the ex-Augustinian, Bullinger the ex-monk at Zurich, and Beza, Calvin's assistant and successor, all expressed their approval of the execution by fire of this dangerous man whom no creed of current Protestantism could satisfy.

For all who were known to doubt the Calvinist faith or disliking its public worship dared be absent from the sermons, Geneva was no "perfect school of Christ"; neither was it anything of the kind to worldly people pilloried for playing cards, for wedding parties, arrested for decking the bride with overmuch finery, for young women banished for singing comic songs, or scourged for setting frivolous words to psalm tunes.

In short, the Geneva of Calvin's rule was, save for the preachers, magistrates, and the cunning who could outwit the severity of the law, an unspeakably sombre place; a community submissive to terror, governed by an authority that held itself infallible in morals as well as in faith. The bleakness of outlook, the appalling cruelty of social and domestic life that followed the acceptance of Calvin's creed, were not always apparent at the time even to the victims of the tyranny. The backward glance, revealed in memoirs and letters of a later generation, disclose the misery inflicted and the lives warped and twisted by the doctrine of predestination and the severity it evoked in its professors.

Calvinism that made religion independent of state control was a development of Lutheranism. The territorial extension of Protestantism in Scandinavian countries was Lutheran. Carried out by kings it was necessarily political. The Lutheran churches in Denmark, Norway, Sweden, and Iceland are state churches. The repudiation of papal supremacy in all these lands was followed by the establishment of a reformed faith that excluded the sacrifice of the Mass and the numerous distinctive Catholic doctrines and practices disallowed by Luther.

DENMARK

Denmark was the first of the Scandinavian countries to suffer the royal supremacy to supersede the pope's. Christian II, violent and murderous in his rage, no friend to higher clergy or nobles but always sympathetic to peasants and to workmen in their contests with rich and powerful overlords, encouraged Lutheran preachers and spoke as frankly of his preference for the gospel of Wittenberg as he did of his contempt for the papacy. But Christian's monstrous tyranny and incalculable devices — many have thought him mad — provoked the nobles and the wealthy landowners to depose him and elect his uncle Frederick I in his stead.

Christian departed into exile to wait for better times.

His successor swore at his coronation to uphold the Catholic Church, swore also that Norway should enjoy the free elective monarchy that Denmark and Sweden possessed. To reassure the Danish nobles that burghers and peasants should neither encroach on social privilege nor achieve any political power through the Church, Frederick gave his word that none but the sons of the nobility should be appointed to bishoprics. In token of his personal orthodoxy Frederick also bound himself at his accession, and later renewed the bond, to refuse permission to any heretic whether "disciple of Luther or any other to preach or teach publicly against the holy Faith, against the pope or against the Church of Rome." In return for this pledge the bishops granted subsidies to the crown from the revenues of the Danish church.

Three years after his coronation, in the year when the Emperor Charles, at war with the pope, sent his armies into Italy and the sack of Rome took place, Frederick decided that henceforth no papal sanction nor confirmation of episcopal appointments was necessary. Pope Clement was of small account to the king of Denmark in whose dominions the Lutheran evangel was gaining ground.

Sweden won its independence of Denmark in the reign of Christian II.

Norway, where the beginnings of Lutheranism were marked by the despoiling and burning of churches and houses of religion in Bergen, was plunged into civil war; Christian II arriving on the scene to retrieve, if it were possible, his loss of Sweden and Denmark by championing the defence of the Catholic Church; thereby gaining the episcopate to his side. The success Christian hoped for was not possible.

As king of Denmark, Christian II had been no lover of bishops, had been indeed no lover of the Catholic order; rather had openly expressed approval of the new evangel of Wittenberg. Now in this last and futile effort to recover a lost kingdom Christian II returned to his early faith. It could not save him from defeat and surrender that brought lifelong imprisonment.

Frederick's Catholic professions did not hinder the Lutheran propaganda. With bishoprics immensely valuable largely held by laymen — appointed to the episcopate but never consecrated — and with constant feuds between the bishops and secular nobles, Frederick generally supporting the latter, it was a matter of course that the message of Luther should receive attention.

Therefore, on Frederick's death when his son Christian III, duke of Schleswig, for some years past a professed Lutheran, was elected king, first of Norway and then of Denmark, the change of religion imposed by the crown met with small opposition in either land. Sweden acknowledged the royal absolutism of Gustavus I in 1527.

The decisive year in the history of the Protestant reformation in Denmark and Norway is 1537.

In Denmark the bishops were deposed by the king's authority — all save two who agreed to conform to the new order of service — and that eminently efficient organiser Jacob Bugenhagen arrived from Luther to give the evangelical church of Denmark a good start. Bugenhagen himself was no bishop nor had he any high opinion of bishops save as overseers, but he judged himself competent to make bishops since the royal will favoured episcopacy. Therefore Bugenhagen laid his hands on seven men nominated by the king to bishoprics, and bishops they became. Their function was to act as superintendents of the new Danish church, to see that the Augsburg Confession was henceforth the rule of faith, the Lutheran service book the only manual of public worship, and to assist the magistrates in putting down heresy and suppressing all furtive attempts at keeping the old religion alive. Toleration was not contemplated but the records of persecution are blank pages. Heresies of Anabaptist, Calvinist, Zwinglian, and Unitarian made no appeal to the Danes. The vitality of Catholic faith and practice was at too low an ebb to withstand the coercion of the law. Lutheranism alone prevailed. The heretic did not intrude. Catholicism faded out.

The Lutheran bishops being men of respectable character, by whom education was encouraged, with first the New Testament and then the whole Bible translated afresh into Danish to be printed and widely read, Protestantism became acceptable. The genius of the Danish people for industry brought prosperity. Denmark was none the worse as far as the goods of this world were concerned for the change in religion. Its people had no reason from the point of view of material prosperity to regret or resist the course of the Protestant reformation. Yet only with difficulty could the nobles be restrained from increasing the number of serfs.

NORWAY

In Norway, Christian's other kingdom, it is a different story. Olaf, Catholic archbishop of Trondhjem, the mainstay of the Catholic cause and president of the national council, unable to prevent the ravaging of churches and convents by Lutherans when Frederick was king (though Frederick had promised to Norway, as to Denmark, support of the Catholic Church) took the side of Christian II in the civil war. The archbishop was no warrior, neither was he an astute politician. When the cause of Christian II was lost, and while the nobles were engaged in faction fights, Archbishop Olaf could but wait the turn of events. The death of Frederick and the election of the duke of Schleswig brought a Lutheran king to Norway and the archbishop had no strength to contend for the old religion. Christian III, in the year that he established Lutheranism as the national religion for Denmark, declared that Norway was from that time to be part of Denmark, the religion of Denmark to be the religion of Norway. Two members of the Norwegian episcopate, Hans Reff of Oslo and Gebel Pederson bishop-elect of Bergen, willingly subscribed to Lutheranism, the rest were deposed.

Pederson went to Denmark for Bugenhagen's laying on of hands.

Olaf departed, when these decrees were being passed, to die in the Netherlands at Lierre in Catholic Brabant a year later. And with his death mortal sickness fell on the Catholic Church in Norway. Christianity became moribund.

For Lutheranism in Norway had no roots in the country. Its adherents were few, no new bishops were appointed, the old clergy were left to carry on as best they could. When they died no new ones took their place. Lutheran ministers sent from Germany or from Denmark were ignorant of the language. Schools and churches fell into ruin. The Protestant reformation destroyed the old faith of the people of Norway; it was long before the new faith was established. No material good fortune accompanied the change.

ICELAND

In Iceland Lutheranism was not imposed on the people till 1554 and then after long and fierce resistance. Christian III, bent on getting rid of Catholicism in all his dominions and resolved on one standard religion, the religion of the sovereign, was determined to bring Iceland into line. Lutherans had not penetrated into that far-off island, its people were resolutely Catholic. But the struggle could only end in one way. Might triumphed. The Catholic clergy were expropriated and in course of time Lutheran ministers took their place.

SWEDEN

Sweden, exhausted and impoverished at the end of its war of independence, was free of the rule of Christian II of Denmark when its nobles chose Gustavus (Vasa) for king, in 1523. Joannes Magnusson, humanist and friend of Pope Adrian VI, was papal legate at the time. The archbishopric of Upsala being vacant, for Trolle the occupant of the see was deposed as a pro-Danish noble in the late war, Joannes was elected. This appointment Pope Adrian refused to confirm and requiring the reinstatement of Trolle was met with a frank *non possumus* by Gustavus: "We shall allow no foreigner to rule in Sweden." But many were ready to disallow the rule of Gustavus in Sweden. Conspiracy followed conspiracy against the king, and Lutheran doctrine emerged, practised by clerics who had visited Wittenberg. Gustavus triumphed over his enemies and encouraged the Lutherans.

Joannes, faced by the choice of king or pope for his overlord, knew that the latter must be for him the supreme authority; without reaching the archbishopric Joannes went into exile at Danzig under sentence of banishment. His brother Peter, consecrated bishop of the important see of Vesteras while in Rome, remained to act in Sweden much as Gardner and Tunstall acted in England under Henry VIII.

For Sweden 1527 is the critical year. Gustavus at the Diet of Vesteras, in the presence of a great assembly of nobles, clerics, burgesses, and representatives of miners and peasants, urged the need of money and plainly said that it must come from the ecclesiastical estates. The higher clergy demurred. Gustavus on that threatened that he would abdicate and leave the country to its fate. The prospect of this retirement, of Sweden deprived of the rule of the man who had delivered it out of bondage to the Dane, of the inevitable anarchy that would ensue, overpowered the opposition. The diet made Gustavus dictator, giving him absolute sovereignty in church and state. This absolute sovereignty resulted in the Swedish parliament, the *Riksrad,* being turned into a king's council, the *Recess* of the diet proclaiming a general confiscation of all church property to meet the needs of the state. Bishop Brask of Linkaeping, long the stalwart leader of the Catholics in Sweden, followed Joannes Magnusson into exile at Danzig. The rest of the bishops acquiesced in the surrender of all church property and conformed to the new order. For by this time Gustavus had decided that Lutheranism was the more suitable religion for his subjects. While retaining much of the old ritual, allowing no general destruction of images or vestments, prudently avoiding all apparent violent break with the past, he required the introduction of the new service books of Wittenberg and the abolition of the Mass. As Luther in Saxony and other parts of Germany advised the clergy who had embraced the new evangel to go slowly in their displacement of the old order and to keep in externals the appearance of the Mass, so in Sweden Protestantism displaced the ancient Faith of its people with no grave disturbance.

Service in the vernacular was not unwelcomed; that the clergy should make wives of their mistresses seemed not improper. New bishops were consecrated by Peter Magnusson with the old ritual. "High church" Lutherans in Sweden boast retainment of apostolic succession through this act. No popular rising in favour of the old religion, no particular act of lay or clerical disapproval marks the record of change. Neither was anyone put to death for adherence to the old religion. In no country in that sixteenth century of the

Protestant reformation was the revolutionary change in religion accomplished with so little distress as in Sweden. Gustavus was the national hero, the liberator. What he said and what he did must be right. Lutheranism was established without persecution because general assent was given and there were none to demur. The few members left in religious houses were not roughly expelled; monks and nuns were permitted to live out their remaining years in monastery and convent. Nothing was done to excite alarm or arouse hostility. Sweden was weary of war and rebellion. Gustavus succeeded in the change he desired without losing the faithful submission of his subjects.

Things were not so easy under the kings who succeeded him. Eric XIV was a semi-Calvinist and after more than thirty years of his rule his brothers deposed him and left him to be murdered in prison. Eric's brother, Johan III, the next king, was pro-Catholic, had married Catharine of Poland, sister of Sigismund II, and was anxious to welcome the Jesuits sent by Cardinal Stanislaus Hosius from Poland. For by this time, 1570, the counter-reformation was at work in Europe. Johan sought a compromise — married clergy, the chalice given to the laity at Holy Communion, and other matters. But Rome, through Pope Gregory XIII, declared no concessions to Lutheranism possible, and on that Johan III gave up his dream of a national church, Catholic in character, but with qualities that allowed room for Protestant scruples; a generally comprehensive church not too inquisitorial into the beliefs of its members.

The next king, Sigismund III, the son of Johan III, was a professed Catholic and within a year of his ascent to the throne the final settlement of religion in Sweden took place at the historic Upsala mote in 1593. There it was decreed that Lutheranism, embodied in the Augsburg Confession, must be the religion of all Sweden, that no deviations towards Calvinism or Catholicism must be tolerated in the pulpits or public worship of the Swedish church.

The Protestant reformation had at last come to a standstill in Sweden. And no voice expressed dissent.

Common features may be noted in this passage to Protestantism in the Scandinavian countries:

1. The supremacy of the king and displacement of papal authority anticipates the departure from Catholic faith.

2. The riches of the church, in especial the wealth that belonged to the episcopal estates, attracted the king hard pressed to find revenue and preferring to confiscate property where least resistance could be made.

3. An indifference to religion among nobles and their serfs that had its counterpart in a clergy ill educated and unshepherded. The bishops, with a few noble exceptions, more concerned with temporal business and passing pleasures than with spiritual gifts and the eternal things of God.

Lutheranism rather than Calvinism was adopted because it was far the easier of the two. (It was also for worldlings easier than Catholicism.) For Lutheranism made no serious demand on the intellect, it laid down no hard doctrine of predestination, required no militant hostility to all who were not sealed of the tribe of John Calvin, and allowed a gradual, to some an imperceptible, passage to a new church order. Dull apathy in spiritual life, ignorance of Catholic doctrine left uncorrected, formalism unilluminated—where these things are found the way is open for Protestant or other innovation; the Catholic Church is in decay; and so destruction follows when ambition, avarice, or absolutism dictates since there is none to check its course.

XIV

Catholic Reform

WITHIN THE Catholic Church reformation and renewal recur throughout the centuries. Moral corruption and decay of spiritual life, visible in every age, witness to the human nature of the Christian body. Certain men and women, canonised saints of the Catholic Church, whose names live for ever, emerge, to witness as visibly to its divine creation. The holiness of these men and women is recognised, their sanctity appraised, their goodness acclaimed. Others, and these the far greater number, live inconspicuously the virtuous life; their merits, often hidden from the eyes of neighbours, known only to God. The saints uncanonised must necessarily outnumber the saints officially honoured by the Church. Others again serve faithfully the cause of Christ in their day and generation, rendering valiant service to truth, distinguished for their love of justice, yet their character flecked with obvious disfigurements. Such men and women, lacking that richness of supernatural grace discerned as holiness, being in short defective in humility, are never mistakenly called "saints" either by contemporaries or by posterity.

The witness to the renewal of the spirit of Christianity, to the reform needed within the Catholic Church is not confined to the great historic names — St. Benedict in the sixth century, St. Francis and St. Dominic in the thirteenth at once occur to the mind — every land has its sacred memories of saints and scholars; martyrs "of whom the world was not worthy." But these Catholic reformers of all ages are marked off from the Protestant reformers of the sixteenth century by their complete and reasoned loyalty to the faith of the Holy, Roman, Catholic, and Apostolic Church. For the Catholic reformer there was but one Church of Christ, there could be but one; that built on the rock, founded in this world on the papacy; against which the gates of hell could not prevail. Divine promise assured the presence of Christ in this Church, no matter how grave the corruption, until the end of the world. The unity of the Church — one Lord, one Faith, one Baptism — was the doctrine stressed continually in the New Testament. Separation from this Catholic unity was schism to the Catholic reformer, the rending of the body of Christ. To impose a new doctrine was heresy. (Heresy, of course, is something quite different from error. In all good faith, walking by the light received, men and women may at times live in error, unaware that the Truth is something quite other than what they have been taught to believe. Error in religious belief, as in scientific knowledge, is commonly due to ignorance; not culpable ignorance but an ignorance so rooted in prejudice, often inherited, and fostered by environment, that enlightenment is humanly speaking impossible. Heresy is deliberate action of the will; the setting up within the Church of personal opinion on matters of faith or morals above the official doctrine of the Church; declaring in fact that the Church, that is the rest of Christendom, is wrong and that the innovator alone is right. And heresy being a form of pride leads ultimately to disaster, wrecking the souls of men.)

Development of Catholic doctrine, fresh illumination of Christian morals, new expressions of devotion — on all these manifestations of the Spirit of God within the Christian

Church, Rome, the centre of authority, is apt now, as through the centuries, to bestow no hasty approval. Rather is it her wont to examine the facts, and consider the evidence before giving judgment. The Catholic reformer patiently awaits the authoritative decision, knowing with confidence that the will of God must be done.

So far from inclining to heresy or desiring to separate from the Church, or diminish the pope's prerogatives, the Catholic reformer has more than once sought to increase the papal power, and in no case has contemplated the bare possibility of a Christian and Catholic Church outside the unity of the Holy Roman Church.

The Protestant reformers of the sixteenth century, setting an example to their followers right down to these present days, did not reform the Catholic Church at all. They broke away from it and started new churches. They decided that any Christian man could found a new church with its own creed and discipline. Whereas the Catholic teaching has always been that the Church made the man a Christian by baptising him. It is still held in numerous quarters that we become Catholics and Christians by calling ourselves by these names instead of through reception into the body of Christ, the One, Holy, Catholic, and Apostolic Church, by baptism.

Catholic reform in the Church preceded Luther. It knew the corruption of papal Rome more closely than Luther did, and with not less distress. But the Catholic reformer — and St. Thomas More is an eminent example — thinking of the papacy, distinguished between the man and his office. The man, Pope Alexander VI for instance, was clearly a very poor Christian. But the office he held was the supreme governorship of the Church, it belonged to the vicar of Christ on earth, and no shortcomings of the pope, no glaring scandal of private life could affect the divine institution of that office. No papal misdemeanour could alter two facts, namely, that from the beginning the bishop of Rome had been reverenced as the successor of St. Peter, that to depart from communion with the pope was to depart from the Catholic Church of Christ. Luther unable to distinguish in the papacy the man from his office departed from the Church, denied the truth of the alleged facts, and carried his followers with him.

The Catholic reformers, remaining within, brought new life into the Church.

That famous group of English Catholic reformers, which included Dean Colet, St. John Fisher, and St. Thomas More, laboured before Luther to make the spiritual life a deeper thing, to diminish the formalism that many substituted for religion, to educate both clergy and laity in the knowledge of God by study of the New Testament. To that end did Colet and St. John Fisher preach and set up schools and colleges as places of learning, the former establishing St. Paul's school in London, the latter founding through the Lady Margaret, mother of Henry VII, the Cambridge colleges. (And much disapproval did Colet earn from illiterate clergy for his pains.) To that end was the household of St. Thomas More trained in the lore of Christ. Yet these reformers, far from thinking it possible or desirable to depart from the Catholic Church and start new churches, though the papacy of the time was the papacy of the renaissance, were content when the issue was set to go to the scaffold rather than allow that a king of England could displace the pope — be he the Borgian Alexander VI or the Medicean Leo or Clement — in the headship of any part of the Church Catholic on earth.

Erasmus, no saint, but in all Europe the most eminent scholar of his age, shared the ideals of his English friends (and the closest of these friends was St. Thomas More), seeking reform within the Church as they did; publishing his Greek Testament at Basle while Luther was lecturing at Wittenberg, before the eruptive challenge of the Ninety-five Theses against the Tetzel indulgence business — and in the same year of Sir Thomas More's *Utopia.* In the preface to this New Testament there are words that express, as Protestants after Erasmus have expressed, how strongly the Catholic reformer desired that all should read and value the New Testament for themselves:

"I would have these words [i.e., the New Testament] translated into all languages, so that not only Scots and Irishmen, but Turks and Saracens might read them. I long for the ploughboy to sing them to himself as he follows the plough, the weaver to hum them to the tune of his shuttle, the traveller to beguile the dullness of his journey with them.

"We may regret having undertaken other studies, but happy is the man whom death overtakes when he is engaged in these. These sacred words give you the very image of Christ speaking, healing, dying, rising again, and make Him so present that were He before your very eyes you would not more truly see Him."

Erasmus wrote of the Scriptures with an enthusiasm that later no Protestant could surpass, pleading for and urging a more general study of the New Testament in the Christendom that was to pay for its neglect by the unending vagaries of private interpretation. Erasmus was for reform within the Church. Love and knowledge of the New Testament did not require hate of Catholic things. Rather with love of God and our neighbour deepened by knowledge of the New Testament there would be less room for hate.

The saints and scholars of Catholic reform were men and women of prayer and of the Sacred Scriptures. Far was it from them to think of a new church outside the papal communion, a new Protestant church that had neither Mass nor pope, a church devised by men and no more than one of the many inventions of mankind. Critical as Erasmus was of current practices in the Church he never faltered in loyalty to the Mother of God, to the Mass, to the papacy.

Erasmus is the mouthpiece of Catholic reform when he

speaks of the New Testament. Earlier must be recalled the labour of Cardinal Ximenes for Biblical scholarship, and higher education of the clergy. But in the south, in Spain and in Italy, it is the deepening of the spiritual life by prayer and contemplation that is more evidently the work of the Catholic saints of the reform.

In Italy, at the Lateran Council (1512–1517) assembled by Pope Julius II and continued under the patronage of Leo XIII, much was said of the need for reform within the Church and corruptions were freely denounced; by no one more earnestly than by the general of the Augustinians, Giles of Viterbo. But the papal court during its period of renaissance laxity was as hard to reform as the nineteenth-century court of chancery in England, and the decisions and decrees of the council were a dead letter — this on the very eve of the revolt at Wittenberg.

Nevertheless it is in Rome that the inspiration for Catholic reform had its source; in that group of clergy and laity united in the Oratory of Divine Love. The renaissance had passed into its last phase, pagan and degenerate, to perish in papal Rome when the imperial army made Pope Clement a fugitive and plundered and wasted the city taken by the sword. The Oratory of Divine Love, with its membership of between fifty and sixty humanists and scholars, men of prayer and devotion, could not save the eternal city from the appalling doom that fell upon it. Their work was not political, it was spiritual. Giovanni Pietro Caraffa, bishop of Theate, with Gaetano of Thiene, are associated in the education and training of the secular clergy; establishing for that purpose a new order — the Theatines. Caraffa became Pope Paul IV; the latter canonised is known to us as St. Cajetan. Sadoleto, bishop of Carpentras, friend and correspondent of Erasmus, a man of letters, learned, and with all his desire for the deepening of religious life, appreciative of the encouragement given to scholarship by the Medici popes, must also be mentioned here, and with him Giberti, active with

Caraffa and St. Cajetan in the organisation of the Theatines. He was recognised at the court of Clement VII as a prelate of singular wisdom and holiness, and was made bishop of Verona. To these four, after the sack of Rome, when many of the Oratory moved to Venice the names of Pietro Bembo, Contarini, and Reginald Pole, the Englishman, may be added. All these became cardinals when Alexander Farnese, last of the renaissance and first of reforming popes (for Adrian VI could do nothing effective), was elected in 1534. To this same group the pope turned and with their numbers increased by Aleander[1] and others, he made it the commission to advise on the reform necessary in the Church (1535), the commission that subsequently published its report — the *Consilium delectorum cardinalium et aliorum praelatorum de emendanda ecclesia.*

These cardinals of the Oratory of Divine Love and of the reforming commission were respected by their contemporaries as God-fearing, God-loving men. They saw more closely than Luther saw the ill doing in Rome, because they lived in Rome. They were at the very centre while Luther was away in Germany. In their earnest zeal for reform of morals they began with themselves. They, too, like St. Thomas More, however great the financial corruption of the papal court, however low the spiritual life, never confounded the man with his office in their attitude to the pope. Because the renaissance brought a return to paganism they were not persuaded the best of Greek and Latin thought was to be shunned. Rather in their affection for the classics was the conviction that the literature they delighted in revealed a way to God; because its authors were gifted by God to prepare by philosophy and poetry the coming of the Saviour of the world.

They were Italians and Romans — all but Reginald Pole

[1] Aleander was the papal nuncio at Worms when Luther was put to the ban of the empire. Morone, Contarini, and Aleander were all three *en rapport* with affairs in Germany.

the Englishman — these Catholic reformers; they walked humbly before God, knowing their need of salvation, believing that Christ had died for their salvation. Yet believing no less that in the Catholic Church of Christ was the way of salvation and that the papacy was of divine institution. Princes of the Church were these Italian reforming cardinals, their scholarship adorned with humility, their charity, in those disturbed years of the Wittenberg revolt, unfailing.

Other manifestations of the revival in Italy apart from the Oratory of Divine Love may be observed. Within the religious orders the Camaldolese monks, founded by St. Romuald in the eleventh century, renewed their ancient discipline and as a reformed congregation settled at Monte Corone. The Franciscans in 1528 sprang a new branch of their order, the Capuchins, so called from their habit, and this new branch was the effective instrument for ministering to popular audiences and recalling multitudes to the practice of the Christian religion. At Milan a new congregation of secular priests, the Barnabites, bound by the familiar vows of poverty, chastity, and obedience, worked as successfully as the Theatines. Clerical reform was essential. But education was no less necessary for the laity and St. Angela Merici (1540+) was moved to do something for the education of women, founding the order of Ursuline nuns whose schools are found all over the world to-day. In Venice St. Jerome Aemilian gave himself to the education of boys.

Naples was another centre of Catholic reform. There a Spanish layman, Juan de Valdès, formerly a papal chamberlain under Clement VII, spent the last eight years of his life. Prayer, meditation, confession, and Holy Communion were the means, Valdès taught his friends, for the cultivation of the inner life; mortification of self was the way that opened the soul to the Divine illumination. With an increasing influence, for men and women, ecclesiastics, nobles, scholars were drawn within his circle, Valdès himself never strayed into heresy, nor was his mysticism tinged with the new evangel of Wittenberg.

But others were affected in Italy by the Lutheran teaching. The Catholic doctrine concerning man's justification by faith in Christ was not defined till the Council of Trent. Luther's insistence on faith *alone* as the true dogma, leading no man could tell whither, since on that fundamental belief each one could fashion what creed he would, brought conflict, suspicion, and distrust in Italy as elsewhere.

Catholic reformers long associated in the fellowship of the Oratory of Divine Love were divided on this question.

Cardinals Morone, Pole, and Contarini held profoundly to the preaching of salvation through faith in Christ; nor were they prepared to minimise this belief because Martin Luther and the Protestants of Germany and Switzerland held an exaggerated doctrine of justification by faith alone. Salvation through faith in Christ remained true though Luther's doctrine led multitudes out of the Catholic Church, led to the spurning of the pope's authority, to the overturning of altars in contempt of the Mass and the priesthood.

Caraffa, on the other hand, seeing even in Italy, inroads of Lutheranism, feared any preaching of justification by faith; since to him it seemed this preaching was bound to be misunderstood and therefore liable to bring destruction on the faithful; on the simple, too ill prepared theologically to refute false doctrine.

Venice particularly was susceptible to Protestant invasion. Swiss and Germans were both at hand and Lutheran and Zwinglian literature was conveyed across the frontiers for sale and circulation in very considerable quantities. Melanchthon, in 1539, wrote an earnest appeal to Venice to embrace the new evangel but met with no response. Luther, attributing the Venetian coldness to the intrigues of Zurich, sent a letter of characteristic violence a few years later, three years before his death, warning the people of Venice against the Zwinglians, since the latter were "enemies of the sacrament, drunkards, supporters of a doctrine more intolerable than the popish tenet of transubstantiation." Ubiquitous and itinerant Anabaptists arrived, inevitably they would, and formed a Unitarian society in Venice.

Defections among the clergy in Italy were reported, Bernardino Ochino, formerly provincial of the Franciscan Observants then leaving them for the stricter Capuchins to become Vicar General, was for a season closely associated with Valdès in Naples. Soon Ochino became restive; his ascetic life, his considerable reputation as a preacher could not hinder reports reaching the inquisition that his doctrine was unsound. Caraffa saw no means to stop the flow of heresy into the land, the dissemination of heretical publications, save through the holy office of the Inquisition. Ochino, however, rather than argue the matter, departed from Italy only to find no satisfaction in the various Protestant churches of Zurich, Augsburg, and Geneva. They in their turn expelled him for too free opinions on marriage. Geneva would not tolerate him because Calvin would not allow Unitarians to live within that city. Finally, Ochino died alone in Moravia, since even the Unitarianism of his last phase melted into something too intangible for the Polish Unitarians to accept.

Peter Martyr of the Vermigli family, prior of the Augustinian canons at Lucca, was as notable a man as Ochino and more learned. When he fell away from the Catholic reform movement it was to marry and to embrace the Zwinglian confession. Like Ochino, he too departed from Italy on receiving a summons of the Inquisition to appear at Rome; thereafter, enjoying on Cranmer's invitation a professorship of divinity at Oxford; to resign this on the accession of Mary Tudor and die quietly at Zurich, not without leaving his mark on newly born Anglicanism.

Others left Italy, clergy of the religious orders chiefly, drawn by the Swiss forms of Protestantism. And this exit, which after all was but a small affair numerically, helps to explain why Protestantism had no success in Italy. Counting neither bishops nor nobles among its adherents, winning no approval from local rulers, without any resident clergy to preach the new evangel to a people the least likely in Europe to favour the bleak and bare confessions of Zurich and Geneva, the Protestant Reformation naturally failed in Italy.

The Inquisition also played its part in averting the northern heresy (1542). For under Caraffa's diligent care the prohibition of all heretical literature became a reality and the issue of an index of books forbidden to be read by the faithful had a powerful effect. Clergy, the younger men in holy orders more particularly, were restrained from the expression of opinions judged by authority contrary to Catholic faith and Christian morals.

It must not be inferred, though many writers have inferred it, that the spirit of persecution was the impulse that moved Caraffa and the Inquisition to the defence of Catholic doctrine. The Inquisition was a court of appeal in Rome. The accused were delated to it and required to answer the accusation. The aim of the Inquisition in Italy was to stop the utterance by clergy, or, in the second place, by laity, of vague and misleading theological expressions; to exclude vernacular translations of the New Testament embroidered with notes and comments directed against vital articles of Catholic belief. Ochino, the ex-Capuchin, Peter Martyr, the ex-Franciscan, were living examples of men lost to Catholicism through the inroads of heresy.

What had resulted in Germany and Switzerland through promiscuous Bible reading and private interpretation of the Sacred Scriptures was all too plain. The division of Christian men into all sorts of new churches. The destruction of the Catholic unity. Loose thinking concerning the sublime mysteries of the Christian religion, substituting "I feel this to be true, therefore it is true," for "This is revealed truth and therefore I believe it" was bound to bring disaster; had brought disaster. Loose thinking that found expression in vague and ambiguous phrases, positive only in falsehood, the Inquisition judged not incurable. The return to reason not impossible. Scholastic philosophy — neglected, despised, gone to seed — must be restudied. The theology of St. Thomas Aquinas was the cure for priests and laymen inclined to follow any fancy that appealed to the heart.

Caraffa and the Inquisition went to work.

More potent than the Inquisition was the influence of the Catholic Reformer.

The flight of Italian clergy drawn to Lutheran or Swiss confessions of faith is but a negative and partial explanation of the failure of Protestantism. Catholic reform, growing and expanding in that sixteenth century, accounts beyond everything else for the fact that no variety of the Protestant creed took root, still less could fructify in Italy. The soil was not receptive. The seed sown was not fertilised. Lutheran "no popery, no mass, no priesthood — only believe" alienated the devout laity of the Catholic reform, much addicted to attendance at Mass and frequenters of the sacraments. Calvinistic and Zwinglian dogma that demanded stark exclusion of all ceremony in public worship, that allowed no prayers to the saints, no invocation of the Mother of God in time of trouble, seemed a dreadful affair to Italian people. The prospect offered on acceptance of Protestantism was by no means congenial. Repellant rather than alluring.

Catholic reform was the saving of Italy. Reginald Pole at Viterbo was the centre of a group that kept numerous persons, men and women, seriously attentive to personal religion, loyal to the pope and the faith of the Holy Roman Church. Caraffa shook his head at the piety of Cardinal Pole, mistrusting profoundly all talk of justification by faith, holding such talk dangerous to the unlearned, even when the speaker was as sincere a Catholic as Pole believed himself to be. The Viterbo circle was suspect because of the intensity of its convictions. It was not in the least heretical in reality, for all Caraffa's doubts and misgivings. But it included men and women of distinguished gifts and ancient family — Vittoria Colona not the least remarkable member of the group — who because they were zealous readers of the New Testament, zealous also for the welfare of their neighbours and for the Christian life, set their faith sternly against the paganism of intellectual society and remained loyal to papal authority. These friends of Pole at Viterbo simply would not depart from the Catholic Church. Could in fact no more do it than Pole himself. Other groups — in the academy at Modena and that at Ferrara where Renée, daughter of Louis XII of France held her court — were certainly inclined to dally with Protestant opinions, and justify inquisitorial suspicions.

St. Philip Neri in Rome, with his band of disciples to become a new congregation, the Oratorians, always to be freshly remembered by English-speaking people because of the nineteenth-century membership of Cardinal Newman and Father Faber the hymn writer, kindled a fresh and burning charity. That was after Cardinal Pole had gone to England as papal legate, to die as archbishop of Canterbury (1558), the last Catholic archbishop, when Mary Tudor died.

St. Charles Borromeo, archbishop of Milan (d. 1584), had a wider and as deep an influence in the north of Italy; founding Sunday schools and recalling the indolent to a knowledge of God. Three other men of heroic virtue, to be acclaimed as saints, are found in Italy before the close of the sixteenth century. The Spanish grandee, St. Francis Borgia, duke of Gandia, great-grandson of Alexander VI and third general of the Jesuits;[2] St. Aloysius Gonzaga, a marvellous youth of twenty-two, also a Jesuit; and St. Pascal Baylon, the Franciscan, who came from Aragon.

---

[2] For the most recent and fullest biography, see *The Greatest of the Borgias,* by Margaret Yeo, 1936.

While St. Ignatius Loyola and the activities of his Society of Jesus belong rather to the story of the counter-reformation, yet the conversion of St. Ignatius and the constitution of the society must properly be included in Catholic reform.

Contrasted with Germany or with Italy, the standard in Spain and Portugal of Christian morals and Catholic Faith within the religious orders and the ranks of the secular clergy was, in the years of Luther, immeasurably higher. The great Franciscan Cardinal Ximenes stimulated the intellectual life, promoted in every way the education of priests, and compelled the fulfillment of clerical duties. The works of Erasmus, in the pre-Luther years, were read and discussed with immense interest in the universities of Spain.

The Spanish Inquisition, independent of Rome, and kept by the king outside all papal interference with its management, had been in the main formerly occupied with cases of pseudo-Christian Moors and Jews. Now its energies were directed to check the circulation in Spain of Lutheran and other Protestant publications, discharged from the printing press in Germany and Switzerland and brought into every land of Europe where readers and purchasers could be found. The Spanish Inquisition also kept a close eye on the writings of ecclesiastics and lent an attentive ear to spoken words. Neither learning nor holiness could save a priest or nun from being delated to the holy office. Both Ignatius Loyola and St. Teresa attracted its attention. Carranza, Dominican archbishop of Toledo, known for his scholarship and reverenced for his way of life, was actually kept seven years in prison before being cited to Rome and eventually released.

Catholic reform in Spain and Portugal, then, was not directed to reform of morals, or improved education, exposure of financial corruption, or dethroning of paganism. It is a purely spiritual movement; the awakening of many through the burning faith of a few great souls.

Five names stand out; names of untarnished splendour

— two at least of the names — Teresa of Avila and St. John of the Cross to be held in honour wherever Christian mysticism is known and valued. They are for all time the glory of the Carmelite Order. Their writings relate the high adventures of the soul seeking union with God, abound in the richness of experience in the spiritual life, and belong to the imperishable literature of complete sincerity.

The call to both these saints was total submission to the will of God; to both came the vision of God that summons men and women in every age to leave all and follow Christ. They were not in any way directly concerned with events in Germany. The reform of the religious order of the Carmelites, to which St. Teresa and St. John of the Cross belonged, engaged their attention not because laxity was flagrant but because love had grown cold. Without charity what did it profit — the triple vow of poverty, chastity, and obedience? The spirit of the world had invaded the cloister, as it always tends to do. Its expulsion was stoutly resisted. In the case of St. John of the Cross persecution by his brethren was the reward for seeking within the cloister closer union with God. Neither persecution nor neglect could turn the soul of this great saint from the upward path. Poet no less than saint ("No one is a true son of wisdom if he be not also a son of poetry," said Welsh St. Cadoc in the sixth century), demanding nothing but to follow the way of the Cross, because in that following came the knowledge of God that is eternal life, the Carmelite St. John poured out with marvellous literary skill — his poetry a joy for ever, his prose the ablest exposition of spiritual progress — a flaming manifesto of Catholic reform.

St. Teresa, commanding administrative abilities that so often belong to the soul deeply immersed in communion with God, proved her capacity for the work of reform within the order in her own lifetime. "Ignorance and stupidity cloaked by the names of simplicity and innocence" were noted by St. Augustine as depressing evils of his time. St.

Teresa found them in Spain and in many a Carmelite convent. Unable to uproot these distressing encumbrances in the houses of religion St. Teresa started her reformed convents, removing or getting round every obstacle. Intolerable to this intrepid and intensely warm-hearted woman was the thing we call "humbug." The spirit of the world in the cloister was for her an unclean spirit to be exorcised by the love that transmutes. More than that, the work of St. Teresa and of St. John of the Cross was to bring the spirit of the cloister, the finely ordered contemplative life, the regular life of prayer and devotion, into the world. Against the fiercely controversial writings turned out by the Protestant printing press, the gross invective of partisan pamphlet, are contrasted the letters and autobiography of St. Teresa, the mystical works of St. John of the Cross.

Time has withered and staled the once respected and widely circulated productions of Wittenberg, Zurich, and Geneva, accounted "best sellers" in their day; the fragrance of the sixteenth-century Carmelite writings remain as sweet as ever, the freshness undiminished, the originality without blemish of eccentricity, uneclipsed, the purity of language unspotted by time. Far beyond the visible boundaries of the Catholic Church are the works of Teresa of Avila and St. John of the Cross esteemed. Massive illuminative volumes in the library of mystical theology, the source of strength and comfort to multitudes learned and unlearned who seek to walk more closely with God in their passage through this world.

Catholic reform in Spain means St. Teresa and St. John of the Cross, who in fulfilling the immediate task of driving the spirit of the world from the cloisters of their order brought the spirit of the cloister into the world, the spirit of fair love, and of fear and knowledge and holy hope, to transform and regenerate whom it touched.

Yet Catholic reform does not originate in Spain with the Carmelites. The figure of St. John of God (d. 1550) is emergent. A wealthy man of Portugal who in early middle age was impelled to give all he possessed to his poorer neighbours. This was not enough. He must needs do what he could for the sick, get hospitals built in Granada, and start the society known as Brothers Hospitallers to tend and minister to the wounded and diseased of mankind.

St. Thomas of Villanova (d. 1555) was his contemporary. He, too, moved by compassion at the destitution around him, surrendered earthly treasure to join the Augustinian Hermits, the same order that Luther joined in Germany. The cathedral chapter made St. Thomas archbishop of Valencia, much against his will and after he had refused the archbishopric of Granada. The revenues of the archbishopric went the way of his private income—to relieve the distress around him and mitigate the miseries of the poor. It was said, when he died, that Archbishop Thomas had not a penny left to call his own, that even his bed had been given away so that another bed was borrowed for the dying man.

Finally there is Peter of Alcantara, the friend and supporter of St. Teresa; anticipating her in the pursuit of the mystical life of contemplation, the union of the soul with God, and leaving a treatise on "Prayer and Meditation" that has been translated into all the languages of Europe and is still read with profit. In boyhood Peter of Alcantara turned from the life and society of the nobility to which he was born and entered the Franciscan Order, restoring to primitive observance the Friars Minor. For him the ascetic life gave the environment for the true contemplative. He would not be entangled with the world, nor concerned with the distractions of bodily pleasure; and so lived to be an old man of eighty, to die as he had lived, suffused with charity.

The distinctive thing about these Spanish saints of the Catholic reform is the wholehearted and complete surrender to the will of God. It was all or nothing with men like Ignatius Loyola and Francis Borgia. There is no holding back, no turning back. Christ must be all in all. Humility is no mere passive virtue with them. It is humility that finds outlet in love. Whether like St. Peter of Alcantara, St. Teresa, and St. John of the Cross the spirit life of the contemplative is the ideal; or like St. John of God and Archbishop Thomas of Villanova, the call is to minister to the bodily needs of their neighbours, the call comes and is obeyed to the uttermost.

Catholic reform, the amendment and sanctification of personal life within the Catholic Church, preceded and made possible the movement to recover the ground lost in the spread of Protestant teaching, to check further inroads of that teaching. The movement is known as the counter-reformation.

XV

The Counter-Reformation

THE REFORMED papacy of Alexander Farnese, Paul III, initiated the counter-reformation. Catholic reform, the quickening of the spirit within the Church, gave the material; the papacy, and the papacy alone, could employ that material, directing the work of reconciliation and recovery. Protestantism was the revolt from the authority of the pope; a denial of all papal claims; an emphatic and vehement declaration that the salvation of mankind must be found outside the Catholic Church of Rome, since the pope so far from being Christ's vicar on earth was anti-Christ and all who were joined with him in communion were joined in the worship of idols. Protestant vituperation, uttered in all sincerity, assured the world that the faith of the Holy Roman Church would soon be no more, being but a jumble of superstition; and the head of that Church, being no better than an agent of the devil, would soon be deposed. It was the business and duty of all Protestant governments to hasten the end of papal authority and exterminate from the face of the earth the Church ruled by the pope.

To this challenge, neglected as a thing of small account by his predecessors, and now heard in uproar and tumult all over Europe, Pope Paul III, scholar and humanist replied.

The papacy was denounced as the head and front of offence; the papacy must counter-attack. It was time, fully time. The pope had the instruments at hand, he had but to use them. No one else could set the forces in motion for the recovery of lost ground. (This is seen very clearly in the case of the Society of Jesus. It was the pope who approved the society as a new religious order, endorsed the despatch of St. Peter Canisius to Germany, and thereby gave to the Jesuits the work they most successfully performed. Ignatius Loyola, at the outset of his converted life, was not interested in Protestantism in Germany or elsewhere. Like St. Francis of Assisi before him, St. Ignatius was at first more concerned with the state of the Mohammedan and heathen world. It was the papacy that used the society for the counter-reformation. In the pope's service it was to be used according to the will of its founder.)

But the Catholic recovery in Germany and Poland is the third phase of the counter-reformation. Two earlier events, it may be said, made that recovery possible; two gravely important events; and for both these events the pope was directly responsible. The first of these events was the papal commission appointed to report on the reforms needed within the Church and the report issued by the commission.

The second great factor in the work of Catholic recovery and renewal was the Council of Trent and its decrees.

All these events, or rather series of events, are part and parcel of the progress of the counter-reformation. They belong in order of time to the work of their originator, Pope Paul III.

Reform must begin in the papal court itself. Paul III was aware of that when he made cardinals of the finest spirits in Italy and invited them to report on the condition of things in Rome. The report *Consilium delectorum cardinalium et aliorum praelatorum de emendanda ecclesia* (or for short *Consilium de emendanda ecclesia*), issued in 1535, found the ill conditions at the papal court flagrant and notorious. It pointed out the glaring abuses that followed the general system of money payments, and the scandal given to the faithful everywhere by the deplorable laxity of the clergy in Rome. Money payments were really at the bottom of all the corruptions that were rife in the Catholic Church according to this report. Contarini supplemented the report with certain papers of his own on the responsibilities of the papacy and the need for stopping the iniquitous traffic in holy things. In no place does he insinuate any doubt that the papacy was of divine institution. But the financial methods of the papacy, flagrant and unconcealed acceptance of money extorted as fees from every kind of office, the sale of dispensations, and the gross misuse of power by recent occupants of the throne of St. Peter, these were the shameful things that cried out for reform.

Of course Contarini made enemies by these outspoken words. Officials long entrenched in comfort at the papal court were shocked and alarmed at a program of reform that threatened their livelihood. As for the *Consilium*—what it said of the state of things in Rome made it eminently desirable that such a document should not be published. Nevertheless being privately printed it somehow happened that a copy was taken to Germany; there to be reprinted and circulated far and wide, with comments justifying Protestants for leaving the sink of corruption described in the report.

Pope Paul III encouraged Contarini and the other reforming cardinals to continue in the good work. Commissions were appointed to reform the papal chancery, the offices of the *penitentiaria* and other highly lucrative departments of papal administration. Ciberti was brought to Rome from his diocese of Verona to assist the counsels of the pope. Paul III himself found nothing new, nothing startling in the *Consilium de emendanda ecclesia,* and the papers of Contarini. Had he not been made a cardinal by Alexander VI? Had he not sought to gain the papacy when

Clement VII was elected? Farnese knew the worst of the papal court. Now in his old age he did what he could to bring a better mind to the central government of the Church, choosing for cardinals scholars and men of spiritual power. With the aims of such men Paul could sympathise. He had the understanding that discerned the truth in the indictment of the papal court. But he was an old man, hard to move when ready action was needed, slow to enforce the reforms he approved.

His cardinals proclaimed to the world the rottenness of things in Rome, the pope decreed commissions of reform. He did more than that, he summoned a general council of bishops of the whole Church to meet at Mantua in May, 1537. That council never assembled — there were too many political difficulties; neither did the council summoned by the pope for the following year at Vicenza. The obstacles and obstructions seemed to compel abandonment of the idea of a general council. Only the pressure of the Emperor Charles made Paul III resume the attempts, hitherto frustrated. Once more in May, 1542, a bull was issued calling a general council, to meet at Trent in the following November.

At last the Council so long demanded met. Though the sessions are spread out over eighteen years, finally closing at the end of 1563, in three distinct periods the Council of Trent accomplished its work.

Nothing could be done at the first sessions, the attendances were too small; merely a handful of Italian prelates with Cardinals Pole and Morone as the pope's representatives. So the council adjourned, to reassemble in 1545 and get to work the following year. As far as numbers went it was not an impressive gathering — twenty-five bishops, the majority from Italian sees, five heads of religious orders, with the papal legates, and a certain number of theologians — among them Laynez and Salmeron of the Society of Jesus. Neither the high feelings aroused by the political affinities of Spanish and Italian bishops, nor the old distrust between pope and emperor which never was completely allayed, could prevent agreement when it came to the final drafting of decrees on doctrinal matters. It was essential that a final and unalterable decision should be published to the world, an answer given to the various points raised by Protestants; that all Christendom should be told what was the teaching of the Holy Roman Catholic and Apostolic Church, and wherein all who differed from that teaching were in error.

So the true doctrine of justification by faith was defined; tradition was declared to be of equal authority with the Sacred Scriptures and the Church alone the true interpreter of Scripture; the canon of the Sacred Scriptures was re-affirmed, disallowing the exclusion from the Bible of the Old Testament books dismissed as apocryphal by Protestants. At the same time the existing Latin version of the Bible, called the Vulgate, was pronounced to be the best Latin version and the only one to be used.

None of these decrees favoured compromise or reconciliation with Lutherans, and the emperor found no signs of the necessary reform in church discipline. Religious unity within the empire was for Charles V the essential thing. He had looked on a general council as the proper instrument for restoring unity. Instead of this the decree on justification made reunion impossible.

Relations between Charles and Paul III were strained. The latter saw the possibility of the emperor moving on Trent and by sheer might overawing the council, compelling ecclesiastical reforms and obtaining some modification of the decree on justification. To remove the council from the reach of imperial influence the pope authorised the legates to propose departure from Trent and adjournment to Bologna, which was within the papal states. A few cases of plague having been reported in the city of Trent the council agreed to the adjournment by 38 votes to 14.

But nothing was done at Bologna, and Charles had insisted that the Spanish bishops must stay where they were at Trent. After the death of Paul III and the election of Cardinal del Monte, who took the title of Julius III, the council went back to Trent to resume its decisions. Fresh obstacles were created to prevent a full attendance, when Henry II of France refused to allow any French bishops to appear. However certain Protestant delegates, invited to attend under safe conducts, came as the representatives of Elector Maurice of Saxony and the duke of Wurtemberg to put before the council the doctrines that separated them from the Catholic unity. For a year the council was in session (1551–52) and its decrees dealt with the theology of the sacraments of penance and extreme unction and enunciated various reforms. Then the military advance of Maurice of Saxony made the council fearful of capture. Feelings of uneasiness suggested retirement. The council was suspended — not to meet again for ten years.

Caraffa, who succeeded to the papacy after the few weeks reign of the exemplary Mercellus II, was always in earnest for reform. As Paul IV he at once decided on active measures. But he was an old man now — nearly eighty — and at the mercy of favourite nephews. Also Paul IV, being fiercely the enemy of Spain and all things Spanish, would not tolerate any reassembling of the council at Trent. On Caraffa's death came the election of Pius IV. The wishes of Francis II, stimulated by the demands of the French government to the French bishops to call a national council if the general council was not summoned by the pope, raised the immediate question: Was the assembly which the new pope willingly ordered to meet at Trent a new general council, or was it a continuation of the old? Not a new council but the same council was the decision when at the end of two years' work the Council of Trent was finally closed in 1563.

Apart from a number of regulations for the amendment of clerical life and practice, with reform of abuses by raising the standard of training, the council in these last sessions defined absolutely the doctrine of the Mass, of holy orders, and holy matrimony. It also fixed for all time the supreme power of the pope — so that in a very real sense the definition of papal infallibility in faith and morals at the Vatican Council of 1870 was but the fulfillment of the Tridentine decrees. Luther's old grievance of the scandal of the sale of indulgences or pardons was also, forty-five years after the challenge of the Ninety-Five Theses at Wittenberg, met and remedied. Henceforth the pardoner with his scrip of pardons from Rome was to follow his occupation no more. Bishops and bishops alone were authorised to issue and dispense indulgences to the faithful, and so they issue indulgences to this day.

It was left to the papacy to enforce throughout the Catholic Church the many reforms enjoined at Trent.[1] Succeeding popes, the Dominican St. Pius V, the first canonised pope for many centuries, Gregory XIII who reformed the calendar (a reform ignored by the British government to the inconvenience of the British people for more than a hundred years), the Franciscan Sixtus V, were all engaged in the good work. The very music of the Church was changed when Palestrina became director of music at Rome; the old ribald and florid stuff was prohibited — to the distress of its admirers and the indignation of singers and choirs who revelled in its performance.

---

[1] The various Protestant bodies as a matter of course ignored all that was done at Trent. Bishop Jewel, the Elizabethan apologist of the Church of England, explained why:

"We have not indeed expected the authority or consent of the Council of Trent. . . . According to the practice of the holy fathers and the customs of our own ancestors we have reformed our church in a provincial synod; and according to our duty we have cast off the yoke and tyranny of the bishop of Rome, who had no just authority over us."

The unity of Christians this same Anglican bishop quite frankly abandoned: "Unity and agreement do excellently become religion; yet it is no certain and proper sign of the church of God."

A new age dawned on Rome with the cleansing and renewal of the papacy. The papal court, no longer a place of luxury, a centre of money getting, was filled by prelates of upright life. Rome once more sent forth its legions throughout the world to conquer, in the name of Christ crucified and through the power of the Cross, the lands of the heathen, to recover in Europe vast territories lost to the Protestants.

The counter-reformation, prepared by Catholic reform and the deliberations of the Council of Trent, was carried out by the men whom St. Ignatius Loyola had enrolled in the Society of Jesus.

Luther only eight years older than Ignatius[2] had a long start in the battle for the faith of the Germanic peoples. The year of the cannon ball at the siege of Pampeluna, when the soldier of the viceroy of Navarre turned on a sickbed from the youthful ambitions of a Spanish cavalier to a higher standard, was the year of the excommunication of Luther at the Diet of Worms; the year of the rewarding of Henry VIII of England with the title, "Defender of the Faith." Luther was already a European figure when Ignatius entered on the fourteen years' training for his lifework. When the vows were taken at Montmartre, Lutheranism had been accepted in Prussia, had won supporters throughout the empire. Catholicism was visibly in defeat.

Pope Paul III gave the new religious order of the Society of Jesus full papal recognition, but nothing was suggested immediately of work *contra* Luther. Francis Xavier, the most distinguished member of the little band that joined itself to Ignatius in Paris, was sent by the founder of the Society to the Far East, there to labour and die in the mission fields of India and beyond.

In Italy was the need that particularly presented itself to the society. In Italy (and in Spain and Portugal) the fol-

[2] Their lives are remarkably parallel: Luther, 1483–1546; Loyola, 1491–1556.

lowers of Ignatius — himself established in Rome — preached. To arouse Catholics themselves to the responsibilities they neglected was a most important task, although the missions were not overlooked. The new society won members at once. At the Council of Trent the pope's theological representatives, Laynez and Salmeron, were conspicuous. When its founder died in 1556 the Society of Jesus had fifteen hundred members, and nine provinces in Europe, and this but sixteen years since the order was formally approved by Paul III.

The man who stands out beyond all others on the Catholic side in the counter-reformation is St. Peter Canisius; claimed as a German because the town of his birth, Nymwegen, was in the prince-bishopric of Cologne; claimed more positively as Dutch because Nymwegen is in Holland. Canisius accepted indifferently either nationality. "Call me German or Netherlander — what you will," are his recorded words.

St. Ignatius had not drawn together the men who constituted the Society of Jesus in order to combat the still rising tide of Protestantism. Neither had he planned a new religious order to undertake the business of education. To "the greater glory of God," and "the greater good of our fellow men" was the sole and whole purpose of the Society. The military nature of the new religious order is apt to be exaggerated.[3]

Obedience was not the foundation of the Society. "The interior law of charity and love which the Holy Ghost is accustomed to write and imprint in the hearts of men" was

[3] "It is well to remember that Ignatius Loyola was strictly a soldier only during the last three of the thirty he lived in the world. That he was a soldier in the spirit of his time and country is true; it is also true that he was full of the spirit of chivalry; but chivalry is a very different thing from soldiering, as soldiering is understood to-day. He may have been an Arthur in the midst of his knights of the Round Table; he was certainly not a Napoleon, with his marshals and legions around him." — Archbishop Alban Goodier, S.J., in *The Jesuits*, London, 1929.

counted upon by St. Ignatius "rather than any exterior constitutions" to preserve, govern and advance in God's holy service the Society of Jesus. Yet constitutions were a necessary aid. The vow of obedience had entered inevitably with the formal institution and the election of the general of the society for life. That was five years after the vows taken in the chapel of Montmartre.

Character, trained and directed "for God's greater glory and the universal good," selfless, single-hearted, on that is the emphasis laid in the formation of the Society. "For the greater glory of God"; over and over again does the phrase recur in the Book of the Constitutions — the one book St. Ignatius wrote with the exception of the Spiritual Exercises — it is the end and the ideal. Love and love alone, calling for the most complete self-surrender, would find the way to achieve the perfect loyalty demanded.

The readiness to undertake whatever was asked of the society, to carry out whatever was imposed by the pope's authority, to spend and be spent in the service of God and in obedience to the general, "to go forth into all lands, among Turks, heathens or heretics," wherever the pope might be pleased to send them, "without hesitation or delay as without question, condition or reward" — in this spirit the Society of Jesus manifested itself. Building up the faithful in Spain and Italy, preaching and baptising east and west, in the Indies, in Mexico, and South America, counteracting the Protestant heresies in Germany and Poland by demonstrating that the old Catholic way was the better way, and drawing into its ranks by a common training in the "Spiritual Exercises" men from all over Europe.

Since much of that falling away from Catholicism in northern Europe was the result of sheer ignorance, of dreary apathy and utter neglect, education was obviously necessary; for the clergy no less than for the laity. Therefore education by means of sermons, lectures, schools, colleges must be the work of the Jesuits. It was the work laid upon St. Peter

Canisius, who from the universities of Cologne and Louvain came under the influence of Peter Faber at the age of twenty-three and so joined the Society. At Cologne he withstood Archbishop Hermann's Lutheran propaganda. The early reputation of preacher and writer brought Canisius to the Council of Trent as the bishop of Augsburg's procurator. Next came a summons to Rome from St. Ignatius; then a short spell of professorial work at Messina and the return to Germany.

First to the University of Ingoldstadt, for Duke William I of Bavaria, watching with despair the ebb of Catholicism, had appealed to Paul III and to the General of the Jesuits to send some theologians to save the situation. Few were the clergy and fewer still candidates for the priesthood in Bavaria. It was the same melancholy story all over Germany. Catholicism was dying for want of teachers. The clergy themselves were untaught. At Ingoldstadt, in the very heart of Catholic Bavaria, Canisius found that everybody had left off going to Mass, and wrote: "We couldn't get two people to come to Mass if we paid them."

Quietly and confidently Canisius effected a change. In two years he could leave Ingoldstadt for Vienna to revive by preaching and teaching the apparently moribund Catholicism of that imperial city. From Vienna to Prague, where the prospect was even more desolate, since not a single Catholic bishop remained in all Bohemia. Nothing but education — and prayer — could bring people back to the Faith they had lost through ignorance. So at Prague Canisius started a college which was to become in due time a university. With the appointment as Provincial of the Society of Jesus in South Germany, an office held by Canisius for thirteen years (1556–1569), came still wider scope; for the province included Austria, Bohemia, Tyrol, and Switzerland. Seminaries and colleges for the clergy, schools and colleges for the laity, wherever he went Canisius strove to get these built and equipped.

And he would have no charge made for education. The municipal authorities, the civil government must see to the cost. Catholic princes and Catholic cities yielded, but yielded reluctantly, to the arguments and pressure of this man of God. Only as he made them realise the all-importance of true belief, of the right conduct that follows true belief, did persuasion come that education for all was worth paying for.

Not that Canisius valued education for its own sake, or as the humanist valued it, for the pleasure it brought, the cultural advantage. As Canisius saw it, education like everything else was for the greater glory of God and the universal good. Otherwise what did it profit? Learning and scholarship divorced from religious teaching would not bring souls to heaven. Such learning and scholarship, displayed so triumphantly at the renaissance, had nearly brought Rome itself to destruction; in Germany it had left Lutheranism a free field, with the result that the Protestant schools were everywhere held up as the only schools worth attending. Thirty years later, and the position was reversed. Schools and colleges started by Canisius and conducted by the Jesuit fathers were by consent far and way the better, so that Protestant parents were glad to send their children to the Jesuit colleges.

As an organiser of education Canisius could see in his own lifetime the fruitful results of schools and colleges. The tide of Protestantism was no longer rising. Outside the realms of Protestant princes the Protestant tide visibly ebbed. As preacher and writer Canisius was the same educational force. Ignorance was the enemy. Knowledge of God was eternal life, and knowledge of God was open to all through the teaching of the Catholic Church. To bring men and women of Germany back to the truth, the truth they had forgotten, the truth they had never learnt, was for Canisius the allotted task; task of divine insistence. He used the pulpit as he used the printing press to this one end, the casting out of ignorance by means of instruction.

At Augsburg Canisius was cathedral preacher for seven years, and that in addition to his responsibilities as Jesuit provincial. Lutheranism had early taken root in the city and in 1559 Protestantism of one kind or another was the prevailing and predominant belief. The Catholics were but a small and unimportant minority. It is said that not fifty people were present in the cathedral when Canisius preached his first sermon. Patiently he set out the truth — there is no evidence that suggests Canisius was highly emotional or rhetorical in his sermons — expounding the doctrines affirmed at the Council of Trent, entering into the hearts and minds of Protestants, understanding the causes that had led them away from the Catholic Church, never attempting to excuse or qualify the unchecked abuses in the Church that had been the stumbling block to many pious souls, freely admitting the honest grievances of Protestant reformers — thus he preached and thus it was that all Augsburg, it was said, thronged to hear him.

It is certain the Catholic revival in Augsburg dates from the sermons of Canisius; and what happened in Augsburg happened in other cities. Travelling as he needs must, Canisius preached in the cathedrals of Vienna and Prague, Strassburg and Cologne, and always to the acceptance of the crowds that heard him. Nor was it only in cathedrals. His journeyings to the various Jesuit houses and colleges of his province became missionary journeys. In the numerous parishes of Austria that were without priests — the figures of the clergy presented for ordination in the diocese of Vienna were notoriously low — Canisius on his arrival would preach and administer the sacraments. Children were drawn to him, as they were to St. Francis Xavier in India. It was to the youth of Germany that Canisius turned for the restoration of the Catholic Church.

But what the children and younger people particularly

needed, and the clergy needed it no less, was a plain and adequate statement of Catholic doctrine in Catechism form. There were plenty of catechisms. Luther's was not the first, but it was so vastly superior to anything of the sort in existence that it swiftly won its tremendous popularity. Several attempts had been made to answer the Lutheran catechism but they were, unhappily, dull. Dullness is fatal to a catechism. Indeed it takes a man of genius to write an efficient catechism. Luther had the genius for popular writing and so, combined with finer scholarship, had St. Peter Canisius.

He wrote it first in Latin, the Canisius catechism, for the high schools. Then it was translated into German and issued in simpler and shorter form for younger people. Again Canisius revised it to serve in all schools. Finally he brought out a fresh edition, enlarged with notes and references, for the use of the clergy and for all who gave instruction.

The success of the Canisius catechism was immediate. It caught the attention and went through edition after edition, besides being translated into most of the European languages as well as into Japanese and certain Indian languages. The explanation of this success was the universal character of the Canisius catechism. It was not a piece of anti-Protestant pamphleteering. The note was affirmative not controversial. The purpose was to declare on the authority of the Bible and the writings of the Fathers what the Catholic Church was, and what it taught. The quotations from the Sacred Scriptures number 2,000, from the Fathers, 1,200.

The Canisius catechism was written by a man of genius to one end — the greater glory of God and the greater good of our fellow men — and to a wonderful degree it achieved that end. The astonishing vigour of this son of St. Ignatius, his solicitude for the education of clergy and laity, the fervour of his preaching, and his immense industry brought about the triumphs of the counter-reformation in Germany, because he was recognised as a man entirely disinterested; seeking nothing for himself and inspired by supernatural charity. Many who remained unconvinced that his message was true testified to the nobility of his character. Protestants who hated his catechism and all his works admitted the personal holiness of Peter Canisius of the Society of Jesus.

The writing of simple books of prayer, of a Latin Grammar for schools, free from the Protestant comments of Melanchthon's Latin grammar, of a book of explanatory notes on the Epistles and Gospels throughout the Christian year, and of letters beyond count, added to the rest of his work, brought Canisius to enforced retirement in Switzerland at the age of sixty-eight, though not till he had started new provinces of the society in Poland and Austria and the Rhineland. After being relieved of the provincialship, Canisius assisted at the foundation of the Jesuit college at Freiburg, and for years was its principal figure.

Beyond the empire the Jesuits extended the work of education and in Poland in especial the counter-reformation was the fruit of this work.

Poland was at the mercy of its nobles; all semi-independent rulers of their states, nominally Catholic but scarcely Christian in the first quarter of the sixteenth century. Since all but the nobility were debarred from becoming bishops the Polish episcopate consisted of men very similar to the German bishops. Worldlings, very wealthy but even less civilised than the Germans, since further from centres of civilisation. It was natural that Lutheran and every other heretical opinion should find the lands of these unlettered chieftains fertile soil. The jealousy of any encroachment on their rights made the Polish nobles resist all royal enactments. Each one went his own way in religious matters caring nothing for decisions of Church or state. The Polish diet, in fact, decided in 1556 that the principle *cujus regio, ejus religio* gave every noble the right to have any form of public worship in his house that he pleased; always provided such form of worship could be justified from the Sacred Scriptures.

Poland under these conditions became a happy hunting ground for all Protestant sectaries. To Hussites, Bohemian Brethren, Lutherans, and Zwinglians, were added those who denied the very fundamentals of Christian belief. To Poland came the Italian Socinus from Siena questioning most things and leaving his nephew to deny the doctrine of the Trinity and so found Socinianism; whence spread the Unitarianism that is still found in Hungary and among the Czech peoples.

The real barrier to the divided and mutually hostile streams of Protestant belief was set up when the Jesuits arrived in Poland on the suggestion and invitation of Cardinal Hosius, in 1564. Once in Poland, to the Jesuits was entrusted the work of education. Here, as in Germany, under St. Peter Canisius, recovery came surely and steadily. Lutheranism never took root in Poland for all the apparent fertility of the soil. Protestantism sprang up unhindered, manifested itself in strange and unwelcome forms, and having no root — no Luther, no leaders — died down, not through persecution but through the educational efficiency and missionary zeal of the Society of Jesus. Catholic Poland emerged with a reformed clergy and a better instructed laity. The fruit of the counter-reformation was nowhere more abundant.

Prussia, Saxony, and other territories in Germany ruled by Protestant government were not recovered to Catholicism in the counter-reformation. It was Catholic Germany, sunk in sloth, dying in ignorance, that was saved and brought back to life.

Perhaps the last great figures in the story of the counter-reformation are St. Francis of Sales, recovering the country of Savoy from Calvinism (1594–1598), and St. Robert Bellarmine (d. 1621), indefatigable with his pen in the cause of Catholic unity. In St. Vincent de Paul, founding his Sisters of Mercy (1611), we have the abiding witness to the Catholic reform that is for ever renewing and restoring the body of Christ. For the men and women who wrought the Catholic reform and accomplished the counter-reformation, instructed in the kingdom of heaven, may be likened to "the householder who bringeth forth out of his treasure new things and old."

Conclusion

Weighed in the Balance

SEEN ACROSS the space of four centuries of modern history Martin Luther is still a massive figure. Time does not dwarf the stature of the man; neither does it show the results of his work eliminated. Luther cannot be "debunked" — if the expressive slang of these latter days be permitted. He revealed himself in his own lifetime too fully to be divested by posterity of masterful (and other pleasing and less pleasing) qualities known to his contemporaries. Masterful Luther was. Driving a wedge into Christendom, he split the Catholic Church, tore asunder the body of Christ, and left it rent. No man without immense force of character could have done what Luther did and proudly rejoicing in what he did, conceive the overthrow of papal authority and the uprooting of the Catholic doctrine of priesthood and Mass as matter for thanksgiving to God.

Friends and admirers beyond count have extolled from every angle the Augustinian doctor of Wittenberg, heaping superlative on superlative of praise till the portrait, sugared over with adulation, is almost unrecognisable. Hostile critics have as eagerly brought forward their portraits of the man Martin Luther; seeing him entirely repellant and sinister, an agent of the devil — no more, no less. Caricatures, of course, in both cases; but Luther, no utterer of smooth words, is belittled by the unqualified praise of his admirers. He was no apostle of sweet reasonableness. His enemies at least depict him as a giant in wickedness, not a gentle purveyor of sweetness and light.

Graver and more responsible minds urge that Luther, whatever his personal defects, his inconsistencies, vituperative language, and other regrettable failings, is to be honoured by mankind as a liberator of the human conscience. Others, without admitting any truth in the liberation claim, see Luther as Luther himself saw the advancing sultan of the Turks — a scourge sent by God to chastise the Church for its sins, a drastic cure for the moral sickness that had fallen on the papacy. Without Luther and his Protestant reformation, it is contended, the Council of Trent would not have been called.

But this after all is mere conjecture. No man can tell how the world and the Church in the world would have fared if there had been no Martin Luther.

But what of Luther, the liberator, Luther who brought the Israel of God out of the bondage of Egypt — as Protestants are apt to believe and teach? Whither has Luther led his followers? Into what promised land, after the years of wandering outside the Catholic unity, are now brought the Protestants who date their emancipation from Martin Luther? Four centuries of journeying since Luther started the exodus, and yet the promised land of the Lutheran evangel, so often emergent, fades from sight even as the mirage vanishes in the desert. It is the wasteland of doubt that Lutheran Protestants have reached — a wasteland, littered with abandoned hopes and discarded creeds.

First the papal authority was repudiated; then episcopacy and the priesthood given up; next the doctrine of the unity of the Christian Church abandoned; after that the Bible itself, on which all Protestants had once built their creeds and catechisms was, bit by bit, examined by Protestant professors in Lutheran universities and, in the most arbitrary fashion, with hypothesis proclaimed as scientific truth, declared to be for the most part of no historical value — New Testament and Old Testament alike. True it is that German higher criticism in the person of Harnack, that very great scholar, reversed the extravagant assumptions of his predecessors; but by that time educated Protestants had wandered too long in the wasteland, with its twilight of uncertainty, its agnosticism, its vague generalities, to make further possible any rebuilding of Zion on exclusively Biblical foundations.

Men and women were always free to leave the Catholic Church, to excommunicate themselves, to depart from the service that alone is perfect freedom.

Luther was persuaded, and was the persuader of many, that to forsake the liberty of the Catholic for the service of the new evangelical church, and to deny the freedom of the will, was a liberation of the soul. But of what use to mankind is this Protestant liberation that leaves men and women wandering in a wasteland of despair, all hope abandoned of God's sure and infallible guidance, all faith in a society divinely constituted dismissed, the notion of the miraculous and supernatural despised as superstition?

If Luther, the liberator, has landed his Protestant followers in a wasteland haunted by metaphysical spectres, a no-thoroughfare, whence the only way out, illumined by the grace given to every man who seeks the Truth to find it, is a return to Catholic unity, what of Calvin with his dictatorship at Geneva which made that city appear to the Scotsman John Knox "the most perfect school of Christ since the days of the Apostles"?

Calvin with all the pride and inexperience of youth decided he could build a permanent city of God; decided with his keen, logical mind that he had built it at Geneva; and that, founded on the *Institutes of the Christian Religion,* it stood firm on the Rock of Ages; that his disciples could go out to all the world and found similar reformed churches, cities of God for God's elect. Explorers of the Calvinist churches of Scotland and Holland report to-day the discovery in those lands of no cities of God. Calvin's city of God appears on disinterment a city of dreadful night.

Similarly with the early Calvinist churches of America; what appalling examples of civil and religious codes, now extinct but once predominant, has the historian brought to light. If the Calvinism of Calvin is now anywhere a vital force it operates in the fog that bedarkens this city of dreadful night.

Wasteland of Lutheranism, city of dreadful night that Calvin built—thus the liberation of the soul proceeds.

But Calvinism commands scanty adherence. It never was a creed that without force of law or compelling power of public opinion could win the multitudes. Calvin himself never imagined that multitudes would go to heaven; he reserved the Beatific Vision for the few choice spirits numbered in the elect of the reformed church. From Calvinism men have turned with horror. With the revulsion from this shocking travesty of the Christian Gospel has come revulsion from all revealed religion. Popular atheism, dating from the nineteenth century, has flourished in lands where the Protestantism of the reform, derived from Calvin, has been the doctrine of the schools.

The free will that both Luther and Calvin denied to man has thwarted and diverted the plans for the conquest of the world and for the subjugation of its inhabitants as elaborated by the German professor of Wittenberg and the young French lawyer, dictator at Geneva.

This free will, influenced often enough and warped by economic and social circumstances, has turned the Protestant Reformation into something quite different from the devices of Augsburg Confessions and Calvinistic catechisms. Over vast areas and in the uncounted numbers of great cities it has undermined and brought to destruction not only all belief in the Christian faith, but also in the faith of Judaism and the monotheism of the creed of Islam. A "liberal" or free Christian, tracing his religious ancestry back to Lutheranism or Presbyterianism, will to-day give no definite assent to the divinity of Christ, will openly question the resurrection of Christ from the dead, and, pragmatist in philosophy, will allow no reality to objective faith nor admit the existence of unchanging and universal moral laws. In fact between the modern Protestant churchman, the Jew of the liberal synagogue, and the progressive Mohammedan educated at a Western university, there is small disparity of creed, and no fundamental disagreement. A mild theism binds them in a simple ideal. Christ is to be honoured as a man of highest virtue, to be respected as a great example. He is not to be worshipped as Incarnate God, very God of very God. Culture and patriotism, education of the mind and national prosperity — to this has the Protestant ideal dwindled. For these by no means ignoble ends was the disruption of the Christian Church accomplished in the sixteenth century. By the adoption of a neo-paganism that rejects the supernatural and finds the miraculous only in the queerest freaks have the descendants of Luther and Calvin justified separation from the One, Holy, Catholic, and Apostolic Church of Christ.

The earnest desire for re-union of all churches outside the papal dominion no longer expresses hope for such reunion on the basis of "One Lord, one Faith, one Baptism." For disagreement on the articles of Faith is taken for granted; and baptism is disallowed by various bodies calling themselves Christian (notably the Society of Friends and the Salvation Army). Reunion for the purpose of worshipping one Lord is all that is left. Simple theism.

The Catholic Church remains, with its old creeds, its sacred scriptures of Old and New Testament, its priesthood and its Mass, unchanging and unchanged, yet ever developing its doctrine and enlarging its devotions, ever carrying its faith to far-off mission fields, ever subject to persecution, now in this land now in that. Given up for dead by what seemed to be the exuberant triumphant Protestantism of the sixteenth-century Reformation, not the Catholic Faith but the Protestant creed it is that has died.

The figure of Martin Luther stands out in all its ruggedness. Monument of defiance; to be gazed upon as one of the world's great iconoclasts; an agency of destruction. Hardly to be classed in the history of mankind with the creative minds. The influence of theological Lutheranism, the Lutheranism of Luther and Melanchthon, cannot be seen as a steady enduring influence in modern times. It is the name of Luther that is cheered, and received in Protestant circles with enthusiastic applause for the destructive work that he accomplished. The successful rebel is the hero. Hero because successful in the overthrow of an authority at the time and to many thoroughly distasteful; still heroic because the authority overthrown remains distasteful. Theological reasons alleged for the revolt, religious dogmas of Lutheranism, these are not the things for which Luther is honoured in Protestant circles.

But while it is admitted that the Protestant doctrine has largely evaporated in the course of four hundred years, has not in fact stood the test of time, Protestants are still apt to claim that material prosperity has attended the adoption of their creed, has followed the rejection of papal authority. Additional argument maintains that such material prosperity, being the outcome of Protestant reformation is a sign and token of the essential truth of Protestantism.

But how far is the evident material prosperity to be judged a product of the Protestant reformation? The spirit of adventure that sent men voyaging round the world was active before Luther's day. The foreign imperialism of Spanish and Portuguese governments preceded the exploits of British seamen. The mechanical inventions and scientific discoveries of the last hundred years — inventions and discoveries multiplied in the twentieth century beyond the wildest imagination of our grandfathers—are not by any means to be set down exclusively to the patience and ingenuity of Protestants.

Again it has been urged that capitalism is the result of Protestant ethics; or if not directly the result, has been so fostered and sanctified by Protestant ethics that it would not otherwise have reached the monstrous growth of the present time.[1] And it was to capitalism nineteenth-century liberal professors of political economy ascribed the vast increase of cheap goods that brought material comfort to nations that had not in many cases been conscious of the need of these comforts.

Capitalism is the production of things by hired labour for the purpose of sale; at a price that will give sufficient profit for the owner of capital, after the payment of wages, to set about making more things for sale. Now this fascinating, and at one time highly applauded, theory did make a direct appeal to fallen human nature because it placed vast powers in the hands of successful capitalists. Since no one can serve both God and Mammon capitalism suited Protestants, to whom were forbidden pilgrimages and other devotional practices that took up time, and for whom all good works to the glory of God and the comfort of departed souls were vain and "filthy rags." Mammon was called "business," and business interests became an absorbing occupation for serious-minded Protestants. Financial prosperity was tacitly, but more often quite vocally, hailed as the just reward of godliness. Statues were no longer carved and set up in honour of saints, since that was idolatry. They were erected to the honour and glory of numerous rich

---

[1] This argument was stressed by Max Weber in *Die protestantische Ethik und der Geist des Kapitalismus* (1920). English translation by Talcott Parsons, *The Protestant Ethic and the Spirit of Capitalism* (1930). Recent criticism based on research and fuller knowledge compels considerable modification of Weber's conclusions. But Max Weber may still be read with advantage.

men, rich men that is who gave a certain proportion of their superfluous wealth to public needs; who with money gained by the exploiting of the labourer — understanding that it is of the essence of capitalism that the costs of production should be brought to the lowest level compatible with efficient minding of machines — endowed schools and colleges, universities, hospitals, and laboratories for the benefit of mankind.

Protestant Dives was no longer imagined in a place of torment after death. A summary of his many virtues and excellent qualities as parent, citizen, and benefactor was engraved on the tombstone of the deceased. To suggest that the soul of the departed Dives might be in want of the prayers of friends or kinsmen insulted Protestant complacency and was "rank popery."

With the exaltation of riches in Protestant lands it was inevitable that poverty should be degraded and the poor man, however humble and meek, disdainfully treated. Protestantism "had no use" for poverty, though its rich men throve at the expense of the poor. Catholics, however, covetous, ambitious, and worldly minded, always knew that poverty when embraced for the love of Christ was the higher life, and recognised the sanctity that preferred poverty to riches.

Capitalism under liberalist control, reduced an honourable poverty to a shameful destitution and then penalised it.

There is nothing startling or unusual in a poor man becoming, in Catholic lands and Catholic times, a priest, bishop, or cardinal; or in a daughter of poor parents becoming a canonised saint.

Neither do we marvel when we read of the heroes of Protestant romance; heroes who grow from penniless boys into millionaires or travel from log cabin to White House.

But poverty for the latter has been triumphantly climbed out of, got rid of as a cast-off garment. For the former it has been the good companion, the cherished bride from whom there can be no divorce, borne into whatever exalted place, throne or scaffold, the call of conscience and obedience has enjoined. (But this is not to deny that pride has walked with poverty into the seats of the mighty, that ambition has not lurked within the heart to the ultimate displacement of the spirit of poverty. History can name too many distinguished Catholics who saw the nobler way and approved it, yet followed the lower.)

Capitalism, as such, not appearing suddenly on the earth as a fresh and startling revelation of the indomitable will of man, but developing gradually, as opportunity and occasion served, claims no direct inspiration from Protestant sources; nor can it boast of condemnation by Catholic authority.

Luther, it has been noted, fulminated with his habitual violence against moneylending and the payments exacted by the moneylender. Calvin with the more methodical mind worked out the conditions that made the taking of interest lawful and prescribed the circumstances, the justice and necessity of moneylending. There was nothing of the modern liberal in Calvin. The laws of usury were neither abrogated nor repealed by the *Institutes of the Christian Religion*. The reasonableness of interest was defended and explained. At the Council of the Lateran, 1515, a modest rate of interest on loans was allowed.

At the utmost it can be said that Protestant teaching encouraged attention to business by prohibiting devotional practices and the ceremonies of public worship; by the discouragement of good works, not obviously of practical service to mankind; and by its attitude to the common recreations of mankind. It frowned upon leisure, and made idleness the mortal sin.

In any case, who in these years of recurring economic depression, and the nonemployment of millions of honest men and women has a good word for capitalism and the capitalist? What if capitalism has achieved the flooding of all the world with cheap productions of doubtful utility? It has provoked in its rise internal social strife, bringing riches beyond the dreams of avarice to the few and bitter poverty to the many, with international jealousies and enmities. The civil war of strike and lockout is the price paid for the advance of the capitalist. Revolutionary communism now watches throughout the world what it takes to be the deathbed of capitalism. "Where the carcass is, there will the vultures be gathered together." The reconstruction of the social order on a truly Christian basis is the program drawn up in the great papal encyclicals on labor.

Capitalism grew up for good, and for ill, with the centuries of Protestantism. That is the conclusion of the whole matter.

Protestant ethics found the capitalist system not uncongenial. Catholic ethics detected no violation of Christian principles, saw nothing to be condemned in manufacturers producing for profit rather than for use, buying in the cheapest market to sell in the dearest, though insistence was placed on the ethics of the just price, while the old moral principles were still reiterated. These, however, needed to be newly applied to the newly arisen conditions. Unfortunately, the influence of Catholicism had been set back by the Reformation and its children were infected by the false practices, if not also the erroneous economic theories of their times. Material prosperity is naturally held of more account when men and women find their happiness in the accumulation of earthly treasures, in the gratification of bodily desire, in the manipulation of machinery and its gadgets.

If material prosperity has been encouraged or hastened by the teaching of Luther and is a result of the Protestant reformation, as many allege, this same material prosperity has in later days spread social discontent that refuses to be satisfied by Protestantism. Christian ethics, once the strength of Protestant churches, are now frankly displaced by a code enjoining obedience to the law of the tribe, the herd, the nation, the public school. Neo-paganism provides the fashionable morality in some quarters. Mere hedonism —"a little of what you fancy does you good"—is the prevailing "form" elsewhere.

Since Luther taught that truth was to be sought within, and that what a man felt to be true was true provided it coincided also with what Luther felt to be true, his doctrine obviously implied a reversal of the old order which called on the Christian to seek and find the revelation of God contained in the Gospel, and to follow it because here was the Way, the Truth, and the Life. Under such circumstances it is not to be wondered at that the same process should play havoc with Christian ethics.

No longer is a thing judged to be right because of divine command, and so requiring consent of will and conscience because of its rightness. It is judged right if and when it is agreeable to personal taste. Protestant ethics go the way of Protestant faith.

Sed nondum est finis. Not yet is the end. The Catholic Church remains. The One, Holy, Catholic, Apostolic Church. Assured as of old that its Creed is true, that the morality it teaches is God's natural law sublimated to the ethic of Christ. Convinced that the divine promise abides, that until the end of the world and the consummation of all things it will endure. Protestantism passes as other human uprisings pass. The permanence of the Catholic Church is guaranteed by God. So Catholics are assured.

FINIS

Appendix

Table of Dates

The Papacy

1503	Julius II (Rovere)
1513	Leo X (Medici)
1522	Adrian VI (Boyers)
1523	Clement VII (Medici)
1534	Paul III (Farnese)
1550	Julius III (Monte)
1555	Marcellus II (Cervini)
	Paul IV (Caraffa)
1559	Pius IV (Medici)
1565	St. Pius V (Ghislieri)
1572	Gregory XIII (Buoncompagni)
1585	Sixtus V (Peretti)
1590	Urban VII (Castagna)
	Gregory XIV (Sfondrati)
1591	Innocent IX (Facchinetti)
1592	Clement VIII (Aldobrandini)

The Empire

1493	Maximilian I (Hapsburg)
1520	Charles V
1556	Ferdinand I
1564	Maximilian II
1576	Rudolf II

APPENDIX

Kings of France

1498	Louis XII (Valois)	1560	Charles IX
1515	Francis I	1574	Henry III
1547	Henry II	1589	Henry IV (Bourbon)
1559	Francis II		

Kings of England

1509	Henry VIII (Tudor)	1558	Elisabeth
1547	Edward VI	1603	James I (Stewart)
1553	Mary		

Saxony (*Wettin Family*)

Elector		Duke	
1492	Frederick III (Ernestine)	1500	George (Albertine)
1525	John (Ernestine)	1539	Henry (Albertine)
1532	John-Frederic (Ernestine)	1541	Maurice (Albertine)
1548	Maurice (Albertine)		
1553	Augustus		

Electors of Brandenburg

1498 Joachin I
1535 Joachin II
1571 John-George

Kings of Sweden and Denmark

1513 Christian II, king of Sweden

SWEDEN		DENMARK	
1523	Gustavus I (Vasa)	——	Frederic I
1560	Eric XIV	1533	Christian III
1569	John III	1559	Frederick II
1592	Sigismund III	1588	Christian IV

Kings of Spain

1504 Ferdinand
1516 Charles I (the emperor)
1556 Philip II

Kings of Poland

1501 Alexander
1506 Sigismund I
1548 Sigismund II
1573 Henry (Valois)
1575 Stephen Batheri
1587 Sigismund III

Year	Italy	England and France	Germany
1483	....	....	Luther b.
1491	....	....	....
1495	....	....	....
1498	Savanorola burnt	Erasmus in England	
1502	....	....	Wittenberg University founded
1505	....	....	Luther enters Augustinian Order
1506	New cathedral of St. Peter at Rome begun	....	Frankfort on the Oder University founded
1508	....	....	Luther appointed professor at Wittenberg
1509	Papacy at war with France and Venice		
1511	Luther in Rome		
1512	Lateran Council (ends 1517)		
1515	....	....	Luther lectures on Epistle to the Romans
1516	....	More's **Utopia**	
1517	....	....	Luther issues **95 Theses** contra Tetzel
1518	....	....	Melanchthon, professor of Greek at Wittenberg
1519	....	....	Luther's antipapal writings. Bull of
1520	Oratory of Divine Love in Rome		excommunication burnt by Luther
1521	....	Henry VIII defender of the faith for writing contra Luther	Luther at the Diet of Worms: after sentence of outlawry remains in safety in the Wartburg. Translates New Testament.
1522	....	....	Returns to Wittenberg ....
1524	Theatine Order founded	....	Erasmus writes versus Luther
1525	....	Beginning of Henry VIII's negotiations for divorce	Luther marries. Peasant War. Albert of Brandenburg establishes Lutheranism in Prussia
1526	....	....	Catholic league of Dessau and Lutheran of Torgau
1527	Rome taken and sacked by imperial troops		Diet of Spires drops the edict of Worms against Luther
1528	Capuchin reform of the Franciscan Order		
1529	....	....	Diet of Spires annuls edict of 1526. Minority protest. Hence Protestant

Switzerland	Spain	Scandinavian Countries	Hungary and Austria
....	Ignatius Loyola b.		
....	Ximenes archbishop of Toledo		
Zwingli begins reform in Zurich and Oecolampadius in Basle			
....	....	Lutheranism established in Sweden	Hungary invaded
....	....	....	Siege of Vienna

	Italy	England and France	Germany
1530			Augsburg confession presented at diet
1531			Protestant league of Schmalkald. Peace of Nuremberg
1533	Valdès' circle at Naples		
1534		Vows of Ignatius Loyola and companions at Montmartre. Calvin becomes Protestant	Anabaptist rising at Munster
1535	Council of Cardinals for reform. Angela Merici founds Ursuline Order for education of girls	Henry VIII head of the Church. Martyrdom of SS. Thomas More and John Fisher, Carthusians	
1536			
1537	Jerome Aemiliani in Venice		
1539			Bigamy of Philip of Hesse condoned by Luther and Melanchthon
1540	Society of Jesus constituted		
1543			Archbishop of Cologne deposed for Lutheranism
1545			Council of Trent
1546			Death of Luther. Beginning of civil war
1547			Rout of Schmalkaldic league
1548			Diet of Augsburg. **Interim**
1549		English Book of Common Prayer issued by Parliament	
1550			Peter Canisius at Ingoldstadt
1551 } 1552 }			Council of Trent
1553			
1554			
1555			Diet of Augsburg **"cujus regio ejus religio"**

Switzerland	Spain	Scandinavian Countries	Hungary and Austria
Geneva becomes independent Zwingli killed in war of Cantons, succeeded by Bullinger			
Calvin established at Geneva: publishes **Institutes of Christian Religion**			
		Lutheranism established in Denmark and Norway	
Servetus burnt by Calvin			
		Lutheranism established in Iceland	

Notes on Authorities

A FULL or adequate bibliography is obviously impossible. This short list with the books mentioned in the text, will enable the reader to check the statements I have made and judge their accuracy. Also it will help the student to pursue the subject and enlarge his knowledge.

Armstrong, E., *Emperor Charles V* (London, 1910).

Barraclough, G., *Papal Provisions* (Oxford, 1935).

Böhmer, H., *Luther im Lichte der neueren Forschung*. English translation E. S. G. Potter, *Luther and the Reformation in the Light of Modern Research* (1930). (Lutheran standpoint.)

Denifle, O.P., H. S., *Luther und Luthertum* (Mainz, 1904).

Eels, H., *Martin Bucer* (Yale, 1931).

Febre, L., *Un destin: Martin Luther* (1928). English translation: *Martin Luther: a destiny* (1930) (Agnostic).

Grisar, S.J., H., *Life and Work of Martin Luther*. German edition, 3 vols. (Freiburg, 1924–25). English translation, 6 vols., by E. M. Lemond (London, 1913-17).

Hunt, R. N. Carew, *Calvin* (1933).

Janssen, J., *History of the German People at the Close of the Middle Ages* (Freiburg, 1893–1911). English translation M. A. Mitchell, and A. M. Christie (London, 1896–1910).

Kidd, B. J., *Documents of the Continental Reformation* (Oxford, 1911).

Pastor, L., *History of the Popes from the Close of the*

Middle Ages. English translation edited by F. J. Antrobus (St. Louis, 1891–1933).
Weimar edition of Luther's works, 1883 and onwards.

CATHOLIC REFORM AND COUNTER-REFORMATION

Allen, P. S., *Selections from Erasmus* (London, 1906).
——— *Age of Erasmus* (London, 1914).
Brodrick, J., *Saint Peter Canisius* (London, 1935).
Dudon, P., *Saint Ignace de Loyola* (Paris, 1934).
Fanfini, Dr. Amintore, *Catholicism, Protestantism, and Capitalism,* English translation (London, 1935). This compels revision of Weber's conclusions.
Harvey, R., *Ignatius Loyola* (Milwaukee, 1936).
Kidd, B. J., *The Counter-Reformation* (1933).
Metzler, J., *Petrus Canisius, Deutschland's Zweiter Apostel* (1925).
Ponnelle, L., and Bordet, L., *Saint Phillippe Neri et la societé romaine de son temps* (1928). English translation (London, 1932).

DUCHY OF PRUSSIA
HOLSTEIN
POMERANIA
POLAND
Hamburg
Bremen
BRANDENBURG
Berlin
Brandenburg
Frankfurt
NETHERLANDS
Magdeburg
Dessau
Wittenberg
Munster
SAXONY-Electoral
Eisleben
Torgau
Merseburg
Meissen
Leipzig
Naumberg
Dresden
HESSE
Eisenach
Gotha
Erfurt
SILESIA
Cologne
Marburg
Wartburg
Schmalkald
SAXONY-Ducal
Fulda
Coburg
Frankfurt
Mayence
Bamberg
BOHEMIA
FRANCONIA
Worms
Nuremberg
Heidelberg
Ratisbon
Spires
SWABIA
Ingolstadt
AUSTRIA
BAVARIA
LORRAINE
Augsburg
Vienna
Basle
Zurich
SWISS CANTONS
GERMANY
1525 A.D.

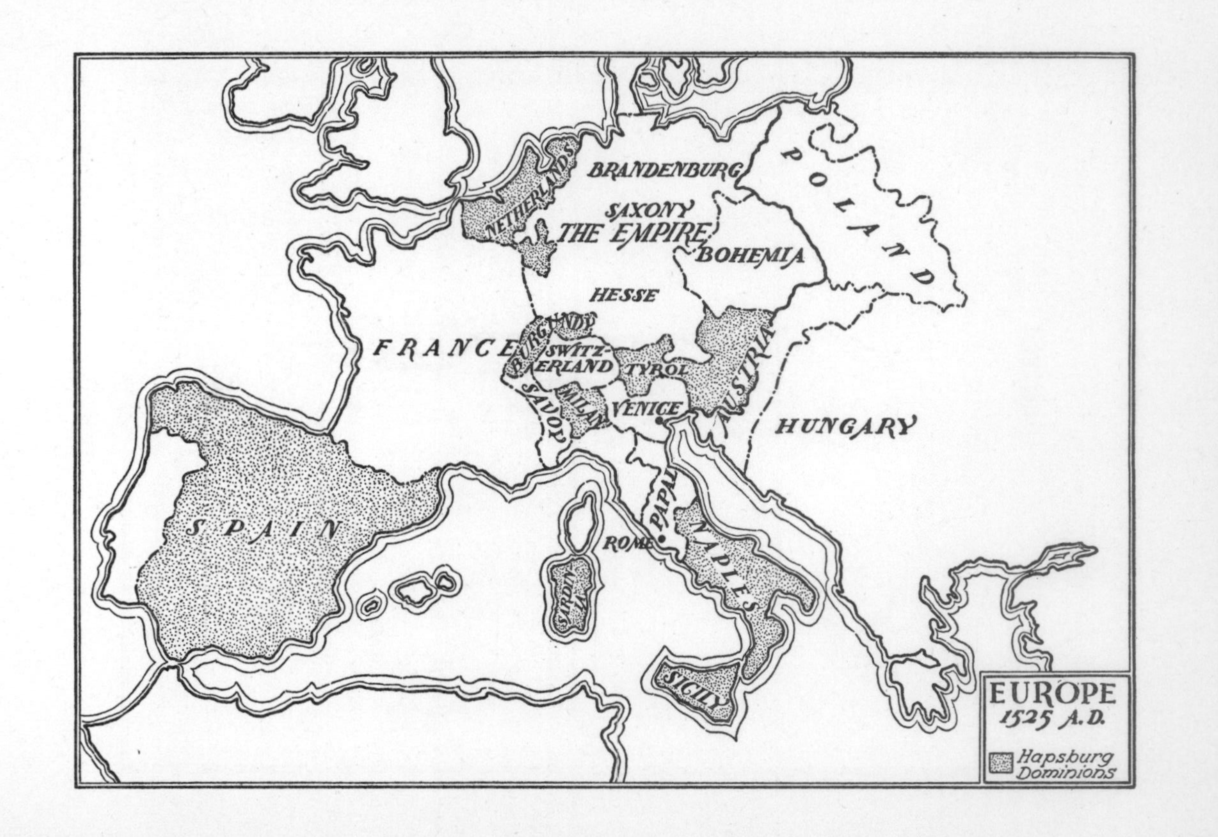
EUROPE
1525 A.D.
Hapsburg Dominions
POLAND
BRANDENBURG
NETHERLANDS
SAXONY
THE EMPIRE
BOHEMIA
HESSE
FRANCE
BURGUNDY
SWITZ-ERLAND
TYROL
AUSTRIA
HUNGARY
SAVOY
MILAN
VENICE
PAPAL
ROME
NAPLES
SARDINIA
SICILY
SPAIN

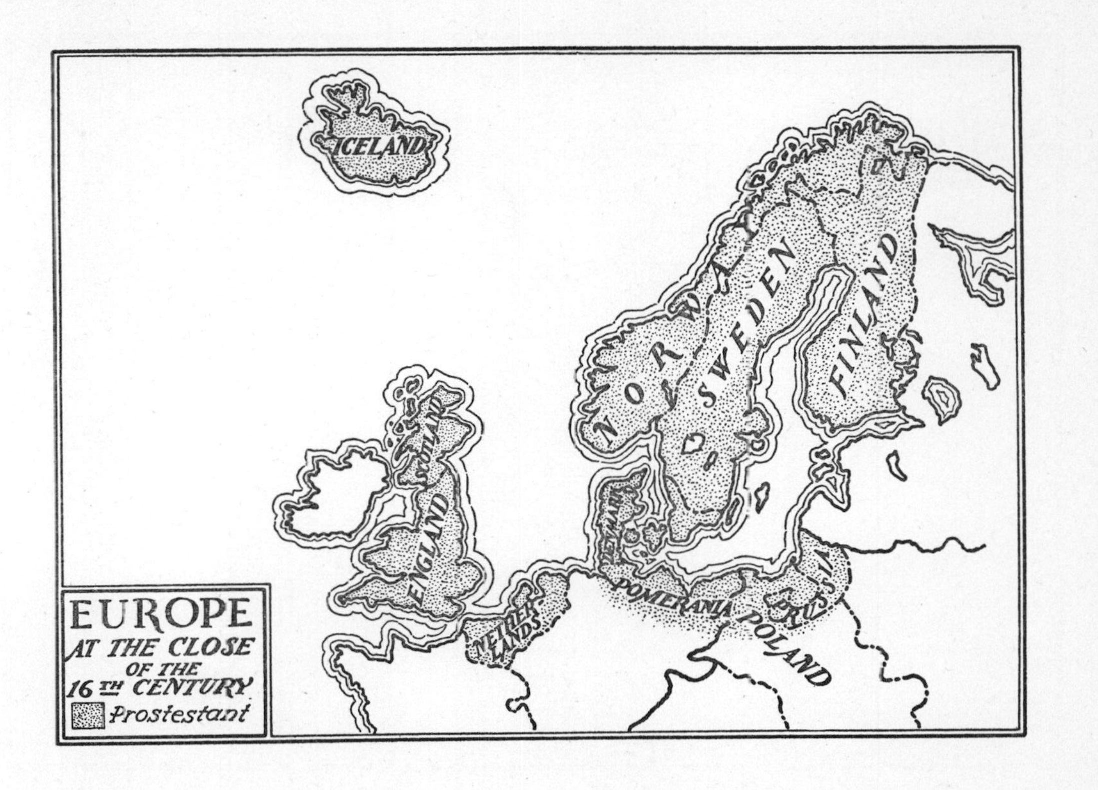

ICELAND
NORWAY
SWEDEN
FINLAND
ENGLAND
NETHER LANDS
POMERANIA
PRUSSIA
POLAND
EUROPE
AT THE CLOSE
OF THE
16 TH CENTURY
Prostestant

Index

INDEX

INDEX

INDEX